The 1996 Wiles Lectures given at The Queen's University of Belfast

THE CONSTRUCTION
OF NATIONHOOD

THE
CONSTRUCTION OF
NATIONHOOD

ETHNICITY,
RELIGION AND NATIONALISM

ADRIAN HASTINGS
University of Leeds

Christopher & Anthea
with love —
Adrian.   1. June 2000.
                Whitby.

CAMBRIDGE
UNIVERSITY PRESS

PUBLISHED BY THE PRESS SYNDICATE OF THE UNIVERSITY OF CAMBRIDGE
The Pitt Building, Trumpington Street, Cambridge, United Kingdom

CAMBRIDGE UNIVERSITY PRESS
The Edinburgh Building, Cambridge CB2 2RU, UK   http://www.cup.cam.ac.uk
40 West 20th Street, New York, NY 10011-4211, USA   http://www.cup.org
10 Stamford Road, Oakleigh, Melbourne 3166, Australia

First published 1997
Reprinted 1999

Printed in the United Kingdom at the University Press, Cambridge

Typeset in Bembo

A catalogue record for this book is available from the British Library

Library of Congress cataloguing in publication data
Hastings, Adrian.
The construction of nationhood: ethnicity, religion and nationalism / Adrian Hastings.
p.   cm. – (The Wiles lectures given at the Queen's University of Belfast)
Includes bibliographical references and index.
ISBN 0 521 59391 3 (hardcover)
1. Nationalism – History. 2. Nationalism – Religious aspects.
3. Hobsbawm, E. J. (Eric J.), 1917– . Nations and nationalism since 1780.
I. Title.   II. Series: Wiles lectures.
JC311.H346   1997
320.54–dc21   97–7039   CIP

ISBN 0 521 59391 3 hardback
ISBN 0 521 62544 0 paperback

CE

For
Janet Boyd

Contents

Preface

This book is based on the Wiles Lectures which I had the honour to give at The Queen's University of Belfast in May 1996. I have first to thank the Vice-Chancellor and the Wiles Trustees, in particular Professor David Hempton, head of the Queen's School of History, Professor Terence Ranger, Professor Ian Kershaw and Trevor Boyd for the invitation to deliver them. It is the particular attraction of the Wiles Lectures that a group of distinguished historians from other universities are invited to Belfast for the week in which they are given, to discuss each lecture after dinner that evening with the Trustees and selected members of Queen's academic staff. The guests for 1996 were Professor Tom Bartlett, Dr Kim Knott, Professor Hugh McLeod, Professor John Peel, Dr Eamon Duffy, Dr Scott Thom.s, Professor Sean Connolly and Professor Mark Noll. Discussing nationalism in Belfast, especially if one is an Englishman, might be compared, I remarked at the beginning of my second lecture, with the situation of Daniel in the den of lions, but, as I added, the point of the Daniel story was that the lions proved wonderfully friendly and so did the academics of Belfast. Their discussion was no less stimulating for that.

I am most grateful to Dr Ian Green and Professor Peel for subsequently letting me read chapters from forthcoming works. I must also express my most sincere thanks for comments, advice and information provided by Branka Magas, Noel Malcolm, Tudor Griffiths, Brigid Allen, Lesley Johnson, Frank Felsenstein and Martin Butler. I owe a very great deal to Ann, my wife, for listening over the preceding months, suppertime after suppertime, to my rehearsing the developing argument of the lectures. Ingrid Lawrie, once again, has typed and retyped versions of both lectures and book with a precision, a promptitude and an eye for small mistakes which make it her book as well as mine.

Janet Boyd established the Wiles Lectures forty years ago in memory of her father, Thomas Shires Wiles of Albany, New York, an inventor of genius, to whom we owe the washing machine. They have ever since proved a wonderful enrichment of the culture both of Belfast and of the world. It is a huge privilege to have been brought into the truly ecumenical circle created by this annual series ever since the first were given by Herbert Butterfield in 1954 on *Man and his Past.* If the frontiers of the present book may seem absurdly wide to the eye of the modern specialist historian, I can only plead both that the subject chosen requires this sort of range of comparison across centuries and continents, and that the Wiles Lectures have as an essential purpose the discussion of broad issues relating to the general history of civilisation. Butterfield dedicated *Man and his Past* to Janet Boyd. Since then she has attended every series and for me it added greatly to the occasion to see her, at each lecture, now in her nineties, listening attentively in the front row. Seldom can a patron of modern scholarship have found so continuously creative a manner of furthering the cause, yet the Wiles Lectures are only one of many ways in which her Quaker conscience has contributed to the furtherance of understanding and peace. It is a very great pleasure and honour to be able to dedicate this book to Janet Boyd.

Most of what is here printed was written before the lectures were given, though only parts could be presented in the time. The whole has since been thoroughly revised. Chapter 1 represents the core of Lecture 1; chapters 2 and 3, Lecture 2; chapters 6 and 7, Lecture 3; and chapter 8, Lecture 4.

Only when the revision was finally complete did Lesley Johnson draw my attention to the recent work of Thorlac Turville-Petre, *England the Nation: Language, Literature and National Identity, 1290-1340* (Clarendon Press, 1996), whose profound and subtle learning supports the main thrust of the argument of chapters 1 and 2. While I have altered nothing in my own text, I am very happy to signal here the appearance of this important book.

Leeds
December 1996

CHAPTER ONE

The nation and nationalism

I

Nation, ethnicity, nationalism and religion are four distinct and determinative elements within European and world history. Not one of these can be safely marginalised by either the historian or the politician concerned to understand the shaping of modern society. These four are, moreover, so intimately linked that it is impossible, I would maintain, to write the history of any of them at all adequately without at least a fair amount of discussion of the other three. That is a central contention of this book and it stands in some disagreement with much modern writing both about nationalism and about religion. The aim of this first chapter is sixfold: to set out my own position, to provide a review of recent literature, to establish the sense of an emerging schism in this field between what we may call, for simplicity's sake, modernists and revisionists, to explore the history of the word 'nation' and to lead on from there, through an analysis of the relationship between language and society, to a larger discussion of the nature of both the nation and nationalism.

When I chose this subject I thought that in developing my theme I would be able to begin by largely adopting the viewpoint of recent studies of nationalism and go on from there to insert within it the somewhat neglected dimension of religion. In particular, I naturally intended to take as a starting point Eric Hobsbawm's Wiles Lectures of 1985 on *Nations and Nationalism since 1780*[1] as probably the most influential explicitly historical discussion of nationalism in recent years. However I quickly realised that my own understanding of nationalism differed too profoundly from that of Hobsbawm to make this possible in the way I had hoped. Moreover the very parameters he laid down for the subject effectively ruled out two-thirds of what I wanted to discuss. Far from moving forward from Hobsbawm, I realised that the only course open to me was to attempt to deconstruct his central thesis in favour of a very different one, and this I have endeavoured to do. In consequence, the central topic of this book has become the history of nations and nationalism in themselves. Most modern theorists of nationalism appear somewhat weak on hard history and that is why, in speaking as an historian, it is Hobsbawm that I find myself facing above all. Nevertheless, as he drew quite considerably on several other hardly less influential recent works such as John Breuilly's *Nationalism and the State*, Ernest Gellner's *Nations and Nationalism* and Benedict Anderson's *Imagined Communities*, all of which first appeared just as he was preparing his lectures,[2] I have found it sensible to link the four, while recognising their differences where necessary. Together they represent what has come to be known as the 'modernist' view, the principal current orthodoxy in nationalist studies, but one increasingly challenged by medievalists and others. Thus Keith Stringer recently suggested not only that 'medievalists and modernists have more to learn from each other than has often been thought', particularly in regard to 'the thorny problem of nationalism', but that this may constitute no less than a 'current crisis of historiography'.[3] My discussion of the relationship of religion to nationalism has then had to be done within the course of a larger historical reconstruction, and in the consciousness of speaking across the frontline of an historiographical schism. This is, I have come to be convinced, the best way to approach it, because, while the role of religion has been far from single-faceted in its relationship to ethnicity and the construction of nations, it has been integral to this wider history, perhaps even determinative. The history of religion can never be best understood within a box of its own and that is evidently particularly true in a field such as this where religion, politics and culture so obviously interact. Nevertheless this has meant that I have devoted less space than anticipated to speak specifically about religion.

Let me begin by briefly setting out my central theses, themes to which we will return from one angle or another again and again.

1. For the development of nationhood from one or more ethnicities, by far the most important and widely present factor is that

of an extensively used vernacular literature. A long struggle against an external threat may also have a significant effect as, in some circumstances, does state formation, though the latter may well have no national effect whatever elsewhere. A nation may precede or follow a state of its own but it is certainly assisted by it to a greater self-consciousness. Most such developments are stimulated by the ideal of a nation-state and of the world as a society of nations originally 'imagined', if you like the word, through the mirror of the Bible, Europe's primary textbook, but turned into a formal political philosophy no earlier than the nineteenth century and then next to canonised by President Woodrow Wilson and the Versailles peace settlement of 1920.

2. An ethnicity is a group of people with a shared cultural identity and spoken language. It constitutes the major distinguishing element in all pre-national societies, but may survive as a strong subdivision with a loyalty of its own within established nations.

3. A nation is a far more self-conscious community than an ethnicity.[4] Formed from one or more ethnicities, and normally identified by a literature of its own, it possesses or claims the right to political identity and autonomy as a people, together with the control of specific territory, comparable to that of biblical Israel and of other independent entities in a world thought of as one of nation-states.

4. A nation-state is a state which identifies itself in terms of one specific nation whose people are not seen simply as 'subjects' of the sovereign but as a horizontally bonded society to whom the state in a sense belongs. There is thus an identity of character between state and people. In some way the state's sovereignty is inherent within the people, expressive of its historic identity. In it, ideally, there is a basic equivalence between the borders and character of the political unit upon the one hand and a self-conscious cultural community on the other. In most cases this is a dream as much as a reality. Most nation-states in fact include groups of people who do not belong to its core culture or feel themselves to be part of a nation so defined. Nevertheless almost all modern states act on the bland assumption that they are nation-states.

5. 'Nationalism' means two things: a theory and a practice. As a political theory – that each 'nation' should have its own 'state' –

it derives from the nineteenth century. However, that general principle motivates few nationalists. In practice nationalism is strong only in particularist terms, deriving from the belief that one's own ethnic or national tradition is especially valuable and needs to be defended at almost any cost through creation or extension of its own nation-state. If nationalism became theoretically central to western political thinking in the nineteenth century, it existed as a powerful reality in some places long before that. As something which can empower large numbers of ordinary people, nationalism is a movement which seeks to provide a state for a given 'nation' or further to advance the supposed interests of its own 'nation-state' regardless of other considerations. It arises chiefly where and when a particular ethnicity or nation feels itself threatened in regard to its own proper character, extent or importance, either by external attack or by the state system of which it has hitherto formed part; but nationalism can also be stoked up to fuel the expansionist imperialism of a powerful nation-state, though this is still likely to be done under the guise of an imagined threat or grievance.

6. Religion is an integral element of many cultures, most ethnicities and some states. The Bible provided, for the Christian world at least, the original model of the nation. Without it and its Christian interpretation and implementation, it is arguable that nations and nationalism, as we know them, could never have existed. Moreover, religion has produced the dominant character of some state-shaped nations and of some nationalisms. Biblical Christianity both undergirds the cultural and political world out of which the phenomena of nationhood and nationalism as a whole developed and in a number of important cases provided a crucial ingredient for the particular history of both nations and nationalisms.

I will be suggesting that England presents the prototype of both a nation and a nation-state in the fullest sense, that its national development, while not wholly uncomparable with that of other Atlantic coastal societies, does precede every other – both in the date at which it can fairly be detected and in the roundness that it achieved centuries before the eighteenth. It most clearly manifests, in the pre-Enlightenment era, almost every appropriate 'national' characteristic. Indeed it does more than 'manifest' the nature of a nation, it establishes it. In the words of a very recent writer, Liah Greenfeld, 'The birth of the English nation was not the birth of a nation, it was the birth of the nations, the birth of nationalism.'[5] Moreover, its importance for us lies too both in its relationship with religion and in the precise impact of English nationalism on its neighbours and colonies. Much of this, I will be claiming, was detectable already in Saxon times by the end of the tenth century. Despite the, often exaggerated, counter-action of the Norman Conquest, an English nation-state survived 1066, grew fairly steadily in the strength of its national consciousness through the later twelfth and thirteenth centuries, but emerged still more vociferously with its vernacular literary renaissance and the pressures of the Hundred Years War by the end of the fourteenth. Nevertheless the greatest intensity of its nationalist experience together with its overseas impact must undoubtedly be located in and after the late sixteenth century.

I will argue that there appears to be no comparable case in Europe and that it was this English model, wholly preceding the late eighteenth century, in which this sort of process is held by modernist theory to find its roots, which was then re-employed, remarkably little changed, in America and elsewhere. I will not suggest that English nationalism preceded an English nationhood. On the contrary. However English nationalism of a sort was present already in the fourteenth century in the long wars with France and still more in the sixteenth and seventeenth. Indeed, without the impact of English nationalism, the history of England's neighbours seems virtually unintelligible.

These claims have, of course, to be justified by the evidence. If true, they require a considerable rewrite of the standard modernist history of nationalism. To many people they will seem surprising claims. Perhaps as I am myself so very much an Englishman, they may even seem an expression less of historical enquiry than of English nationalism itself. Yet if there is such a thing as English nationalism it is surely right that an Englishman should explore it, especially as it is undoubtedly a category that many English people have denied to exist. Foreigners have nationalism, which is a bad thing; we English have patriotism, which is a good thing! I do not agree. English nationalism, partially transformed from the eighteenth century into British nationalism, has been a very powerful, and frequently damaging, historical force. Yet historians have made a habit of ignoring it. Thus it is strange that an historian so searching in other fields as Hobsbawm can simply remark in passing that 'the development of nations and nationalism within old-established states, such as Britain and France, has not been studied very intensively . . . The existence of this gap is illustrated by the neglect, in Britain, of any problems connected with English nationalism.'[6] That may be the most remarkable understatement of any Wiles lecture. It is odd that historians of nationalism have managed for long so easily to avert their eyes from what in hard reality, I believe, has been the prototype for the whole story.

It would surely be surprising if England was not in at the start of a process which has been so central to the political development of the modern world, surprising because England did so clearly provide the lead in regard to most other aspects of that development, such as the establishment of a strongly centralised state, the growth of parliamentary government, elective and representative, the early decline of villeinage, the limitation of royal power, the emergence of a powerful capital city, the formation of political parties, the ending of slavery, the emergence of industrial society and of an effective press. Britain has also led the way in the writing of political theory from the seventeenth to the nineteenth century, from Hobbes and Locke, through Burke, Hume and Adam Smith, to Bentham, Mill, Bagehot and Bosanquet. Benedict Anderson's astonishing claim that the English nation was only emerging at the heart of its empire in the later years of the nineteenth century[7] not only goes in the teeth of the evidence but is totally implausible. Only if national identity and nationalism were really marginal phenomena within the modernisation of the world over the last three centuries would it be easily imaginable that they did not affect the country, which had throughout provided the lead for modernisation, until the very eve of its decline. In fact they are central and indispensable elements within that movement and it would be hard to imagine the development of the modern world without them.

This does not mean that the nation-state is the only political form available for the modern world. Far from it. The nation-state does not inherently belong to modernity and if Britain, for long the prototype of modernity, pioneered the nation-state, it also pioneered

the non-national world empire. While France's empire was conceived, if unrealistically, as an extension of its nation-state, Britain's
was not. That does not make it less modern. Indeed it may be the
political reality of Britain's global empire which looks in another
fifty years' time more like the real prototype for the political
structuring of modernity. The nation-state has always been itself to a
very large extent an unrealised myth; it only too manifestly does not
fit the complex reality of human society very helpfully in many
places; its values have often been overplayed in the past hundred
years, its dangers, until recently, foolishly belittled. Nationalism has
been enormously damaging to peace, tolerance and common sense;
and the model of a nation-state, which could seldom fit social reality
without grave injustice to numerous minorities, may well be wisely
superseded by arrangements which stress both smaller and larger
units of power and administration. While nationalism's territorial
form seems vastly preferable to its more ethnic or linguistic form, its
ideal has relied far too heavily on simplistic concepts of the
indivisibility of sovereignty – concepts which have in our time been
in practice increasingly superseded by the working of the UNO,
international law and the European Community. For many people
the structures of a pre-nationalist Habsburg Empire, or an extra-
nationalist British Empire, or a post-nationalist European Community look basically more sane than those of the nation-state. Nevertheless it has to be recognised that the Habsburg or British Empires
were only tolerable, for most of their parts, because of relative
underdevelopment. Once the dominance of Latin as the one
language of civilisation in the West fell before the literary advance of
French, English, German and Spanish, it came to seem inevitable
that any kind of Holy Roman Empire model, whose legacy survived
in the Habsburg Empire, would need to be replaced by one of
'national' states reflecting the more advanced and stable of ethnic/
linguistic identities. One of the functions of this book will be to
explore wherein lay that inevitability but it is quietly symbolic of
what made the Habsburg Empire possible for so long that Latin was
still used as an official language in Hungary in the nineteenth
century. Moreover, as English becomes increasingly a new world
language so do new universalist, supra-national, states edge themselves into existence.

What needs explaining may be less why England, followed by

Spain, France, the Netherlands, Denmark, Sweden and Portugal, moved steadily towards the creation of nation-states, than why Germany and Italy, caught more deeply in medieval structure, imperial, commercial and ecclesiastical, failed for so long to do the same. To this crucially important question we will return. For the moment it is sufficient to recognise that the attractiveness and apparent power of the nation-state, manifest above all in England and then in Britain by the eighteenth century, guaranteed that sooner or later its pursuit would be taken up across the rest of Europe. The heady shock waves of the French Revolution and Napoleonic Wars, followed by a huge increase in printing in many languages, ensured that central, southern and eastern Europe in the nineteenth century, and much of the rest of the world in the twentieth, would endeavour to imitate the political model provided by the apparently most advanced and successful countries of the world.

At this point it is appropriate to set out as clearly as possible the principal lines of disagreement with the 'modernist' view of nations and nationalism as represented by Hobsbawm, Gellner, Breuilly and Anderson. I may repeat, before I do this, that I am not alone in disagreeing. On the one hand one senses a renewed conviction among medieval historians that these are categories fully appropriate for the understanding of pre-sixteenth, let alone much pre-late eighteenth century, history.[8] On the other hand is the school of nationalist studies of a more sociological kind, led by Anthony Smith and John Hutchinson who, however much they acknowledge the inspiration of the masters of 'modernism', appear decidedly unconvinced by its central theses. Smith's most important work, *The Ethnic Origins of Nations*,[9] represents the strongest critique of modernism hitherto presented though it still accepts far too many modernist presuppositions. Equally encouraging, so far as I am concerned, is Liah Greenfeld's 1992 *Nationalism: Five Roads to Modernity*, already quoted, with its explicit recognition that England was 'the first nation in the world, and the only one, with the possible exception of Holland, for about two hundred years'.[10]

Greenfeld's work is a truly major, and originally constructed, contribution to a subject now being heavily overloaded with often repetitive studies. Nevertheless her thesis remains, in my opinion, seriously misleading on several counts. First, it is still in principle

8

within the enterprise of the modernists. Nationalism remains the 'road to modernity', a road which still opens in the late eighteenth century apart from the one privileged exception of England. I am not convinced by the great divide between the pre-modern and the modern and I certainly do not think that nationalism is, as such, a door, let alone the main door, from the former to the latter. It can often be a road in quite the opposite direction, but the recognisable nationalism of, say, early fourteenth-century Scotland cannot usefully be described as either modernising or anti-modernising. Understanding nations and nationalism will only be advanced when any inseparable bonding of them to the modernisation of society is abandoned.

Secondly, she still does not get England right. For Greenfeld, 'the emergence of national sentiment in England' is to be located in 'the first third of the sixteenth century'.[11] I find this decidedly unlikely. For one thing there is really no obvious reason why it should emerge at that point, prior to the Reformation and in a period of peace. For another she, like all other modernists, totally avoids consideration of the medieval evidence. For that very distinguished American medievalist, Joseph R. Strayer, 'England was clearly a nation-state in the fifteenth century.'[12] Yet it would be highly implausible to claim that it was the fifteenth century when this came to be. What happened to English nationalism in the sixteenth century can only be understood, I am convinced, if the pre-Reformation history of the English nation is fully recognised. If Greenfeld is right to claim that England was 'the first nation in the world', it requires demonstration in medieval terms.

The key issue at the heart of our schism lies in the date of commencement. For the modernists, following in this Elie Kedourie's highly influential *Nationalism* of 1960,[13] nationalism is a very modern phenomenon about which you cannot reasonably speak before the late eighteenth century; nationalism, moreover, precedes the nation. 'It is nationalism which engenders nations', declared Gellner.[14] Again, 'Nationalism is not the awakening of nations to self-consciousness: it invents nations where they do not exist.'[15] Hobsbawm agrees. 'Nations do not make states and nationalisms, but the other way round.'[16] 'The nation', he adds, is 'a very recent newcomer in human history . . . it belongs exclusively to a particular, and historically recent, period. It is a social entity only in so

9

far as it relates to a certain kind of modern territorial state, the "nation-state" and it is pointless to discuss nation and nationality except in so far as both relate to it.'[17] 'The basic characteristic of the modern nation and everything connected with it is its modernity.'[18] That is why, of course, Hobsbawm puts 'since 1780' into his title. For him it is 'pointless' to discuss the subject in pre-1780 terms. 'Nations', Gellner agrees, 'can be defined only in terms of the age of nationalism.'[19] For Breuilly too nation-states appear in principle inadmissible before the nineteenth century, anything prior to that being dismissed with remarkably little investigation, as 'prelude' only in a period when anything 'nationalist' is considered by him to be necessarily in opposition to the state.[20] Anderson wholly agrees and his conclusion, faced with the national reality of the American War of Independence, is that it must all have begun there: 'The large cluster of new political entities that sprang up in the western hemisphere between 1778 and 1838, all of which self-consciously defined themselves as nations . . . were historically the first such states to emerge on the world stage, and therefore inevitably provided the first real model of what such states should "look like".'[21] The French Revolution quickly followed in the American wake and in consequence this new entity, the nation, Anderson continues, was 'a complex composite of French and American elements'[22] which became 'available for pirating' by the second decade of the nineteenth century. All our authors follow Kedourie in insisting on this late eighteenth-century date for the start of the whole process (even though Gellner does at one point, self-contradictorily, admit that England somehow became a nation in a much earlier age). On why or where it all began they are not so united. Anderson claims that it was really all a great American invention – 'Nationalism emerged first in the New World not the Old . . . it is an astonishing sign of the depth of Eurocentrism that so many European scholars persist, in the face of all the evidence, in regarding nationalism as a European invention.'[23] For Kedourie, it was Kant and the Enlightenment that must accept responsibility; for others, the political, military and intellectual impact of the French Revolution was the precipitating factor. For Gellner and Hobsbawm it appears to be more an inevitable consequence of capitalism and industrialisation. The problem with that is twofold. First, much of the nationalist explosion in central and eastern Europe has not been in areas noted for industrialisation; second, it does not well explain why the process should begin in America. Anderson has a point in claiming that the first example of this new wave of nation-making was the American; what he does not at all explain is why that should be so.[24] The general explanation given by both Anderson and Breuilly of the rise of nationalism in terms of the decline of dynasties and of religion and the growth in printed literature implies an extraordinarily over-simple picture of both the state and religion in Europe before the late eighteenth century, while Anderson offers no explanation as to why the growth in books did not have in the sixteenth century the effect he postulates for the late eighteenth.

I do not wish to dispute the rapid spread of nationalist ideology and nation-creating movements from that time, nor do I question the sort of Hobsbawmian analysis of why in the nineteenth century this took hold of central and eastern Europe in the way that it did. Gellner and Hobsbawm are in their roots central Europeans and the view from Vienna or Prague is naturally somewhat different from that from London or Edinburgh. But a balanced history of nationalism in its entirety must not be allowed to belittle the primacy of experience of the Atlantic coastal states. The basic question remains whether 1789 or thereabouts is a reasonable starting date for a study of this subject. Hobsbawm wrote a history of nineteenth- and twentieth-century nationalism, but not a history of nationalism, and denial of the first half of the story has inevitably skewed the whole. In particular it impairs an understanding of the nation–nationalism relationship because while in the later period nationalisms may often have preceded nations rather than the reverse, in the earlier period it is far truer to say that nations as they grew more self-conscious, or came under threat, produced nationalisms.

Where, then, did these nations come from? The answer can only be, I argue, out of certain ethnicities, affected by the literary development of a vernacular and the pressures of the state. The second area in which Hobsbawm and Gellner are quite unconvin-cingly negative is that of the relationship between ethnicity and nationhood. Clearly enough, as they so strongly insist, every ethnicity did not become a nation, but many have done so. What has to be asserted counter to modernism is not any kind of primordialism – a claim that every nation existent today, and just those nations, all existed in embryo a thousand or fifteen hundred years ago – but, rather, a finely constructed analysis of why some ethnicities do become nations while others do not. The defining origin of the nation, like that of every other great reality of modern western experience, whether it be the university, the bureaucratic state or individualism, needs to be located in an age a good deal further back than most modernist historians feel safe to handle, that of the shaping of medieval society. I will argue that ethnicities naturally turn into nations or integral elements within nations at the point when their specific vernacular moves from an oral to written usage to the extent that it is being regularly employed for the production of a literature, and particularly for the translation of the Bible. Once an ethnicity's vernacular becomes a language with an extensive living literature of its own, the Rubicon on the road to nationhood appears to have been crossed. If it fails to pass that point – and most spoken vernaculars do fail that hurdle – then transformation to nationhood is almost certain never to take place.

I confess to finding in Hobsbawm as in Kedourie an altogether too negative and derogatory approach to both nations and nationalism. Of course, if they are all only a late arrival in the course of history and, as Hobsbawm also argues, something already out of date in view of the internationalisation of the modern world, then they may perhaps be rather easily dismissed. Yet to look at European and world history in this way is to leave out a central line of meaning and even to misunderstand or denigrate much of what is most valuable in the European cultural and political achievement. For our own islands it is to dismiss, and quite unjustifiably, the creative specificity of Englishness, Irishness, Welshness and Scottishness. Evil and disastrous as nationalism has often been, it relates to values of the greatest importance. Even when we condemn, we need the ability to sympathise.

Finally, there are major omissions in the modernist view. If due consideration of England and related nations, including the making of America, is one of them, the impact of religion in general and of the Bible in particular is another. I believe it to be quite impossible to discuss the subject without careful consideration of the Bible as prime lens through which the nation is imagined by biblically literate people, but I find no reference to this even in Anderson, where it would be most appropriate.[25] Hence, to summarise our schism, in contrast to Hobsbawm's Wiles Lectures on nationalism, mine were at least as much about the period before 1780 as the period after it, and about the way ethnicity turns naturally in certain circumstances into nationhood. They focused upon the impact of vernacular literature; paid large attention to Atlantic countries, above all England; and they were about the influence of the Bible and of religion more generally. On those five points I have put, I think, sufficient clear water between me and Hobsbawm, but I could not have begun to establish a counter-view with the clarity I hope to have reached if I had not had before me, to read and reread, the often enlightening as well as provocative books of these distinguished authors.

I want at this point to refer to one other recent book, Rogers Brubaker's *Citizenship and Nationhood in France and Germany*,[26] not only because I have found it exceptionally convincing but because the contrast he sets out between France and Germany appears to lie at the heart of any wider understanding of the central tension within nationhood. The basic contrast he finds to be one between a French *jus soli* and a German *jus sanguinis*. The French have defined themselves territorially in terms of a country created by a state and then productive of a nation; the Germans have defined themselves ethnocentrically in terms of a community of descent (in theory), of language (in practice), which is then productive of a state. Each arrived at a nation-state but came at it from opposite ends. The one is inclusivist of everybody in a place, the other is inclusivist only of people who share certain ethnic or cultural characteristics. Brubaker establishes this thesis very convincingly but historians need to explain, so far as is possible and more than he does, just why these two central peoples of Europe have had such a strikingly different approach to nationhood and what are the implications of their diversity for other Europeans. All in all France represents in this the earlier 'western' European experience while Germany is the prototype for the later 'eastern' experience. Nevertheless, as we shall see, other west European states by no means followed exactly the French route, nor did east Europeans always follow the German route. All the same this French–German antithesis, as analysed by Brubaker, is, I believe, one of the principal building blocks for a sound analysis of nationalism as a whole.

II

If we are to construct a summary history of the nation and what relates to it, we can well begin by considering the history of the word 'nation' itself. That indeed is what Hobsbawm did in his own opening chapter, using principally Spanish examples to conclude that the word has until quite recently not possessed anything like 'its modern meaning'.[27] Now, undoubtedly, the experience of nationhood has been historically so diverse that it may be expected that the word itself should in different languages have developed with a variety of stresses. Nevertheless if we are seeking to assess the age of a modern word/concept, then it seems most sensible to seek for it where it is likely to have been most long-lived, not where it could be expected to have had a shorter history. The Spanish linguistic community was for too long subordinate to an inter-territorial imperial polity to be a place in which the concept of nationhood would fully flower. The English linguistic community's political experience offered a far more likely milieu in which to find early verbal expression of the modern concept.

A good place to start is Johnson's *Dictionary* of 1755 which defines 'nation' as 'A people distinguished from another people; generally by their language, origin, or government' and quotes a passage of Raleigh: 'If Edward III had prospered in his French wars, and peopled with English the towns which he had won as he began at Calais driving out the French, his successors holding the same course, would have filled all France with our nation.' I see no significant difference between this Johnsonian usage of the word and ours; we are still not so sure whether language, origin or government should be the principal criterion but the sense of a large human community, at once cultural and political, is clearly here. Johnson is no isolated example. He simply represents a standard English understanding of the word, not only in the eighteenth century, but in the seventeenth and sixteenth. When Pitt the Younger appealed to 'our existence as a nation . . . our very name as Englishmen' to define what was being fought for in the war with Napoleon, when Adam Smith spoke of a 'nation of shopkeepers', when Edmund Burke applied the word to the Americans arguing that 'a nation is not governed which is perpetually to be conquered',[28] when the Anglicised African Olaudah Equiano described his own Igbo people

as 'a nation of dancers, musicians and poets'[29] – to take a scattering
of examples from the half century following Johnson's *Dictionary* –
they were all using the word with essentially the same meaning,
which is our meaning. But they were doing nothing new. For the
seventeenth century, take John Milton's 1640s appeal to parliament:
'Lords and Commons of England, consider what nation it is where-
off ye are . . .' or his 'Methinks I see in my mind a noble and
puissant nation raising herself like a strong man after sleep',[30] or
again Francis Bacon's advice to Prince Charles on going to war with
Spain twenty years earlier, 'As for that great body of Germany, I see
they have greater reason to confederate themselves with the kings of
France and Great Britain, or Denmark, for the liberty of the German
nation, and for the expulsion of Spanish and foreign princes than
they had in the years 1552 and 1553.'[31] Both these quotations have a
clear political dimension, suggesting that a nation is a good deal more
than its government, that it has rights of its own and a claim for
'liberty' from tyrannical rule or foreign domination. For the
sixteenth century we can remember Shakespeare's Falstaff remarking
'It was alway yet the trick of our English nation . . .'[32] or Samuel
Daniel, writing late in Elizabeth's reign,

> And who, in time, knowes whither we may vent
> The treasure of our tongue, to what strange shores
> This gaine of our best glory shall be sent
> T'enrich unknowing Nations with our stores?[33]

Go back to the fifteenth century and one can cite Fortescue's 'the
said kynge is compellid to make his armeys . . . of straungers, as
Scottes, Spaynardes . . . and of other nacions', or Fabyan's 'a great
hoost of Danes, and other strange nacyons'. Go further still to the
fourteenth and you have Wyclif's 'The gospels of Crist written in
Englische, to moost lernyng of our nacioun', and, even, a couple of
generations before Wyclif, to the author of the *Cursor Mundi*, 'Of
Ingland the nacion'.[34] The frequency and consistency in usage of the
word from the early fourteenth century onward strongly suggest a
basis in experience: Englishmen felt themselves to be a nation.

One very obvious literary instrument for such consistent usage
was surely to be found in the English Bible, and, from the Reformation onward, its weekly vehicle for public audition, the Book of
Common Prayer. While the stable English usage of the word

'nation' goes far further back, it is, from the mid-sixteenth century, securely anchored for English people in the frequent and emphatic biblical reference to nations and the world as a world of nations. Isaiah's 'nation shall not lift up sword against nation' (Isaiah 2.4), or Matthew's 'nation shall rise against nation, and kingdom against kingdom' (Mt. 24.7) are but two of a vast multitude of texts which it would be tedious to rehearse from both the Old and the New Testament as read in the King James Version of 1611. The King James version is, however, in this no different from the Genevan English translation of 1560, which had over seventy editions between that date and 1611. But again, this usage of the word 'nation' goes back still further to be found in fourteenth-century English translations of the Bible. Thus the translation of a verse in the Book of Revelation (5.9) circa 1350 already has the rendering 'all kyndes & tunges & folkes & nacions',[35] and the Wyclifite Bible a little later 'each lynage and tunge and puple and nacioun', corresponding very closely to the King James version two and half centuries later 'of every kindred, and tongue, and people, and nation'. These can be compared with the 1960s Jerusalem Bible's 'of every race, language, people and nation'. Of the four terms needed for the translation of this verse, only 'nation' has not changed between 1350 and 1960! The English Bible, it is not exaggerated to claim, has ensured a standard use of the word 'nation' from the fourteenth to the twentieth century.

Why did the Wyclifite translators use the word 'nacioun'? The short answer is that they were translating the Vulgate text which used the Latin 'natio'. Where the Vulgate had translated the Greek 'ethnos' as 'natio', it was rendered 'nacioun' in English. That this was not simply a matter of a translator's subservience to the Latin is demonstrated by Wyclif's own wider use of it in the passage already quoted, as again by the prologue to Luke in one manuscript by the 'caityf' who described himself as one who 'writith the gospel of Luk in Englysh . . . to the pore men of his nacioun which kunnen litil Latyn'.[36] Nor were the Wyclifites in fact the first so to translate for we can get back yet another fifty years to Richard Rolle of Hampole who died in 1349. In his edition of the Psalms he used 'naciuoun' in all nine places where the Vulgate does so. Thus Psalm 107.4, 'Psallam tibi in nationibus', becomes for Rolle 'I sall synge til the in nacyuns.'[37] If this is, very probably, as far as we can go on this particular track then the pursuit of the origin of a vernacular 'nation' ends with the words of a Yorkshire holy man.

The intellectual impact of the vernacular 'nacioun' was surely, then, in origin the same as that of the Vulgate's 'natio'. The Vulgate does not in point of fact use the word a great many times – only six in the whole of the New Testament. It prefers 'gens' and 'populus'. There is no clear Vulgate distinction between 'gens' and 'natio'. Nevertheless its uses of 'natio' are often in particularly important texts, including the account of the miracle of languages at Pentecost in Acts 2 followed by the list of nations involved – Parthians, Medes, Elamites and the rest – 'men of ech nacioun that is vndir heuene' as the Wyclifite, Purvey, put it.[38] No other book had half so wide or pervasive an influence in medieval Europe as the Vulgate Bible and it is simply perverse to seek odd meanings for the word 'natio' elsewhere while ignoring its use in this absolutely central text. The psalms were repeated every week by thousands of monks and clerics and, every time they did so, they used the word 'nation'. While the Vulgate certainly does not employ it with any technical precision, the regular implication that the world consists of a number of nameable peoples is clear enough; it is absurd to disregard such usage and refer instead for its Latin medieval meaning to the division of students in various universities into four 'nations'.[39] Universities needed to organise their students into groups, they liked to see the university as some sort of mirror of the world and liked also – in the way of academic societies almost everywhere – to use language to describe their community a little idiosyncratically. When early sixteenth-century humanists in Aberdeen divided their students into the four nations of Mar, Buchan, Moray and Angus, it really tells us next to nothing about the precise way, outside university organisation, a 'nation' was conceived, except that for the Aberdonian his university, as a world of its own, could amusingly be divided into nations to mirror a Christendom divided between Germans, Frenchmen, Italians, Scots and others.

There is in fact overwhelming evidence that 'natio' was regularly used in the Middle Ages in the Vulgate sense of a people distinct by 'language, laws, habits, modes of judgement and customs' – to use an almost defining phrase of Bernard, first Norman Bishop of St David's, when describing the Welsh as a 'natio' to the Pope about 1140.[40]

Mostly, however, the Vulgate uses 'gens' for the Greek 'ethnos' and 'populus' for 'laos'. Both had their equivalents in French and Italian but in English 'gens' produced no derivative. Rolle rendered Psalm 117's 'Laudate dominum omnes gentes, laudate eum omnes populi' as 'Louys the Lord all genge: louys him all folke'[41] but 'genge', a recognised Middle English word for a band or gathering of people, faded from the language and even 'folk' tended to lose its 'Volk' meaning and to survive only with a more local or indeterminate sense. Perhaps this more or less forced a greater use of 'nation' in English. It is not surprising that the King James version of Psalm 117 reads 'Praise the Lord, all ye nations: praise him, all ye people.'[42]

The intention of this excursus into the history of a word is not to demonstrate that in the fourteenth century the word 'nation' had for English people exactly the sense that it may have for a post-nineteenth century nationalist, though it is well worth recalling what Professor Galbraith, recently described as 'a magisterial viewer of the wood on the basis of careful inspection of the few surviving trees',[43] had to say about this over fifty years ago: 'the word "nation" is found in the fourteenth century with something of a modern sense'.[44] What is clear is that there has been a surprisingly firm continuity in usage across more than six hundred years in our language, that the sense of 'nation' was already in the fourteenth century related explicitly to a distinct language group, and that it drew in large part on biblical and Vulgate roots.

The Bible, moreover, presented in Israel itself a developed model of what it means to be a nation – a unity of people, language, religion, territory and government. Perhaps it was an almost terrifyingly monolithic ideal, productive ever after of all sorts of dangerous fantasies, but it was there, an all too obvious exemplar for Bible readers of what every other nation too might be, a mirror for national self-imagining. The point to be made here is that both word and concept were already there from the later Middle Ages at the heart of the English linguistic, religious and cultural tradition, though their influence would certainly become more intense after the Reformation and the vastly increased diffusion of Bible knowledge achieved by Protestantism. In Catholic societies less biblically educated than Protestant ones an explicit verbal sense of nationhood is likely to have developed more recently among ordinary people, but at least for England the presence of the word and the idea behind it in full public consciousness is unquestionable, at least from the latter part of the sixteenth century, but most probably from the fourteenth. This does not, of course, prove of itself that the English were themselves at that time a nation, as we understand the term, though their frequent use of the term shows clearly enough that they thought they were. However, it is one thing to discuss whether the Chinese, say, under the Ming dynasty were a 'nation' when one is taking a word entirely foreign to their society and seeing whether it can suitably be applied to them, and quite another to maintain that a word which we have inherited from our ancestors in continual verbal continuity is not relevant to their society in a way they thought it was, but is one which in terms of historical understanding it is 'pointless' to apply to them. Can the historian validly so redefine people against their own self-understanding?

If a history of nationhood can well start by such, inevitably selective, reflection upon the history of the word itself, that easily leads us into a wider discussion of the social role of language, oral and written, though this in its turn will bring us back once more from a rather different angle to recognise a certain decisiveness of biblical influence within the European context. There are, for our purposes, three sorts of language. First, the purely or almost purely oral; secondly, written vernaculars; thirdly, universal languages. Language is the first great media invention of humankind but for thousands of years it was unwritten and unwritten language alters fast across distances of both time and place. The consequence is a huge diversity of languages, each expressive of a distinct ethnicity, of so-called dialects within languages, and a basic arbitrariness in deciding when a dialect becomes a language. Mutual intelligibility is not much of a criterion, for oral language changes on a territorial continuum so that while dialect A can be understood by a speaker of B, B by speakers of C, and C by speakers of D, A cannot be understood by speakers of D. Are A and D one language? Are their speakers of the same ethnicity? No external categories can in reality do justice to the complexity of social and linguistic experience but the mutability of a purely oral language certainly militates against the development of a clear social identity derived from its use other than a highly local one. But once a language is written down, the process of change becomes far more limited and a degree of linguistic uniformity comes to prevail across far longer distances of space and time. From this can derive an explicit consciousness of community drawn from the unity of what may still be essentially a vernacular language. The mere writing of a vernacular by a handful of people does not establish the enhanced status of a written vernacular of this sort. Its social effect will depend upon the extent to which the written language impinges upon popular usage and becomes something of a recognised standard, a medium that ordinary people can respond to. The more a vernacular develops a literature with a popular impact, particularly a religious and legal literature, the more it seems to push its speakers from the category of an ethnicity towards that of a nation.

Even in the ancient world of the Roman Empire something of the sort was happening. The usage of two written languages, Latin and Greek, each with a vast literature of its own, in fact created two social identities, quite unrelated to any underlying ethnicity, almost two nations, although that was held back by the underlying political ideal of a single 'universal' empire. Some may be disturbed by the idea that, in a sense, texts can produce peoples. But there is really no alternative. A community, political, religious, or whatever, is essentially a creation of human communication and it is only to be expected that the form of the communication will determine the character of the community.

In early pre-modern societies the uses of writing were relatively limited and the advantages of restricting writing to one or another 'universal' language were considerable. In the case of western Europe, Latin was for long both useful and flexible; medieval Latin answered the needs of the church, of learning, of a vague political continuity with the Roman Empire. It was far less its 'sacredness' (as sometimes suggested) than its utility to church and society which for long ensured its living survival. What alternative was there? Were people really to build up centres of scholarship based upon languages in which hitherto very little had been written? The idea is absurd. In many other circumstances too – such as modern Africa – there develops a dual system: a single 'high' language used for literature, government and long-distance trade and a multitude of almost unwritten vernaculars. People normally experience no difficulty with living inside a stable dual system of this sort and there are many advantages. Nevertheless there is also a natural tendency for the vernaculars of large and prosperous groups to push ahead with their written form. Most people, after all, will have a fairly limited grip of the universal language, if any at all, which will in consequence lack for them the richness of vocabulary and meaning of a truly home language. Some education in the vernacular seems sensible in almost any society and books seem needed for this, particularly in a society like early Christian Ireland, one quickly gripped by the excitement of literature but in which knowledge of the universal language was exceptionally restricted for Europe at that time. It is hardly surprising that the vernacular literature of Europe begins here and in Wales – even before the end of the sixth century. They were followed by most of the larger language groups of western Europe before the year 1000. A restricted written use of the vernacular may not greatly alter its social role or lead it to challenge the domination of the universal language but once a lively vernacular literature starts to roll, the pattern easily shifts. The more the vernacular is written, the more stable it becomes, the wider its ability to express current ideas, the larger the number of people who will understand one another better by using it and not something else. This almost of necessity begins to create what one may call at least a 'proto-nation' and its users start to see all sorts of benefits in further retrenching the use of the universal language in religion, government and education. At the same time as challenging the universal language's hegemony, the written vernacular restricts the diversity and divisiveness of purely oral vernaculars or dialects, though it may also leave them in place in the purely domestic arena by simply taking over and expanding some of the duties hitherto performed by a universal language. It becomes in fact – as High German has been for centuries in relation to German dialects of great diversity, some of which still flourish – a sort of new, more localised, but more vibrant, universal language.

Oral languages are proper to ethnicities; widely written vernaculars to nations. That is a simplification requiring all sorts of qualifications, but it is sufficiently true to provide a base from which to work on the refinements. The question we need first to face is what pressures make possible a successful take-off from orality to literacy. The advantages for the state, commerce and religious institutions in a universal language – Greek, Latin, Arabic or, in many parts of the modern non-western world, English, French or Spanish – are obvious enough to make the large written development of a vernacular, let alone a multitude of vernaculars, require explanation where it has actually happened. From our end of the telescope it may seem an obvious enough development, only held up by the intransigence of some backward-looking church, clinging on to a 'sacred' language. Yet the fact is that the immense educational advance of the high Middle Ages through the growth of universities would be unimaginable in the form it took or the speed of its development if Paris, Bologna, Oxford, Cambridge and Cologne could not all have used the same language, the same texts. It was the secular efficiency, not the sacrality, of Latin which ensured its long survival. Exactly the same is true in regard to English in the universities of modern Africa: Ibadan, Legon, Makerere or Nairobi. The advantages were so considerable that Francis Bacon and other savants of the seventeenth century were still writing some of their most important works in Latin.

What then made the anti-universalist breakthrough in early modern Europe possible? Doubtless there were a number of factors involved but a very strong case can be made for the claim that the single most effective factor was the desire of many Christians, clerical and lay, to translate the Bible or produce other works conducive to popular piety. I will return in chapter 8 to the reasons for the deep Christian thrust to vernacularise, a thrust which had been behind the switch from Greek to Latin in the western church many centuries earlier. There appears in this an intrinsic difference between the Christian and the Muslim approach to language use. But once the ball of a vernacular literature had begun to roll, with translations of the psalms, summaries of the gospels, lives of the saints and manuals of morality, it moved naturally enough from fulfilling religious to secular needs and the impact of codes of law in the vernacular – Welsh, Irish or English – could be as nation-forming as anything religious.

One of Benedict Anderson's more interesting arguments concerns the effect of the multiplication of books upon the ability of people to imagine themselves members of a community as large as a nation. Yet it could never be a matter of groundless imagining – rather a growth in realisation of, and preoccupation with, certain important shared characteristics. Print capitalism, he claims, alone made it possible. In so far as this is true it is, nevertheless, hard to see, on his own admission about the numerical growth of books already in the sixteenth century, why this effect of print capitalism should be postponed to the end of the eighteenth. Furthermore, one should not ignore the genuinely capitalistic development of a mass book trade well before the arrival of printing. The effect of a relatively small increase in the number of books in a community which has, hitherto, had none or very few is far greater than people in a world used to a surfeit of books can easily realise, and it extends far beyond the literate. Thus the impact of a vernacular literature in shaping the consciousness of communities hitherto untouched by printing in, say, late nineteenth- and early twentieth-century Africa could be enormous. It is not that everyone, or most people, could read. The social impact of written literature may even be greater when that is not the case. What can be so decisive in such circumstances is the mediation of the authority of the written text across certain privileged forms of orality. Again the extent to which an oral literature too can be the medium for a people's self-imagining is not something, unfortunately, Anderson seems to have considered. Yet the faithful handing on of an extensive oral literature by many peoples is something which of late anthropologists have taken very seriously.[45]

Given these considerable reservations, there is still sufficient force in the main point of Anderson's argument to ask whether the crucial issue arising from it may be just when and where the Bible or its equivalent appeared in the vernacular and circulated in considerable quantities. Evidence of translation alone is not enough or only half enough for our argument. Half enough because Bible translation already indicates a society and a vernacular judged capable of making use of it. Not enough, because it remains less important for us whether a translation was made than whether and how it was used. Only extensive use can bring with it a nationalising effect, and that means use at a popular, and not merely academic, level. In regard to such effective diffusion, the presence or absence of a vernacular liturgy was also of the greatest importance. Even if the number of available copies of the vernacular Bible was small and almost only in the hands of the clergy, if the liturgy was celebrated in the vernacular, its influence was extremely wide. Where it was not celebrated in the vernacular, as in almost all Roman Catholic societies, it might be much smaller.

It is fascinating to know that a complete Bible in Catalan was printed in 1478, preceded in the field of western European vernacular Bibles only by German in 1466 and Italian in 1471. That says a lot about medieval Catalonia. Nevertheless the Catalan Bible was soon ruthlessly suppressed so that not a single complete copy survives. Again, while several Spanish translations of the Bible were printed in the sixteenth century, none was printed in Spain. The existence of a Spanish Bible printed in Amsterdam cannot be taken as likely evidence of its nation-building effect at home. On the other hand, although there was no printed English Bible before 1535, the complete Bible did exist in English, translated by John Wyclif's disciples, from the late fourteenth century and, despite ecclesiastical prohibitions, its widespread use is demonstrated by the survival of over 200 manuscripts. Vastly more striking, all the same, is the diffusion of English printed Bibles in the Elizabethan period. In the forty years from 1570 to the arrival of the King James version in 1611, there were sixteen different editions of the Bishops Bible and seventy-five of the Genevan Bible, an average of more than two a year, a fantastic record. Linked to a vernacular biblically-based liturgy which all English people were legally bound to attend, and to a multitude of catechisms – *The ABC with the Catechisme* was already 'a huge best-seller'[46] by the 1580s – the mass impact of this English Bible in strengthening a common language, installing in all its hearers and readers the idea of nationhood and actually shaping the English of all classes into an awareness of their own nationhood cannot be overstated. Something similar was happening in Holland, Sweden, Denmark, Germany and elsewhere, though it looks as if, with the exception of Holland, these countries were well behind England in the quantitative dissemination of Bibles until the eighteenth century and the impact of Pietism.[47]

While it would be a great over-simplification to regard the vernacular Bible as the sole catalyst for language unification or to claim that the development of a national consciousness could not be achieved through other means, nevertheless as a matter of fact the correlation between biblical translation and what one may call a national awakening is remarkably close across most of Europe and, quite often, for other parts of the world as well. The fact that a string of highly diverse dialects continued to be spoken in Germany long after the huge publication success of Luther's Bible detracts rather little from the nation-making function of the written form of the language, especially when used publicly in a regular way as in the services of a state church. The two could continue in tandem just as Latin and the vernaculars lived together in an earlier age. What, however, significantly differentiated the one case from the other was that in the later one everyone could recognise the bond and underlying unity between their particular oral dialect and the single written form of a language employed by both church and state. Long before the advent of mass primary education vernacular culture and established authority had thus come together again as seed-bed of the nation-state. But this was, as we have seen, principally a Protestant reality.

What is a nation? Anderson makes another valuable point when he suggests that what is most characteristic of a nation is a felt horizontality in its membership – 'the nation is always conceived as a deep horizontal comradeship'.[48] Horizontal images are something we will come back to from time to time as one yardstick of the presence of this sort of society. What we have to look for in nation-spotting is a historico-cultural community with a territory it regards as its own and over which it claims some sort of sovereignty so that the cultural community sees itself with a measure of self-awareness as also a territorial and political community, held together horizontally by its shared character rather than vertically by reason of the authority of the state.

Even when it is the state which has created the nation, it is not a nation until it senses its primacy over and against the state. What its shared character is felt chiefly to consist in is quite another matter and open to vast diversity: the territory itself may provide the basic criterion in one case, language in another reflecting the myth of pure ethnic origin, religion may be effectively decisive in a third. These different criteria do produce very different types of nation and different types of nationalism as well. We have already referred to the contrast as defined by Brubaker between French and German forms. But it would be a mistake to try to categorise nations and nationalism in just two types – 'western' and 'eastern' or whatever. In reality every nation is a unique socio-historical construct. The shaping of Dutchness, of Spanishness, of Irishness has in each case to be examined in its own historical evolution, quite as much as Frenchness, Germanness or Englishness.

Nor is it a simple matter of a nation existing or not existing. Nations grow out of ethnicities, out of wars and religious divisions,

25

out of the emergence of literatures and nationalist propaganda and administrative pressures, but they do so bit by bit, so that at a given point of time one often cannot simply say 'this is a nation' or 'this is not'. Eugen Weber speaks helpfully in regard to France of 'the nation not as a given reality but as a work-in-progress'.[49] Even a process in reverse is possible. Scottish nationhood may have existed, then declined in the degree of its reality, but now be advancing once more. Again, one cannot say that for a nation to exist it is necessary that everyone within it should want it to exist or have full consciousness that it does exist; only that many people beyond government circles or a small ruling class should consistently believe in it. A nation exists when a range of its representatives hold it to exist – clergy, farmers, lawyers, merchants, writers, as well as members of a court or cabinet. The more people of a variety of class and occupation share in such consciousness, the more it exists, but it would be quite unreasonable to establish norms for its existence really only appropriate to a twentieth-century, mass-media society. It appears, rightly or wrongly, to be axiomatic to our subject that an American nation had come to exist in 1776 though the consciousness of being part of it was hardly offered to, or included, black slaves. Equally it does not invalidate the existence of a nation in early modern Europe that many of the peasantry had little sense of being part of it. But, of course, if a specific society was overwhelmingly one of peasants and nobles only, then that might indeed be a decisive difficulty.

The frontiers of a nation are not unalterable. It does not invalidate the existence of a nation in, say, 1700, that it did not then include territory and ethnicities today fully incorporated within it. A nation can grow in size while remaining substantially the same reality. The fact that it was only in the nineteenth century that Switzerland was extended to include the Italian-speaking Ticino and some French-speaking areas, including Geneva, does not mean that the Swiss could not have been a nation before that date. It was perfectly possible for the German-speaking core of the country, existing in a federal and thoroughly horizontalist way far earlier, already to have the characteristics of a nation. Again, true as it is that well into the nineteenth century in large parts of France the majority of the population did not speak French and had little sense of being French, as Weber has demonstrated so convincingly in *Peasants into Frenchmen*, this does not prove that there was not, from a much earlier date, a French nation in existence, centred upon Paris. It would really be very difficult to give a convincing account of the Revolution, if it was not that of a nation, of all classes, sharing a language, culture and sense of territorial and political identity. That nationhood was not created by the Revolution but existed prior to 1789, even if it needed the Revolution fully to actualise itself.

Nations, then, grow in geographical spread and intensity of self-awareness. It becomes a mark of their self-confidence that some can incorporate people, even entire ethnicities, very different from the ethnicity out of which the nation originally developed. They can also decline or even disappear, surviving only as a matter of ethnic or provincial loyalty, though it can also be the case that such disappearances are temporary only and more apparent than real. While ethnicities can fade into nations, nations cannot so easily merge with one another. And even ethnicities do not lightly fade away. Saxon, Dane and Norman could finally merge in England by the thirteenth century with mere minor family, class and provincial divergences, but they had taken their time. The fusion of Walloon and Flemish ethnicities into a single Belgian nation, to take another example, while it may have appeared to be working successfully as long as Belgium had an overseas empire for both to share, can now be seen to have been in part imaginary with an imagination that has lost its magic. In the mid-1970s many a Yugoslav would have asserted uncompromisingly that there was now a Yugoslav nation and Croat, Serb or Slovene identities were mere provincial ethnicities. Today the stress is entirely upon the unbroken national existence of these different peoples.

Nationhood can survive only through an exercise in imagination, both collective and personal, and imagined things can prove very impermanent. Yet some of them can be toughly enduring as well. The history of the way we see ourselves, the interaction of social understanding and the world around us, is never predictable and in the experience of nationhood, as of ethnicity too, the level of unpredictability seems particularly high.

III

Let us turn now from a review of the concept of nationhood to one of nationalism. Early forms of nationalism related to states already in existence, their defence, glorification or expansion. England, as we shall see, was the quintessential example of this, but Scotland already in the fourteenth century provides another example: the wars of liberation to rescue the Scottish state from English dominance produced a recognisable nationalism. In this case, a state preceded the nationalism but the nation may rather have followed it.

Seventeenth-century Holland and Revolutionary France are basically similar. Holland was created in its separatedness by a religious struggle, but, once established, nationalism largely took over from religion. French nationalism in the era of the Revolution presupposed a French state and involved a crusade to carry French values abroad, ensuring their export, as likely as not, by French force of arms. Such state-engendered nationalism turned imperialist triggered a vast wave of new ones, relating to the construction of nation-states which did not then exist. This new wave is said to constitute the 'Age of Nationalism' about which most theorists of nationalism are chiefly concerned. It is this phenomenon, a sort of Mark II nationalism, that we need now to review as a whole. First, we should note the importance of what Anderson calls 'pirating'[50] – the taking over of an attractive model from one society to another, essentially in reality the passing across of an English model, first to Scotland, next to America, and then, with an ever-increasing range of sub-models, to France and elsewhere. It was pirated because it was seen to work, linking together people and state in a manner that produced a great deal of power and some progress. Thus Greenfeld argues that 'the dominance of England in eighteenth-century Europe, and then the dominance of the West in the world, made nationality the canon'.[51] 'The canon' may, again, be quite a useful concept to keep in mind. If eighteenth-century England presented the world with a new 'canon', consisting at once of nation-state, an industrialising social economy and parliamentary government, and the three together appeared to go with social stability, military success and considerable prosperity, then one can expect that other societies will endeavour to pirate this model and reconstruct themselves as parliamentary nation-states. But societies still needed appropriate internal pressures if they were to respond to such a programme in a way capable of arousing the masses or shaking the status quo.

The multiplication of nationalisms from the nineteenth century on derived chiefly from two kinds of pressure. The first lay in the relationship between ethnicity and non-nation-states once they began to modernise. The modern state can be contrasted with the traditional state by the quantity of its interference in local life and culture through administrative developments of all sorts, the enforcement of uniform standards, the control and extension of formal education, the scale of taxation. The traditional state impinged so slightly on the lives of most ordinary people, except in moments of crisis, that it did not disrupt or inflame local ethnic patterns unduly. A state could exist very easily with a multiplicity of ethnicities within it, employing different languages and even systems of local government and customary law. As a state modernises this becomes impossible without a thorough policy of federalism or pluriformity – something exceptionally difficult to achieve to the satisfaction of all sides. The traditional state did not need to turn its people into a nation, it hardly wanted to do so. The pre-Revolutionary French monarchy is a case in point. Very little effort was made to try to ensure that the inhabitants of France could even speak French. Why bother to risk disturbing the tranquillity of Brittany? The modern state has necessarily to do so, to attempt to turn its people into a nation, that is to say a state in which the sense of its history, its law, educational system and patriotism are consciously shared. The language of government inevitably comes to impinge upon countless people who have not hitherto had any need to understand it. Even in so clearly a non-nation-state as the Habsburg Empire, government policies were inevitably taking on the note of those of a nation-state. As the pressure of a state's modernisation mounts, ethnicities which have existed hitherto within its borders in a condition of suspended animation are inevitably drawn into its wider consciousness. They can come to do so willingly enough so long as there is sufficient continuity of culture between one and the other. A multitude of ethnicities may be fused into a single nation. As this happens their differentiating traits necessarily diminish and may either disappear almost completely or become simply a matter of regional survivals or local folklore. They may also survive with clear but limited borders within the nation where a minority language is explicitly recognised.

Switzerland provides an excellent example of the survival of significant ethnic diversity within a single nation. It could hardly have happened without a strong federalist constitution. An ethnicity is of its nature a single language community but a nation, because of its far more self-conscious definition of itself, does not need to be. There is no doubt that the Swiss continue to contain within them a clear diversity of ethnicities marked by four different languages, each with its own area; there can equally be no question that they have made of this a single nation. Such diversity within a nation is evidence not of a diminished, but of a mature, nationhood.

In the Swiss case the nation-state could not have fused the ethnicities with impunity. In many other cases it has tried to do so, sometimes successfully, but often quite unsuccessfully. Fusion may naturally and successfully take place in cases where a group of ethnicities were already fairly close together in language, custom, religion and history, and where the state does not appear to favour one ethnicity and its characteristics against another. But the more a modern state defines itself in terms of a single central authority or in terms which at least appear to exclude or question the identity of one of its constituent ethnicities, the more it blocks the latter from a progressive transition into one national life, and forces it instead to develop a self-protective movement, which we call nationalism, demanding the right of separate self-determination, to be a nation apart.

To put it like that is to define the causative process of nationalism in terms external to an ethnicity, but it needs also a second pressure, an adequate internal dynamism. Small ethnicities easily succumb to the pressures of state construction, however unimaginatively the latter are mediated, if an ethnicity's resources, economic, linguistic, ideological or geographical, are too limited. Its settlement pattern may be too diffuse to provide a viable area of resistance geographically; its members may be so poor as to be swallowed up in the economy of the dominant ethnicity; its language may be merely an oral vernacular, so little used in a literary way that it appears incapable of challenging the claims of that of the state for administrative and educational purposes; it may have no religion, ideology or historical tradition of its own sharp enough to set it apart from that of the state and so provide the imaginative base for resistance. Such is the case for many hundreds of small African, Amazonian and Asian ethnicities, some of which simply disappear within a few years under external pressures.

The sort of ethnicity which is likely to develop nationalism in self-defence is one with control of a clear territorial core, one sufficient in size of population and local economy to be able to avoid economic strangulation; one with something of a literary vernacular of its own; and one which possesses a religion or historical tradition markedly different from that of the majority in the state of which it has been part. The rise of nationalism in any particular group of people is something far less arbitrary than is sometimes suggested. It is rather an almost inevitable consequence of the interaction of a range of external and internal factors of this sort. The less intrusive state formation there is, the less ethnicities will turn nationalist; but, equally, the more they have advanced towards a self-conscious separate identity, an identity of language or religion, the more likely they are to respond to intrusion by adopting the option of nationalism.

The most influential and widespread single internal factor in this is almost certainly, as I have already suggested, the literary development of a spoken vernacular. Arguments for and against the linguistic base for nation-formation almost invariably concentrate upon orality whereas the decisive factor is in reality the literary one.[52] It is when its vernacular possesses a literature that a society seems to feel confident enough to challenge the dominance of outsiders. Moreover the bond between the written language, perhaps used only by the few, with the oral language forms used by everyone, can ensure that a linguistically based nationalism quickly gains support even in largely non-literate communities.

A language, moreover, does not stand on its own. Once a significant vernacular literature exists, it creates a more conscious community of those who read it, of those in whose houses it is to be found and it quickly builds up an enhanced sense of historical cultural particularity. Every ethnicity, I would conclude, has a nation-state potentially within it but in the majority of cases that potentiality will never be activated because its resources are too small, the allurement of incorporation within an alternative culture and political system too powerful. But the intrinsic connection between ethnicity, nation and nationalism is not to be gainsaid. It provides the sole intelligible starting point for a theory of nationalism.

Finally we do, I think, need to remind ourselves that nationalism does not necessarily or always imply that national values are placed above all other values, or that they alone are recognised as real, important and worth defending. Most members of a nation and many nationalists have other communities of loyalty to which they also belong and to which they may, on occasion, give superior recognition – communities of religion, family or class. The extreme nationalist will indeed regard all other values as insignificant compared with the imagined requirements of the nation but many nationalists would see those requirements as limited to some extent by other requirements of morality, religion or even the rights of other communities. Certainly, most members of a nation or potential nation-state are, most of the time, far from being extreme nationalists, or even nationalists of any sort. Nationalism often exists as a latent presence, something which flares up extremely quickly in times of war or some real or imagined threat and can then become overwhelmingly and irrationally strong, to subside in altered circumstances almost as quickly as it has been inflamed. One may well say that its ability to do this is closely linked to the sheer irrationality of its claims for the supreme sacredness of its own particularist values. Far less than any religion or ideology can a nationalism justify extreme claims in rational terms because of its inherent particularism.

I gave my first public lecture in 1955. It was in Rome, in Italian, given to hundreds of my fellow students in the ecclesiastical universities of the city of almost every nationality, and interestingly enough, it was on nationalism. In it I quoted Pierre de Menasce to suggest that the theory of nationalism was 'always based on autarchy – only that which is indigenous is of value, all that is indigenous is *ipso facto* of value'[53] and, I continued, 'They nourish historical grievances, about which other people have long ceased to think; they are intolerant of everything and everyone coming from outside their own national group' and yet in fact, while committed to an extreme particularism, they 'all speak the same language'. Nevertheless then, as now, I wanted to appeal for recognition of the good, as well as the bad, in nationalist movements. The historian, in particular, needs to be fortified not only against defending the claims of an extreme nationalism of any sort, but also against a mistaken distaste for nationalism of any sort.

Rationality is universalist of its nature. The claims of the particular, nevertheless, are not necessarily irrational. On the contrary. The character of human life as experienced in the historical reality of a vast diversity of cultures, languages and beliefs is inherently particularist. The values which most people cherish are largely the values of their own culture and people. We can cherish the cultural tradition of our own upbringing, and even prefer it to any other, while recognising that the totality of human culture is itself of supreme human benefit. The imposition of uniformity, where not genuinely required, is the imposition of a cultural impoverishment often demanded these days with particular arrogance on grounds of economic or political advantage. Such policies go on advancing ruthlessly, in the words of the poet David Jones,

> Till everything presuming difference
> and all the sweet remembered demarcations wither
> to the touch of us.

The positive side of nationalism, undergirded by a profound rationality, is a passion to defend the particular treasures of a given human tradition lying inside 'the sweet remembered demarcations' now apparently threatened by some alien force. It is quite often a lost cause yet it is perfectly possible to mount an essentially philosophical justification of a moderate nationalism as David Miller does very effectively in his recent work, *On Nationality* (1995). Once again I cannot, therefore, agree with Eric Hobsbawm when in the final paragraph of his Introduction he declares that 'no serious historian of nations and nationalism can be a committed political nationalist'.[54] The two are not compatible, he urges, 'any more than being a Zionist is compatible with writing a genuinely serious history of the Jews'[55] unless, he adds, 'the historian leaves his or her convictions behind when entering the library or the study'. That, of course, is not something in one's power to do. Hobsbawm can no more leave his 'non-historical' Marxist convictions behind than I my Christian and Liberal ones. And no historian exists without 'non-historical' convictions, whether or not she or he is aware of them. It is surely better to be aware of them and historicise with them, recognising that they affect our value judgements and that there is no value-free, purely objective, history. The point is that a commitment to Christianity, for example, provides insights which can enrich histor- ical understanding though it may also lead to prejudices and blind- ness. So it is with nationalism. Its worst failing is so to highlight the rights of one particularity as to become blind to those of all others. Nationalism is to be justified as an appropriate protest against a universalising uniformity, dominance by the other, but its consequence is too often precisely the imposition of uniformity, a deep intolerance of all particularities except one's own. But one may actually be best placed to pinpoint its irrational, destructive and truly evil dimensions, if one has shared from the inside and almost nationalistically a specific cultural tradition in all its rich particularity. Nor has one's nationalism necessarily to be only cultural; indeed it cannot be. Public culture implies the political and one can justify being a committed political nationalist in some circumstances just as one can justify being a committed Marxist or Christian. We must not *a priori* place nationalism in a quite different category, but we can and must recognise that just as both Christianity and Marxism have inspired vast human abuses, so has nationalism, particularly forms of nationalism based on criteria inherently productive of intolerance.

A nationalism grounded on *jus soli* can in principle assist neighbours of different languages and cultures inclusively to live together and accept one another as members of a single national society, while a nationalism grounded on *jus sanguinis* is in principle exclusivist and intolerant. Given the fact that in most parts of the world people of quite different backgrounds, races, languages and religions do live cheek by jowl and have nearly always done so, *jus sanguinis* leads logically to ethnic cleansing, *jus soli* to ethnic integration. Nationalisms have to be stringently categorised if they are to be tamed. Remodelling is less impossible than abolition and historians of nationalism have surely some responsibility to examine and help modify its undoubted destructiveness.

CHAPTER TWO

England as prototype

What have I done for you,
England, my England?
What is there I would not do,
England, my own?

William Ernest Henley's poem certainly fits Anderson's dating for a
surge of English nationalism at the end of the nineteenth century.
We may note in passing that it was still England, not Britain, that
Henley hailed as 'chosen daughter of the Lord', but while his poem,
like many others, certainly shows that English nationalism was alive
and well in the 1880s, it does not at all show where it began, and that
is the question which must concern us now. One can find historians
to date 'the dawn of English national consciousness' (or some such
phrase) in almost every century from the eighth to the nineteenth. If
Anderson puts it in the heyday of late Victorian imperialism and
Greenfeld in the early years of the Tudor monarchy, others see it as a
product of Foxe's *Book of Martyrs*, the Hundred Years War, the reign
of Stephen, the Saxon monarchy in the age of Athelstan and Edgar,
or even the Venerable Bede for whom a decisive 'role in defining
English national identity and English national destiny' has been
claimed by Patrick Wormald.[1]

There is, I suspect, a fairly widespread willingness even among
modernists to admit that late Elizabethan England was already
becoming a genuinely national society, with tinges of nationalism
strongly fed on Protestantism. A vague use of the phrase 'early
modern' and equally vague recognition of the Reformation as
'prelude' to modernity may be sufficient to assuage their modernist

suspicions. The nationalism that England would export abroad in the following century and pass on as core to an enlarged British nationalism in the eighteenth was certainly very Protestant, as Linda Colley has stressed, in its self-understanding and sense of righteous mission. But I am afraid it is still not going nearly far enough to admit a post-Reformation beginning to English nationhood. Indeed English post-Reformation nationalism is likely to be itself much misunderstood if it is not recognised to be just a new expression of something already well set several centuries earlier. We may do well at this point to listen to Patrick Wormald and start our pursuit of national identity no later than the age of Bede, even though England in his time was neither a single state nor, except in the eye of Bede himself, at once historian and national prophet, as yet a nation. But with Bede's history firmly behind us we can best approach the late Saxon period and recognise, in the unqualified words of a very recent study by James Campbell, 'the position of 1066'. 'England was by then a nation-state.'[2] Full stop.

Bede wrote his *Ecclesiastical History of the English People* about the year 730 in his monastery of Jarrow near the Northumbrian coast. It is a commonplace that England was united ecclesiastically well before it was united politically, that the Archbishop of Canterbury was primate of all England for centuries when there was no king of England, and that Bede's *Ecclesiastical History of the English* as a single people wonderfully presumes a unity that was far from obvious on the ground. We need, however, to analyse Bede's sense of unity rather more precisely than that.

Throughout the book three different levels of unity are taken for granted. The first, all too easily passed over, is that of Britain, territorially a single island but a unity in ways far beyond that. Britain extends in time as well as in place well beyond the 'gens Anglorum' he is explicitly committed to chronicle. It is the context of the whole story, a Roman context beginning with Julius Caesar. It is extremely symbolic of his thinking that this history of the English people has as its opening word 'Brittania' and, again, that 'Brittania', now united by Christian faith, loyalty to Rome, the leadership of the English and, apparently, even a state of peace and prosperity, is the subject of its final paragraph. The continuity of English history with British history is demonstrated too by the space Bede gives to the story of St Alban, Britain's first martyr, whose cult he seems to suggest continued unbroken at Verulam. Again, Bede is careful to keep, in his story, not only the tiresome Britons themselves but the Scots and Picts as well. Indeed the last pages of his book are largely devoted to Bishop Ceolfrid's letter to the King of the Picts and events on the island of Iona. The ecclesiastical history Bede set himself to write is clearly not just one of the English people in any narrow sense, despite the opening words of the preface, it is a history of Britain and we have already in Bede the possibility of a certain confusion between England and Britain which twelve hundred years later we have not really overcome.

The second level of unity is the specifically ecclesiastical – a unity dependent upon the archiepiscopal see of Canterbury and the most scrupulous obedience to the apostolic see of Rome. A church centred in Canterbury with bishops in London, Winchester, York, Lindisfarne and elsewhere vastly transcended the political divisions of seven or eight petty kingdoms. In his final chapter Bede stressed that the present Archbishop of Canterbury came from Mercia. The British churches, too, were all, at least theoretically, subject to Canterbury, but the ecclesiastical unity maintained by Canterbury was effectively the unity of the churches of the English. That is the point at which Bede's ecclesiastical history becomes almost necessarily a national history, an account of the 'gens Anglorum'.

This represents the third level at which he implies an existent unity. It is the one which most immediately concerns us, though in his view of things it could only make sense in the context of the other two. Yet it is, in a way, the most unexpected. Bede himself insists that three different Germanic peoples came to Britain – the Saxons, the Angles and the Jutes – and that they set up a whole series of distinct kingdoms, the Jutes in Kent, the Saxons in various southern districts, the Angles in East Anglia, Mercia and North-umbria. Nevertheless by the time he is writing – some three hundred years after the early migrations and a hundred years after their Christian conversion – he takes it for granted that this whole medley of peoples and kingdoms has become a single nation, 'gens Anglor-um', the people of the English, and he regularly uses the name 'English' to include not only Northumbrians and other Angles, but Saxons and Jutes. He does not, however, for one moment, think that it includes the other peoples of Britain – Britons, Scots and Picts. Britain is one but it includes four peoples with four languages. The

English, he has no doubt at all – meaning Saxons, Angles and Jutes – are now a single nation with a single language and a single church.

In his preface, addressed to King Ceolwulf of Northumbria, we get the Bede approach at its most succinct. He is extremely respectful in offering the king this history of his people but he makes it absolutely clear that it is in no way a history of Northumbria alone. On the contrary. It is history centred quite considerably on Canterbury, hugely dependent upon information obtained from a priest in London, and yet something not actually presented as a history of the church at all. It is, indeed, an ecclesiastical history but its subject is the 'gens Anglorum'. Its unity is at least as much that of the nation as that of the church, while being implicitly a history of Brittania too. It is particularly remarkable that at this, the book's defining moment, Northumbria, Mercia and the rest are described simply as 'provincia', the provinces of a single country, even though he is addressing the king of one of them. Bede stresses the continuity of this sort of history with the study of the scriptures, on which he had written so many commentaries, and it is hardly imaginable that he did not see continuity between the history of the people of Israel and the history of his own people. Exactly the same spiritual and providential principles were applicable to both. Each was a nation under God. The English would suffer divine punishment, just as the people of Israel, if they deviated from the right path.

Bede, like the Vulgate, normally uses the word 'gens', not the word 'natio', but in his preface's final paragraph he prefers to use the latter when he reaffirms that he has written the 'historia nostrae nationis', the history of our own nation. Here, then, in his preface for King Ceolwulf we see the first verbal appearance of the English 'nation', something we earlier traced back in the vernacular to the fourteenth century. If the nationalism of intellectuals, the Rousseaus, Herders and Fichtes, precedes the existence of nations, as the modernists argue, and it is their 'imagining' which brings a nation into being, then Bede is undoubtedly the first, and probably the most influential, such case. It is just that he wrote his books in the eighth, and not the nineteenth, century. In his Northumbrian monastery he did indeed imagine England; he did it through intensely biblical glasses, but no less through linguistic and ecclesiastical ones, and he did it so convincingly that no dissentient imagining of his country has ever since seemed quite credible. The very considerable number of manuscripts of the history surviving – including four from the eighth century – demonstrate how widely Bede's construction of his country's history was welcomed. When, a hundred and fifty years later, Alfred, most imaginative of West Saxon kings, was endeavouring to create a vernacular literature for his people (rather like President Julius Nyerere creating a Swahili literature for Tanzania eleven centuries later and sitting down himself to translate Shakespeare's *Julius Caesar*), he decided, unsurprisingly, to translate Bede's *Ecclesiastical History* into English.

It is with Alfred that we begin to move from perceiving the nation to establishing the nation-state. It happened between his reign and that of Edward the Confessor. The very perilousness of England's condition was Alfred's opportunity. The Danish invasions which so nearly swamped his own kingdom of Wessex had completely demolished all the other kingdoms. As the reconquest advanced out of Wessex it could, in consequence, unify the English rather easily. But the sense of a deeper unity, even a political unity, was already there. We see it in Alfred's own codification of law, including that of Offa of Mercia and Ethelbert of Kent as well as Ine of Wessex. If medieval society in particular was ruled by law at least as much as it was ruled by kings, then Alfred's uniting of the laws of various kingdoms was a way of saying that they had already been something of a single political community as well as a linguistic one. His quite extraordinarily precocious attempt to establish a vernacular literature with a programme of translation including Gregory and Boethius as well as Bede was no less nation-forging. The elements, then, are already there with Alfred – national language, national literature, national law and that element of horizontality suggested by the characteristically Saxon institution, the Witan: 'I, Alfred, king of the West Saxons, shewed these to all my Witan, and they then said that it seemed good to them all to be holden.'[3]

In Alfred's time, however, a large portion of the English and of England remained outside his kingdom. The unification of peoples is the achievement of his successors, Danish as well as English. What, however, ensured that the unity of a shared vernacular law was reflected sufficiently in the life of the people as a whole to make of late Saxon England a quite unmistakable nation-state was the triple impact of economic life, political administration and religion. The vitality and regularity of the economy is suggested as well as anything by the scale and orderliness of the coinage, with literally millions of coins regularly produced throughout the country with dies all of which were cut in London. The combination of centralised control and decentralised production is remarkable. Thus we know of at least forty-four places in which coins were minted in the short nine-month reign of Harold Godwinson, every coin being identified by both the name of its moneyer and the place where it was struck. The late Saxon currency is proof both of the country's economic vitality and of the government's administrative efficiency. When a regular currency was introduced in the Scandinavian countries of Denmark, Sweden and Norway, in every case it was modelled on the pennies of Aethelred II.

When speaking of commerce, it is also appropriate to refer to London, already the country's economic capital. The role of London in creating a nation-state can hardly be overemphasised. It was already the heart pumping the economy, but it was more than that. There was no other town of remotely comparable size, but London's national unifying role was so effective because it was neither a regional nor a royal one. London was not Wessex, nor Northumbria, nor the Danelaw. It was only, very marginally, even Mercia. Its identity was very much its own, the point where Saxon, Angle and Jute met but no less the point where the English encountered the continuity of Roman Britain. Nor was London in principle a royal city. The early kings of England are buried at Winchester. Even after the Conquest, Westminster was only one of three places in which the king wore his crown at a major feast, and it is noteworthy that the royal palace developed at Westminster well to the west of the city. Eleventh-century London was also already playing a major independent role in military and political history. Theoretically we cannot as yet call it the capital. In reality, it was so much the capital that it was both creating and sustaining the country around it.

To turn to administration. I have long thought that if there was one institution which produced the English nation it was the shire. The shires were already in place (except north of Tees and Ribble) by the early eleventh century. They were ideally constructed to develop both the reality and the consciousness of a united country. Royal creations, neither feudal nor tribal in origin, they were too small to be seriously separatist yet important enough to focus loyalty in an essentially horizontalist and healthily emulative way, with the shire courts bringing a great many people regularly together, as did service in the local fyrd. The shires – backed by that parallel Saxon institution, the boroughs and borough courts – were to provide the building blocks of the nation for a thousand years.

To commerce and local administration add the church and books, the start of whose impact goes back, as we have seen, to a far earlier date than the political unification of the people. The church of the age of Dunstan was a highly national institution, its life integrated with that of the state in countless ways and productive of a vernacular theology unparalleled elsewhere in pre-twelfth-century Europe. But the English vernacular writing of the tenth and eleventh centuries was by no means all by clerics or for clerics. The scripture translations should have for us a particular significance on account of what we may best call their ideological influence. They included the Gospels and large parts of the Old Testament; with these may be included the Rule of St Benedict and other major ecclesiastical works. To them add the laws, the chronicles, the poetry (30,000 lines of Anglo-Saxon poetry are still extant), the sermons, the medical texts, and the range and quantity of vernacular literature appears quite remarkably rounded and functional for the needs of a nation. As Dorothy Whitelock insisted thirty years ago, 'The glory of the late Anglo-Saxon period was its English writing. At a time when no vernacular prose of any distinction had appeared on the Continent, the Anglo-Saxons had developed a language of great copiousness and flexibility, capable of rendering Latin works on theology, philosophy and science.'[4] Much of this was clearly written for a lay clientele as well as for the clergy. If the equation of a significant vernacular literature and a nation bears any weight at all, it must be applicable here.

Unsurprisingly, it is hard to find explicit expression of nationalist feeling in surviving texts from the old English state but it is worth pointing to a few suggestive passages. National feeling is most manifest in war and it was the Danish invasions which produce here and there a more distinctly national note. One sees it in brief remarks in the chronicles such as the admiring sentence in the account of English resistance in 1010, 'Then stood Cambridgeshire firm',[5] or in many a phrase in *The Battle of Maldon*, that most stirring of war poems. Here, despite the poem's rather old-fashioned stress on loyalty to the eorl and the duty of dying where he died (which may be seen, though perhaps mistakenly, as a vertical rather than horizontal bonding) the principal message is simply that of the heroic defence by a mixed band of Englishmen of 'their land, the land of Ethelred the King, the place and the people'. The poem goes out of its way to stress that thanes were fighting side by side with churls, Mercians with East Saxons, a poem about national horizontality, the bonding of men who had 'rallied each other in the wide room where we met at mead, making each man a bigger boast than his brother of the wine-bench'. Byrhtnoth, the doomed earl of Essex, began the battle by rejecting the Viking terms: 'Shall our people, our nation, bear you to go hence with our gold?'[6] *The Battle of Maldon* was surely an appeal to the nation to stand firm against invasion. A third, final, example, comes from the pen of Aelfric, the leading ecclesiastical writer of his time. In a letter to a nobleman named Sigeward he explains the purpose of his translation of the Book of Judith in similar terms: 'It is set down in English in our manner, as an example to you people that you should defend your land against the invading army with weapons.'[7] These examples illustrate well enough national sentiment in the old English state when under attack. England is seen in biblical terms, a nation to be defended as the Israel of the Old Testament was defended. One feels aware of the sense of a people, kingdom and land, something regularly called 'England' though sometimes more grandly 'Britain', holding together local loyalties – old ones to Mercia, new ones to Cambridgeshire – all of which can contribute to the national defence in which Dunnere, 'undaunted churl', deserves mention as much as Elfwine, the thane 'of mighty stock'.

I do not really think one can fault James Campbell's claim that England is to be reckoned a nation-state before 1066. It would certainly seem to possess all the characteristics required for nationhood by Anthony Smith.[8] Perhaps a chief reason why it was at this point centuries ahead of any other west European society lay in the assistance it had received from the clear territorial delimitation granted by an island and a fairly small area, things which the French and the Germans, whose advance in vernacular literature was partially comparable, manifestly lacked. Yet Ireland was more compact territorially and also had a far greater homogeneity of population than England, but it quite failed to develop in the same sort of way. It was not that eleventh-century Ireland lacked the consciousness of its own specific ethnicity, a people distinct from

others, but that this did not lead on, as in England, to the development of a nation-state. The benefits of a defined territoriality, the
politically unifying impact of ecclesiastical unity, the contribution of
two geniuses, Bede and Alfred, the stabilising of an intellectual and
linguistic world through a thriving vernacular literature, the growth
of the economy and of an effective professional royal bureaucracy, all
these are contributive to a firmly affirmative answer to 'Was England
a nation-state in 1066?' When one surveys such a range of factors
behind the English leap into early nationhood, it would be arbitrary
to regard any one on its own as necessarily decisive.

What happened at the Conquest? For many commentators,
Norman rule is held to have wiped out whatever there was of
nationhood existent in the preceding age. The wholesale substitution
of a new ruling class, the replacement of the English language by
French among the rulers and, eventually, for the law; the near
disappearance of English literary writing; the fact that England was
ruled by people whose political interests lay equally in France; the
imposition of feudalism – all this may seem more than enough to
demonstrate the absurdity of claiming any sort of nationhood for the
England of the post-Conquest period. Not until the fourteenth
century, we tended to believe, did anything reasonably describable as
the English nation begin to re-emerge. Yet one of the most
interesting things in recent medieval historiography has been the
increasingly emphatic rejection of such a conclusion.

A number of closely-argued studies by John Gillingham in
particular[9] demonstrate, to the contrary, how rapidly the conquered
digested the conquerors. If the men were disinherited, their daugh-
ters married Normans and taught their children the meaning of
Englishness. Of course there were huge changes – one sees it very
strikingly in Christian names – nevertheless it looks as if by the
middle of the twelfth century an English identity was very clearly
being re-established among the country's ruling class. Only rather
few of the most powerful men had landed interests on the continent
to divide their loyalty, while the structures, administrative system,
ecclesiastical order, myths of origin of the country the rest had made
their own, remained essentially those of pre-Conquest England.
Even the cults of Anglo-Saxon saints, initially under Norman
suspicion, had largely survived. The speed of this resurgence and the
fact that by the second half of the twelfth century the invaders of

Ireland could be so generally referred to as 'the English'[10] demonstrate as well as anything how thoroughly a sense of English nationhood had taken root in pre-Conquest society. In the reign of William I the English could feel themselves an oppressed people, but by the reign of Henry II or even earlier one has a strong sense in writers like William of Malmesbury, Henry of Huntingdon, Geoffrey of Monmouth and Aelred of Rievaulx that national identity is being reasserted, an identity tied to the land, 'most noble of islands', and incorporating everyone from Romans to Normans. If Edgar was the model of modern kings and Arthur of ancient ones, everyone could find a place within an ongoing national epic. The Normans were now no different from earlier immigrants. Like the Danes a couple of generations earlier, they might conquer in war but in societal and intellectual terms they were effectively and quickly absorbed. They really had no alternative, given their limited numbers and institutional inferiority. Inside England their survival depended less on domination than upon assimilation.

One thing alone they clung to in some measure for 200 years – the use of French as a language of culture. The near disappearance of literary English for 150 years has been the chief misleader for the evaluation of twelfth- and thirteenth-century Englishness. Undoubtedly the introduction of French and the enhanced use of Latin had a crippling effect on one side of national identity. It did not mean that English as a spoken language was in any danger of abandonment and most people of Norman descent knew it and used it within, at most, two generations. But it would be foolish to doubt that the distinct, self-conscious national identity of England was temporarily weakened by the use of French – even though French could certainly be used for English nationalist purposes, as it was in Geoffrey Gaimar's *Estoire des Engleis*, which could even glorify the resistance fighter, Hereward the Wake. All the same the renaissance of English writing in the fourteenth century parallels a wider renaissance in the self-consciousness of nationhood.

The Norman infusion into English identity does, however, seem permanently to have modified it in one quite serious way. The English were not dynamically aggressive and the general picture of the relationship of the old English state with its Celtic neighbours was a relatively pacific one. Cornwall was quietly absorbed more than it was conquered. The Normans were different. The one thing

44

they were really good at was conquering people – in England, Sicily, Palestine, Wales or Ireland. And very brutally. As they fused with the English, they turned the latter into potential imperialists, and English nationalism would ever after have an imperialist tone to it, as it did not have before. Bullying does not always work. The Cornish became English without for centuries forsaking their own vernacular; the Welsh never did. From this point of view the Norman infusion was, nevertheless, fateful for our story. If the English gave the world the model of a nation-state, the Normans ensured that it would be an aggressive model, and necessarily productive of counter-nationalism among the ethnicities it overran. They also taught the English the skill they chiefly needed for military success, that of archery.

In 1295, Edward I needed money. He was at war with France, at war with the Welsh and shortly to be at war with the Scots. He was a decidedly imperialist monarch, but when imperialists are in trouble they almost invariably seek to rally support by stirring up nationalism at home. The letters summoning Parliament asserted emphatically that the King of France was planning an invasion and intended to wipe out the English language – a truly detestable plan which may God avert.[11] Who imagined this extraordinary piece of nonsense one does not know, but it is in itself something quite remarkable. The likelihood of the King of France, even if he were to conquer England, wanting to abolish its spoken vernacular is extraordinarily slight given that he already ruled a kingdom of many languages. A few years later Edward's government played the same card again when in 1305 William Wallace was accused at his trial of refusing to spare the life of anyone who spoke English. As Wallace most probably did so himself, as well as many of his soldiers, the charge tells us nothing about him but a lot about England. Though the literary revival of English was still only just beginning, Edward could all the same hardly have been mistaken in thinking that such accusations were likely to raise the hackles of any honest Englishman and produce generous financial support, or show what a dangerous man Wallace was. Language is here quite clearly back at the heart both of national identity and of nationalist fervour.

So is it seventy years later in the Statutes of Kilkenny (1366) though the context is very different. Insistence on the obligation of speaking English in the Irish Pale was partly a matter of desperation – the English grip on Ireland was slipping badly. Control of much of the country had been lost already and what remained was at risk to the English crown, if its cultural and linguistic Englishness could not be preserved. The Gaelic revival, decreed the Statutes, was to be countered by the cultivation of the English language, English surnames, and of archery, the prohibition of hurling and other Irish sports. Here again the language is recognised as crucial for the survival of English identity and as a usable tool for policies of state.

If in Ireland English could be genuinely at risk as the settlers were gradually Hibernianised, at home the pressure was all the other way. French was fast declining in England just as English was in Ireland. To many people the primacy of a written French seemed increasingly anomalous, indeed insulting. Thus Robert of Gloucester, writing just at the time of Edward I's appeal to save the language from the King of France, complained sadly that there is no land 'that holdeth not to its own speech save England alone', and the anonymous author of the long narrative poem, *Cursor Mundi*, justified in its Prologue his use of the 'Inglis tung' out of love for the 'nacioun' of England, adding that it is little likely that English be praised in France and it is no outrage to give a people its own language.[12] The linguistic nationalism of Robert of Gloucester and the *Cursor Mundi* are all the more important for coming from insignificant clerics in the west and north of the country, and well in advance of the literary revival of the fourteenth century. They are evidence for a continuity of English national consciousness reflected in language comparable to the continuity of English prose about which R.W. Chambers wrote a memorable essay.

A generation later Ranulph Higden complained that it was 'against the usage and manner of all other nations' for children in school to be compelled to leave their own language. By 1385, however, John Trevisa could comment that a change was now general: 'in all the grammar schools of England children leave French and construe and learn in English'. Trevisa pointed out that this had its disadvantages as well as its advantages – they learnt more quickly but if they went abroad they no longer knew the language![13] In 1362, four years before Kilkenny, an English statute had ordered, probably ineffectually, that English should in future be used in the law courts while the following year the Chancellor had opened parliament with a speech in English for the first time.[14] All this suggests a quite rapid shift in the public sense of what was linguistically appropriate, coinciding with anti-French sentiments stimulated by Edward III's wars.

We have already in chapter I discussed the translation of the complete Bible into English a few years later. Its impact was considerable, despite Archbishop Arundel's condemnation of it in 1408, as the multitude of surviving manuscripts – copied both before and after 1408 – makes clear. One has the impression that the importance of the Wyclifite Bible has been unduly played down by Protestant and Catholic alike – by Protestants anxious not to weaken the picture of the vernacular Bible as brought to England by the Reformation, by Catholics because it was the work of people suspected of heresy. Yet for our purposes the best literary expression of national maturity to be found in the fourteenth-century English renaissance may still be its most widely read product, the Prologue to the *Canterbury Tales*. Here you find a thoroughly horizontalist portrait of the nation, people 'from every shire ende of Engelond', professedly brought together by religion, on pilgrimage to a great national shrine, but in fact having a whale of a time, listening to the very best of stories, some of them decidedly risqué. They appear as a remarkably literate group. Doubtless the 'Clerk of Oxenford' was unique in spending all he had 'on bookes', but it is noticeable that the village parson is also characterised as 'a lerned man' yet his brother was the plowman. The Monk, Friar and Prioress represented the traditional clerical end of the social spectrum as did, on the lay side, the Knight and the Frankeleyn, the latter a regular judge in local session and representative of his shire in parliament. But it is all those other people, the Serjeant of the Law, the Doctor of Phisik, the Marchant, the Reeve, the Sumnour and the Pardoner, whose work no less required a functioning literacy. Probably even the members of the urban confraternity – the Haberdasher, Carpenter, Webbe, Dyere and Tapyer – were at least marginally literate. One may recall that the Reeve had in youth, Chaucer tells us, been apprenticed as a carpenter. The Prologue is exciting because it fills out for us so imaginatively the working corps of a nation of a largely middle-class kind – industrial, agricultural, bureaucratic, academic – meeting appropriately enough in London, England's literary as well as commercial and political capital, the home of Chaucer and Gower as it would later be of Thomas More and Ben Jonson, Marlowe and Donne, even of born Midlanders like Shakespeare and Johnson.[15]

The age of Chaucer undoubtedly represents one of the high points in the consolidation of national consciousness and image-making, even architecturally and artistically. It was the age in which Perpendicular architecture – the most purely English style ever practised – was perfected. Superb in technique, buildings like the octagon at Ely, the cloisters at Gloucester, or Westminster Hall, reflect a confidently insular approach, symbolic of an increasingly nationalist culture. Again it was the age of the Wilton Diptych, perhaps the earliest genuine portrait of an English king, depicting the young Richard II kneeling before the Virgin, sponsored by his two patron saints, St Edmund and St Edward and suggesting thereby the symbolic unification of the nation, Angevin dynasty and English past, because both patrons were Saxon kings. Nevertheless it needs to be remembered that the one major factor which frequently made a negative contribution to the ideology and consciousness of the English nation was the monarchy itself. From the twelfth to the fifteenth century its mind was bewitched again and again by the mirage of ruling France and it clung to the use of the French language when it was largely abandoned and even disliked by the nation. It is ironic that the Hundred Years War so greatly increased English national sentiment and anti-French feeling because the purpose of the war was to make the King of England King of France. Despite the far greater strength of the English experience of being a nation-state in the later Middle Ages, the claims of its kings in fact inhibited a convincing assertion of English nationalism in international debate comparable with the French or the Spanish,[16] and while France's favourite national saint was a king, St Louis, England's was an anti-royal hero, Thomas of Canterbury. To put it simplistically – in France, as in Scotland, the kingdom precedes the nation; in England, the nation both precedes, and can even see itself as contrasted with, royal power. We have to find its strengths elsewhere, in such things as parliament and the long bow.

The Statutes of Kilkenny stressed archery as well as language for the making of a true Englishman. That, after all, is how he won his wars – over the Scots, the Irish, or, still more important, the French. The long bow was absolutely vital for both the construction and the achievement of English late medieval nationalism, whipped up particularly by the exertions of the Hundred Years War.[17] If 'One Englishman can annihilate many Scots', as a patriotic song of Edward

I's reign put it,[18] how still more exhilarating it was to discover that he could also annihilate plenty of Frenchmen, particularly if they were nobles. A poem written just after Agincourt puts the following words into Henry's mouth: 'thenke be Englysshemen that never wold fle at no batelle, for azenste one of us thowthe there be tene, thenke Christe wil help us in owre ryght'.[19] The English armies of the Hundred Years War were commoner armies of foot soldiers, paid directly when abroad by the king, and they won their battles, Crecy, Agincourt or wherever, largely through use of the long bow. Essentially Shakespeare's patriotic description of Agincourt, with its contrast between the common man on the English side pitted against the feudal nobility on the French, is good history. The English, like the Scots or the Swiss, were nationalised by the very way they fought while the French were not. As May McKisack concluded in her *Oxford History of England* volume on the fourteenth century forty years ago, 'the most lasting and significant consequences of the war should be sought, perhaps, in the sphere of national psychology . . . the victories were the victories, not only of the king and the aristocracy, but of the nation'.[20] And they were victories which generated both Francophobia and a belief in English invincibility – 'il leur est avis que il ne poeent perdre'.[21] Shortly after Crecy some clerical writer composed a poem of anti-French vitriol as exemplific of intense nationalism as anything a later age can manage. It survives in three manuscripts. French and English are contrasted thus:

> Francia, foeminea, pharisaea, vigoris idea
> Lynxea, viperea, vulpina, lupina, Medea . . .
> Anglia regna, mundi rosa, flos sine spina
> Mel sine sentina, vicisti bella marina.[22]

The author loaded France with every nasty adjective he could think of, while adorning England with similes of beauty.

The archers who won the battles were not, of course, the same people who represented their shires and boroughs in parliament: Chaucer's Yeoman did the one, his Frankeleyn the other. But each was necessary for the confident horizontality of achievement which constituted the nation's public experience. From our point of view the precise powers of fourteenth-century parliaments matter less than the fact of their frequency. In a general way the calling of parliament already represented recognition that royal government needed to be national government, that laws and taxes would not function without assent, that the underlying principles of the Great Charter had regularly to be reaffirmed.

It is not fanciful to locate Magna Carta near the heart of the political development of England as a mature nation-state. Consider the comments of Bishop Stubbs that 'The Great Charter is the first great public act of the nation, after it has realised its own identity', and that 'the English nation had reached that point of conscious unity and identity which made it necessary for it to act as a self-governing and political body, a self-reliant and self-sustained nation'.[23] This may be to use rather too mythological a language in regard to the Great Charter and it has been much criticised. Yet, in the words of Professor Holt, 'Stubbs nevertheless grasped the essentials.'[24] This is undeniably true in terms of both content and reception: in content because of its crucial stress on the rights of the non-baronial 'free man', something unparalleled in contemporary continental documents; in reception because the circumstances of Henry III's reign produced a repeated confirmation of the Charter and insistence on its annual reading in shire courts which came to endow it with a symbolic significance, almost as object of the kingdom's ultimate loyalty. In a very real way parliament grew naturally and inevitably out of the political ethos generated by the Charter, and when in the seventeenth century it appealed against the king to 'the most fundamental law of the kingdom'[25] it was doing little more than explicate in altered circumstances the underlying principle of the Great Charter, a principle which subordinated the monarchy to the nation and its legal structure. Basically that principle was common to both sides in the Civil War.[26] It was a national presupposition.

While the claim found in the fourteenth-century document entitled *Modus tenendi Parliamentum* that the Commons were the essential element of parliament because they alone 'stand for the Community'[27] may seem a little fanciful, the fact that such a claim could seriously be made in a document of the time is what really matters to us. But it was the sheer experience of very frequent parliaments for which commoners had to be chosen anew in shires and boroughs throughout the land from Newcastle-on-Tyne to Truro almost every year which seems so important in nation-building. There were 118 separate parliaments between 1307 and

1422.[28] If most were held in London, quite a few met elsewhere in places like York, Lincoln, Gloucester and Cambridge. The parliament of the fourteenth century could hardly have developed as it did except on the already well-established local foundation of shires and boroughs. One advance in nation-building prepared the way for another. In a typical parliament of the period the Commons included two knights from each of thirty-seven shires and two burghers from each of some seventy towns with four from London. While many of these men were returned a number of times, the majority were not. They included a number of rich and powerful people but most were very minor local worthies of no national importance. What mattered was the regular meeting together of chosen representatives from every community of any possible weight in the country. It was an on-going experience inherently constructive of a political nation and represents in terms of national government a very considerable advance in horizontalist and participatory terms on anything that went earlier.

This concentration on the later fourteenth century has been grounded on the conviction that it represents the very latest point at which it is plausible to claim that the English nation-state had gelled so decisively that no imaginable circumstance could later have diverted English society into some quite other form. This steady enhancement of national identity and nation-state institutions owed, however, very little to religion. It was a quietly secularising process which actually went parallel, not with any hostility to religion or to piety, but with a growing resentment towards its more powerful institutional forms. The early English nation owed a very great debt indeed to Catholic Christianity and the papacy in particular and it was for long almost over-deferentially grateful in return. On the one side, as we have seen, the church and leading churchmen did much to unite England and provide English people with a sense of their unity as a nation; indeed it was a Pope, Gregory I, who, we may claim with tongue just a little in cheek, invented not only the English nation but also its uniquely favoured status by declaring that Angles were Angels. A much later Pope, Hadrian IV, and the one Englishman ever to be Bishop of Rome, conveniently bestowed Ireland upon the King of England – or so it was claimed. Papal Bulls in the twelfth century were not insignificant things; whether or not the Bull *Laudabiliter* is genuine, Hadrian IV's encouragement to

Henry II to possess himself of Ireland is certainly historical, though he died years before Henry's invasion began. One can see why he encouraged him. The Church in England, reshaped by busy archbishops like Lanfranc and Theobald, was becoming a model of modern catholicism along the lines of high Gregorian principle. The Church in Ireland was certainly not. The establishment of English rule in Ireland must have seemed the quickest way of bringing an area of rather backward religion into the full blaze of Roman Christianity. As Professor Davies remarked in the Wiles Lectures eight years ago, the conquerors were anxious 'to explain and justify their activities, in part at least, as a campaign of ecclesiastical reform and spiritual regeneration'.[29] Gerald of Wales rather let the cat out of the bag when, in comment on the Synod of Cashel of 1172, he remarked that 'in all parts of the Irish Church all matters . . . are to be conducted hereafter . . . in line with the observances of the English Church'.[30] Thus the early export of English nationalism could like its origin still be linked with, and benefit from, the very *romanitas* which it would later repudiate so emphatically.

Church support for the nation had, on the other hand, for centuries been balanced by its restraining insertion of the nation within a wider moral community. At Canterbury Greek archbishops like Theodore, Italian archbishops like Anselm, Norman archbishops like Theobald, even mere English archbishops like Langton or Winchelsey, were anything but nationalists. On the contrary their principal role was much more to internationalise a narrow church both spiritually and institutionally. Authority within the church of such men could never be seen as a merely national one. For them national sovereignty, or whatever phrase you choose, must have its limits, and tension between the national and the international was already present. We see it, for instance, in Bishop Grosseteste's attempt to get English common law brought into line with canon law over the matter of legitimacy and the famous reply of the barons at Merton in 1236, 'Nolimus leges Angliae mutare'. Until the close of the thirteenth century church leadership had stood for the restraint of the national principle quite as much as for its enlargement.

From then on the role of religion changed and its independence declined. Boniface of Savoy, who died in 1270, was the last foreign archbishop. Hostility to foreigners was growing. The Jews were expelled twenty years later. The rise of nationalism went with a decline in wider loyalties and tolerances. Moreover, from then on nearly all senior bishops were men who had made their careers in the echelons of the burgeoning royal administration and they remained uncreatively absorbed within the national political system, the validator of national wars. At its heart the growth of late medieval nationalism within a society where everyone was a Catholic could owe little to religion until that religion itself came under renewed scrutiny, a scrutiny that the very rise of the nation-state would eventually require.

When Henry VIII sealed this development by formally asserting in the Act of Restraint of Appeals of 1533 that 'This Realm of England is an Empire and so have been accepted in the world' governed by one sovereign in matters both spiritual and temporal, only a handful of people had retained the conviction or clarity of mind to stand against the triumph of the nation-state over the church which had fostered it. Thomas More, lawyer, civil servant and philosopher, went to his death precisely because he could not accept the unlimited claims of national identity: England cannot legislate against the world – 'For this one kingdom I have all other Christian realms.'[31] Western medieval Christendom had both encouraged the nation and restrained it. From now on, for England at least, the national principle alone would reign supreme.

This forced march through eight centuries of English history from Bede to Henry VIII has had a range of purposes. First, it has sought to summarise the case study of a particular medieval nation and nation-state – in fact by far the best example that we have – to demonstrate that the modernist claim, to quote Hobsbawm, that it is 'pointless' to use such terms except in regard to an 'historically recent period' simply will not do. Moreover the history of English national consciousness down the centuries is so valuable for nationalist study generally just because it is so extended, the material available for its analysis is so vast, and one can in consequence distinguish phases and factors in a way far harder to do with shorter timescales. It is, I have been trying to demonstrate, a many-layered reality, growing in depth and extent in time yet capable of significant setbacks too as well as of alterations in direction, something in which the Bible, ecclesiastical organisers and early historians, vernacular literature, myths of origin, early names for territories, shires (and the jury system as well), parliamentary elections and attendance, wars and weapons all have to find a place. Secondly, it is only within a context where one is aware of such things as long bows and the election of knights of the shire to parliament that one can evaluate with realism any specifically religious factor. Thirdly, there is a danger at present among those who have rejected the shallowness of the full modernist thesis that they all the same refuse to go back beyond the watershed of the sixteenth century. We have noted it already in Greenfeld. One can see the same in Anthony Smith, a modernist whose consideration of ethnicity has forced him to abandon the full orthodoxy of late eighteenth century origins but who refuses quite to grasp the nettle of medieval nations. Thus he has very recently written that 'It is only from the late fifteenth century that we can confidently speak of a growing sense of English national identity, in a wider national state.'[32] There is in fact absolutely no reason to single out the late fifteenth century as crucial for a 'growing sense of English national identity'. Quite the contrary. A period of civil war and its aftermath and few parliaments, it has little special claim to any major notice in a history of the nation and its nationalism, any more than Greenfeld's equally arbitrary selection of the first third of the sixteenth century.[33]

I would like nevertheless to take one fairly early fifteenth century text to illustrate the character of medieval English nationalism, particularly because it suggests such close continuity with the post-Reformation form. It is entitled 'The Libel of English Policy', was written in 1436–7, probably in the Cotswolds, and presents a striking impression of economic nationalism: the nation of shopkeepers seems already upon us. Dick Whittington is its hero –

> . . . penne and papere may not me suffice
> Him to describe, so high he was of prise.[34]

The writer is concerned principally with control of the sea, especially the Dover–Calais crossing, and he is decidedly irritated by what he sees as unfair foreign competition. After describing at length the content of international trade and the chief nations England trades with, he focuses his worries upon Ireland. It is a fine country, productive of hides, fish and woollen and linen cloth. Moreover, Waterford has an excellent harbour and the land as a whole could produce a good deal more. Alas, however, its inhabitants are extremely unsatisfactory: 'the wylde Yrishe', he always calls them. Ireland is by rights an English possession but control is being sadly lost. If things go on as at present, they could soon have a king of their own. The English have already been pushed into 'a lytelle cornere'. The result of a complete loss of Ireland could, in the author's eyes, be positively catastrophic:

> . . . if it be loste, as Christe Jhesu forbede,
> Ffarewelle Wales, than Englond cometh to drede
> Ffor alliaunce of Scotelonde and of Spayne.[35]

Here are the concerns of late sixteenth-century English nationalism clearly present in the first half of the fifteenth. English security and trade require the control of Wales and Ireland. Scotland is seen as a natural ally of continental enemies ready to pounce. All we can rely upon is divine help and naval supremacy. It is important to recognise that attitudes of this sort were not simply the product of the post-Reformation situation but were already present a hundred years earlier, even if Protestant–Catholic conflict could greatly exacerbate them. The grounding of late medieval English nationalism lay in economics, geo-political facts, the maintenance of power both at sea and over England's first empire – its Gaelic neighbours. All this precedes the sixteenth century.

Nevertheless the Reformation brought an undeniable change in intensity through a series of events beginning with Henry's well-orchestrated but thoroughly secularising anti-Roman assertion of absolute sovereignty in the 1530s, the subsequent swing to state Protestantism, Mary's brief but bloody persecution and the threat of conquest from Philip of Spain, Mary's erstwhile husband. There was nothing inherently nationalist about Protestantism. The linkage was largely fortuitous. The excommunication of Elizabeth by Pope Pius V in 1570, the Massacre of St Bartholomew two years later, the Armada, Foxe's *Book of Martyrs* and Gunpowder Plot combined to heat up English nationalism from the middle of Elizabeth's reign while reshaping it as a thoroughly militant and Protestant force determined to take on the Spanish threat not only in the Straits of Dover but in the Netherlands, Ireland and the New World. When the danger from Spain receded, that from France replaced it and the liberation struggle – as English people saw it – against foreign political and religious tyranny went on. The revocation of the Edict of Nantes, the arrival of thousands of Huguenot refugees in England, the Trial of the Seven Bishops and the whole Catholicising policy of

James II, the wars with Louis XIV and the exiled Stuart court set up in Paris itself, all ensured that a great fear of Catholicism would continue to dominate English consciousness for a century and a half, until well after the 'Protestant Succession' was firmly established in the eighteenth century. In the course of this long period, Ireland would be settled and devastated, America colonised, England itself for a time wholly disrupted. The Protestant nationalism which unifies this whole sequence of events would become, partially tamed and secularised, the British Protestant nationalism of the eighteenth century which Linda Colley has described so persuasively. To this vast development we have now to turn.

Even Hobsbawm reluctantly admitted that in Tudor England we have to recognise a case of proto-nationalism or even 'something close to modern patriotism' though he added that while 'it would be pedantic to refuse this label to Shakespeare's propagandist plays about English history . . . we are not entitled to assume that the ground-lings read into them what we do'.[36] Whyever not? The nationalist message of Shakespeare's histories from *Richard II* to *Henry V* is anything but obscure and they were all written within ten years of the defeat of the Armada, when the sense of national struggle against the greatest power of the age was at its height. What is noteworthy in the Shakespearean histories, as also in a poem like Michael Drayton's *Agincourt*, is both what is there and what is not. Shakespeare revels in the history of what we have already seen as a major nationalist period – the late fourteenth and early fifteenth century – as evidence of England's uniqueness from John of Gaunt's dying speech in *Richard II* to Henry V's near miraculous victory at Agincourt. But what is most striking in the more mature plays – *Henry IV* and *Henry V* – is his preoccupation with the common man: Falstaff, Bardolph, Judge Shallow, John Bates, Michael Williams and the rest. The Englishness which Shakespeare and Drayton celebrate is that of 'true English hearts stuck close together' in Drayton's words, or Shakespeare's 'on one pair of English legs did march three Frenchmen',[37] the superiority of a nation of commoners over an army of feudal lords and peasants. Nothing is more significant than the contrast implied between French anxiety lest, even in death, 'our vulgar drench their peasant limbs in blood of princes'[38] and the comradeship between the English king and his largely plebeian army. Here again a suggestion of horizontality predominates.

To deny the nationalism of Gaunt's 'This blessed plot, this earth, this realm, this England', or Henry V's speech, 'On, on, you noblest English'[39] before the walls of Harfleur would seem as absurd as to deny the nationalism of the poem of Henley with which we began. But what throughout is absent in Shakespeare is the slightest hint of a nationalism Protestantly inclined. Of course, one may answer that this really would be too anachronistic in plays set in the early fifteenth century, though if Shakespeare had a mind to do so he could well have brought Wyclif or some later Lollard in to provide an additional theme. Even the final history, *Henry VIII*, written many years later, has an ambiguous note to it. It does end prophetically with the baptism of 'the high and mighty princess of England, Elizabeth' and yet it is striking how the play's tragic heroine is undoubtedly the rejected Catherine, seen at the end of her life with the Spanish Ambassador. Shakespeare is reasonably credited with being at least a little of a recusant. Whatever the reason, it is not with him but with Milton that the full force of the new form of England's nationalism appears.

Several years before Shakespeare penned Gaunt's 'This England', John Lyly had already expressed what was to become a commonplace of the next century, 'So tender a care hath he alwaies had of that England, as of a new Israel, his chosen and peculier people.'[40] So Milton sixty years later: 'The favour and the love of heaven, we have great argument to think in a peculiar manner propitious and propending towards us. Why else was this Nation chosen before any other, that out of her as out of Sion should be proclam'd and sounded forth the first tidings and trumpet of Reformation?'[41] Milton had Wyclif in mind. 'Peculiar', a word that frequently recurs in such contexts, is biblically orientated, identifying the English by its very usage with God's 'peculiar people' of 1 Peter 2.9.

Every year after 1605, 5 November was the nearest thing England ever had to a national day in which the preservation of parliament was recalled, effigies of the Pope and Guy Fawkes burned in the bonfires of popular liturgy. Burning an effigy of the Pope was not a piece of naughty fun but the fiercest rejection possible of what was widely seen as Anti-Christ, someone directly and personally responsible for every crime against Protestants from St Bartholomew's Massacre to the Gunpowder Plot. 'This bloudye monster of Rome', wrote Francis Hastings in 1598 in his *Watchword to all religious and true-hearted Englishmen*, 'doth not stay here, but having alreadie stirred up Spaine to set upon us both in Ireland, and in England, doth still whet them on by his unholy provocations, to invade.'[42] Remember too the special prayers recalling God's 'marvellous loving kindness to our Church and Nation': 'Be thou still our mighty Protectour, and scatter our enemies that delight in blood. Infatuate and defeat their Counsels, abate their Pride, asswage their Malice and confound their Devices . . . ' Which brings us back to the Book of Common Prayer and the vernacular Bible. The impact of the two books on the intensification and re-formation of English consciousness cannot be overemphasised. Over one hundred editions of the Bible in English between 1560 and 1611 and no fewer than 140 of the Authorised Version between then and 1640 make it absolutely clear that it was reaching very far indeed into the community, but it was the compulsory weekly attendance at the parish church to hear the services of the Prayer Book which ensured that almost everyone was permeated both ideologically and linguistically with Bible and Prayer Book religion. The very 'Catholic' shape of Anglican services with their repetition of finely expressed formal prayer rather than sermons and informal rantings ensured the breadth and depth of their impact, unachievable by either the Latin services of Roman Catholicism or the less structured services of pure Protestantism. Nevertheless the formal sermons laid down in *The Book of Homilies* included a certain amount of anti-Catholicism which also had its effect. The very real and prolonged threat from overseas, its express linkage with religion and the sheer success of England in providentially warding off attack from apparently far greater powers provided the ideal context for a nationalist biblical interpretation which did not require the under-girding of any special theology.

To Bible and Prayer Book were, moreover, joined two other classics for the construction of a history of Christian nationalism. The first was Foxe's *Book of Martyrs*.[43] Its enlarged edition of 1570, the year of the Queen's excommunication, was ordered to be set along with the Bible in all churches. It was second only to the Bible in the number of copies printed to the end of the seventeenth century and it continued to be frequently reprinted often in cheap instalments to enable the poor to buy it, through the eighteenth century. Thus, the *Book of Martyrs* could be treated as a sort of additional biblical testament. It provided a complete history of the church in England, an account of struggles against the papacy of medieval kings, of Wyclif and of national liberation achieved under Henry VIII. The seven hundred pages devoted to the Marian martyrs were thus firmly placed within a national Christian history, a sort of English Book of Maccabees, and later editions carried on the story to the Armada and beyond. Foxe's martyrs were very ordinary people, men and women; the book was graphically illustrated and there was considerable stress upon Queen Mary being the wife of Philip of Spain. The dedication to Elizabeth likened her to Constantine and the book as a whole became for generations of ordinary Englishmen their national history *par excellence*, an explanation as to why they were indeed a 'peculiar' people set apart for divine purposes. To Foxe we may add Hakluyt, whose *Principal Navigations, Voiages and Discoveries of the English Nation* was first published in 1589 and included, of course, 'the memorable defeat of the Spanish huge Armada'. Further enlarged editions followed. Froude described the *Principal Navigations* as 'the prose epic of the modern English nation' and G.M. Trevelyan called Hakluyt the 'most influential writer in the age of Shakespeare, if it was not Foxe'.

The internal construction of the Protestant nationalism which came to dominate English history for a highly decisive century and a half when England moved from being a small nation-state to being a highly successful, aggressive, imperialist power is clear enough. But it needs to be stressed once more that this was a redirection in a situation providing heightened consciousness of something which had long existed, and it was a redirection which took time to be assimilated by the nation at large. Even the sense of England as a chosen nation with a providential role can be found in sixteenth-century Catholics like Cardinal Pole as well as Protestants like Foxe and it goes back, at least implicitly, to pre-Norman times. If Shakespeare and Drayton were appealing in post-Armada days to the nationalist epics of the later Middle Ages, Archbishop Parker was at the same time appealing to a still earlier phase in English nation-building when he printed the Anglo-Saxon gospels (1571) and made an appeal to old English tradition a major element in the Anglican case in his *De Antiquitate Britannicae Ecclesiae* (1572). It was because the English nation-state, its history, structures and self-consciousness had been so long and so firmly in place that they could both be used extremely aggressively by Protestant propagandists and proto-imperial apologists on the one side and be taken for granted by people with very different stances. The virulence of Protestant nationalism should not deceive one into thinking it affected everyone or in the same way. Probably only a small minority were infected with it as decisively shaping their outlook in the age of Shakespeare. One may call that minority Puritan. A century later, Puritan theology had been watered down but the sense of a Protestant national identity had taken root in the vast majority of Englishmen.

The obvious exception is that of English Catholics. However much they were denounced as crypto-traitors, most Catholics were not the less patriotically nationalist. They would again and again feel themselves forced to be 'Englishmen in vaine'[44] but almost ostentatiously English for all that. They could do so without difficulty precisely because English nationhood preceded the Reformation. A very different example is that of seventeenth-century radicals of various sorts, both religious and secularising, such as the people who surfaced so vividly in the Putney debates of 1647. We should not forget in this regard the huge outpouring of newspapers and pamphlets in the 1640s. The year 1645 saw no fewer than 722 different cheap newspapers representing more than every conceivable viewpoint. For no year between 1643 and 1649 did the number fall below 400. In the same years more than a thousand pamphlets were published annually.[45] Here, if anywhere, is a case of the intensification of national consciousness through the printed page. Much of it was intensely Protestant but it was of its nature also highly horizontalist, and productive of a much enlarged political nation. Colonel Rainborough's famous words at Putney, 'The poorest he that is in England has a life to live as the greatest he', were not so much more than a contemporary application of the principles of Magna Carta, especially clause 39, 'nullus liber homo capiatur, vel imprisonetur . . . nisi per legale judicium parium suorum vel per legem terrae'. What was new was to find it so clearly required by the Bible: 'I do not find anything in the law of God', remarked Rainborough, 'that a lord shall choose twenty burgesses and a gentleman but two, or a poor man shall choose none.'[46] Frequent Leveller talk of 'England' and 'the free-born Englishman', however seemingly impractical in its applications, was fiercely horizontalist and nation-conscious. It was biblically-based yet, curiously, it proved also distinctly secularising.

The really important point about English nationalism regarded internally is that it encompassed just about everyone. The celebration of English national excellence was common to both sides in the struggles of the seventeenth century.[47] If Milton and the radicals saw the political implications of England's peculiar election one way, Tories saw it another. Edward Chamberlayne wrote a kind of guidebook to England in 1669, 'a necessary book for all Englishmen at all times'. For Chamberlayne, England 'excels all other nations' in almost every imaginable way — even if, he admits, the enemy had sowed a few tares of late. Even 'good nature' he could claim is 'a thing so peculiar to the English nation and so appropriated by Almighty God to them . . . that it cannot be well translated into any other language'.[48] But it was Defoe who may express best the mature essence of English nationhood as it moved into the eighteenth century and not just because of his satirical poem *The True-Born Englishman* of 1701. As a dissenter in politics, a prolific journalist, a common man, the son of a butcher and himself a hosier as well as author of *A General History of Trade*, he represented the inherently secularising process within the English nationalist drift, the prophet of the trend to become a nation of shopkeepers. His very mockery of the Englishman as a 'heterogeneous thing', a mix of numerous ethnicities, was possible just because he and his society were in fact so confident in their national self-identity.

But by the time Defoe died in 1731, was it still an English identity or a British one? We have now to face the Colley thesis. The impact of Linda Colley's *Britons, Forging the Nation 1707–1837* has been a very considerable one, almost acceptable even to modernists because it still seems to retain nation construction within their orthodox eighteenth-century parameters. Of course, that was not her intention and she recognises explicitly that the British nationalism whose construction she demonstrates with such detailed evidence for the eighteenth century was indeed the revamping of a much older English one. 'The invention of Britishness', she has no doubt, was 'closely bound up with Protestantism, with war with France and with the acquisition of empire.'[49] The need to plug Britishness was obvious enough after the 1707 Union with Scotland. Englishmen expected the Welsh to see themselves as really just part of the English but, in theory, the Scots could not be made to do the same. There had to be some give and take and an official substitution of 'British' for 'English' was an important part of it. *Rule Britannia*, written by a Lowland Scot in 1740, proclaimed the new identity. In official vocabulary 'English' and 'England' were regularly being replaced by 'British' and 'Britain' by the 1750s. Isaac Watts had already produced a translation of the Psalms in 1719 in which the word 'Israel' was regularly and ludicrously replaced by 'Great Britain', and forward-looking citizens debated about how best to express themselves so as not to give offence to other groups within the United Kingdom.

All that is well enough and it was particularly important for the Scots. Nevertheless there is a real danger of overdoing its significance so as, in modernist talk, to conclude misleadingly that Britain is an invented nation, not so much older than the United States. It would be far truer to say that it was a renamed nation and not so much renamed as all that. 'For many poorer and less literate Britons', writes Colley, 'Scotland, Wales and England remained more potent rallying calls than Great Britain, except in times of danger from abroad.'[50] It is the 'except' clause in that conclusion to which we have to take exception. 'Rule Britannia' is arousing enough but its flamboyant nationalism suggests a certain artificiality reflective of something not quite believed. Yet the occasional use of the word 'Britannia' was not new in the eighteenth century. English people always liked to play on the Greater Britain theme when it suited them. Bede began the practice and Saxon kings had regularly continued it. From the time of Geoffrey of Monmouth, King Arthur had been medieval England's hero. When a troublesome Frenchman at the Council of Constance in 1417 argued that the Welsh should vote separately from the English because they were a distinct 'nation' ('natio particularis'), the English replied that Wales, both spiritually and politically, was simply part of the 'natio Anglicana alias Brytannica'.[51] Camden's *Britannia* was first published well before James VI became James I, and the female figure of Britannia began to appear on the English coinage in Charles II's reign, well before the Union. Even the verbal use of 'Britain' was, then, as much a piece of traditional English mythology and expansionism as any deference to a new post-Union nation. But the fact remains that 'in times of danger', when a 'rallying call' was really needed, it was 'England' not 'Britain' that was used. What did Nelson say at the crucial moment in the war with Napoleon? 'England expects that every man will do his duty.'[52] Or the Prime Minister, William Pitt, confirming that the decisive battle had indeed been won? 'England has saved herself by her exertions and will, as I trust, save Europe by her example.'[53] Not much sign there of referring to Britain in times of danger. But the verbal dominance of England over Britain remained a striking characteristic of the nineteenth century. Even David Livingstone, that most Scottish of missionaries, was subject to it. After sixteen years in Africa, when he returns to this country, it is 'dear old England' he speaks of, glad of 'so hearty an English welcome'.[54] The emotional supremacy of England is no less clear in the poets, whether it be Blake, Browning or Keats: 'Oh to be in England'; 'Happy is England! I could be content to see no other verdure than its own'; 'Till we have built Jerusalem in England's green and pleasant land'.

I do not think that the Colley thesis adequately respects the continued emotional, intellectual and political dominance of the concept of England over that of Britain. If in 1870 Newman could find it natural to write 'Englishmen feel that war might break out between England and France any day'[55] he was only expressing himself in the way that anyone would. The political nation he felt he belonged to was English. And how could anyone easily have felt otherwise when the history of their nation was so overwhelmingly and explicitly formulated in terms of the 'History of England' from Macaulay, Gardiner, Green and Lecky in the nineteenth century to Trevelyan, the Oxford History of England and so much else in the twentieth. As David Cannadine has commented, 'The word Britain did not appear in the title of any of the series that have been mentioned. These years may have witnessed the zenith of the British nation-state . . . but the nation whose history they recounted and whose identity they helped to proclaim was England.'[56] The word which most needs stressing in that quotation is 'may'. But it is in Kipling that the primacy of England over Britain remains most striking, just because here at the end of the nineteenth and into the early twentieth century we are at the heart of the poetry of British overseas imperialism at its 'zenith'. It is true that Kipling occasionally speaks of Britain and the British, as in the poem *The Young British Soldier*, but what comes naturally to him is, undoubtedly, England and the English: 'For Allah created the English mad – the maddest of all mankind'; 'O thirty million English that babble of England's might'; 'Troopin', troopin', give another cheer – 'Ere's to English women an' a quart of English beer.' In lines like these, English nationalism turned imperialist, self-critical yet infinitely self-assured, is creatively re-imagined and demonstrated simultaneously to be alive and well.

Great Britain, Colley concludes, 'as it emerged in the years between the Act of Union and the accession of Queen Victoria . . . must be seen both as one relatively new nation and as three much older nations'[57] with a frequently changing, indeed uncertain, relationship between the two. Whether the Welsh can quite be called an 'old nation' or a nation at all we will discuss in chapter 3; and then, don't forget, by the accession of Queen Victoria there had been a further Act of Union and the Irish were within Great Britain too, which further complicates the issue as to whether it could possibly be called 'one relatively new nation' in 1837. 'Identities', Colley quite rightly insists, 'are not like hats. Human beings can and do put on several at a time.'[58] I suspect that for most English people throughout this period 'English' and 'British' were hardly two identities; 'British' was merely an additional name for a single identity. For the Scots and the Welsh, on the other hand, they were indeed two different, but not opposed, realities. For the Welsh who had long if unenthusiastically accepted that they were in a way part of England, the new stress on Britain could only be welcome. They, after all, remained the lineal representatives of the Britain of the past. For them the resurrection of the term in common currency could actually also help resurrect Welshness as a fully respectable identity and make it possible to contrast it with Englishness without appearing disloyal. For the Scots the formal recognition of Britain was really a condition for the Union. While their internal institutional differences – ecclesiastical, legal and educational – were guaranteed, the advantages of being British as well were manifest – both parliamentary representation at Westminster and the chance to be a partner in a rapidly expanding empire. Between 1760 and 1820 some two hundred Scots were elected for seats outside their own country while the new commercial wealth of Glasgow would be unimaginable outside the imperial context. To Scots Britishness mattered more in practice than to anyone else, as providing profitable membership of what could for them be conceived as genuinely a new nation, but it was clearly additional to the national identity they already possessed. For most Irish, the United Kingdom's fourth people in 1837, Britishness was far more problematic, involving a sense of not only distinct, but almost incompatible, realities, but to that we will return.

One reason why I say 'almost' and not necessarily quite 'incompatible' realities was that the anti-Catholicism within Britishness was rapidly declining by the time of the Union in 1800. There was no longer a point to it. In 1707, as Colley rightly stresses, Britishness seemed almost intrinsically bound up with Protestantism. Wales and Scotland could go along so easily with English nationalism because they shared a Protestant consciousness and, at the lay and popular level, there seemed very little religious difference between the three. Faced with the armies of Louis XIV and a Stuart Catholic court in Paris, one could hardly lower one's anti-Catholic guard. But a century later, any threat from Catholicism had wholly disappeared. English Catholics survived as a powerless little group, Ireland seemed pretty safely in Protestant hands but the overseas enemy, if still France, was no longer Catholic France. The anti-Catholicism of the Revolution made Catholicism more acceptable this side of the Channel. There was no problem in Catholic institutions, housed for two centuries on the continent, moving quietly back to England. Still more important, a great empire could not afford to be too discriminating in matters of religion. Ireland was no longer the only place where the crown had numerous Catholic subjects. The Quebec Act of 1774 was probably the deciding moment when British nationalism, turning imperialist, recognised that an overt anti-Catholicism was better abandoned. The decision to guarantee the rights of the church in Quebec did in fact upset plenty of people whose minds were still set in the Protestant nationalist mould of an earlier age both in Britain and in America. But there could be no turning back, especially when Malta and Trinidad were added to the empire. The rather raucous Protestantism of the Irish Ascendancy would from then on be increasingly irritating to policy-makers in London. Of course, popular anti-Catholicism survived in England throughout the nineteenth century, despite the Emancipation of 1829.[59] Britain remained in many ways both a Protestant state and a Protestant society, but its relationship to Catholicism from now on was a more ambiguous one. English nationalism had been determinedly Protestant for a century and a half. British nationalism was essentially secular.

CHAPTER THREE

England's western neighbours

This chapter will briefly consider ways in which English nationalism impinged upon Cornwall, Wales and Scotland before turning, via America, to its principal subject, Ireland. Cornwall is an interesting but little considered case. Here was a Celtic ethnicity absorbed within the West Saxon kingdom well before the Conquest. Its elite was habituated to speak and write the national language and it is intriguing that in the fourteenth century it was actually Cornishmen – John Cornwall, Richard Pencrych and John Trevisa – who pioneered and proclaimed the replacement of French by English in the teaching of Latin grammar. No significant Cornish literature seems ever to have appeared, yet Cornish remained for centuries the common woman's vernacular. As such it raised no more problems than the oral dialects of other shires. One crucial factor within Cornwall's relatively successful integration seems to be that it did not begin with a ruthless and long-contested conquest of the Norman type, that it happened while the nation as a whole was itself coming into existence, a nation in which Cornishmen were no more alien to Englishness than Danes, and that Cornwall participated in the institutional development of England at every point. It was in fact almost excessively well represented in parliament from the four-teenth century, with the enfranchisement of no fewer than six boroughs: Bodmin, Helston, Launceston, Liskeard, Lostwithiel and Truro. The fate of this identity in ethnic-national terms was, it would seem, finally decided by the Reformation. While Latin was the language of the liturgy, Cornish had remained that of the community, and, doubtless, also that of many sermons. With the Reformation, Latin was replaced by English, despite Cornish protests that many people could not understand it. No attempt was made to provide a Book of Common Prayer in Cornish. The effect was a very rapid decline in the use of Cornish, and, in consequence, of the singularity of the Cornish ethnic identity within England. The springboard for any pursuit of independent nationhood was effectively removed. Nevertheless there remained a stronger sense of separate identity and common purpose, a greater willingness to rise in revolt, among the people of Cornwall than in any other southern shire: 'Here's twenty thousand Cornishmen will know the reason why!'[1] Such potentially politicisable ethnicity could hardly be found elsewhere.

For Wales, Scotland and Ireland too, let us place ourselves for a moment about the middle of the eleventh century and survey the scene at that point. In England, Edward the Confessor was in the middle of his long and peaceful reign over a nation-state which, as we have seen, had attained a degree of cultural, economic and administrative unity unique in western Europe. How far had its neighbours developed in any way comparably? A simple answer is that they had not done so, but a better one is that the issues involved are too complicated to be dealt with by an unequivocal answer. Wales and Ireland had much in common. They were both old Celtic ethnicities with, by the eleventh century, a very long history behind them of which they remained extremely conscious. Each was united by a shared language despite inevitable differences of local dialect and also by both a vernacular law and a vernacular literature possessed as a common tradition.

Extensive written use of the vernacular had, one can presume, been almost forced upon them by their very isolated situation within the Christian world. When Patrick presided over the first conversion of the Irish in the fifth century, he had come from a British Christian Church in a crumbling corner of the Roman world. His Latin was poor and the Irish Church was not assisted in subsequent generations, so far as one can see, by distinguished foreign scholars as was the English Church with men like Theodore of Tarsus and his friend the Abbot Hadrian. It seems unsurprising that Irish monasteries should so soon have begun to experiment with writing in the vernacular, though that writing was initially chiefly a matter of recording Irish oral law and literature, praise poems and myths of origin. The situation of the Welsh was little different. They had not forgotten that they were the survivors of the Roman Province of

Britain and Latin continued to provide an important mark of group identity, surrounded as they were to begin with by illiterate pagans, Saxon, Dane and Irish, but here as in Ireland their very isolation helped stimulate the development of what has been claimed as Europe's earliest surviving vernacular literary tradition.

The ground of nationhood for both Welsh and Irish lay then in a common ethnicity, a common history, a clearly delimited territory and a shared medium of communication, both oral and written, which differentiated them from all outsiders, something of which each was well aware. It did not, however, lead noticeably on towards an English type of statehood. We do indeed see some shadowy recognition in both societies of a common state in the periodic existence of a 'High King'. What is striking, however, in comparison with England (or even Scotland) is the lack of state formation. Century after century both societies remained a network of small dynastic princedoms, territorially identified but highly unstable in both frontier and administration. In terms of an African comparison they correspond to the Azande where England corresponds to Buganda. Bureaucracy was not a mark of the Celt as it was of the Saxon. Gwynedd, Powys, Gwent, Deheubarth, Dyfed; Ulster, Leinster, Munster, Connaught, Dublin. These were not well-run little states, often hardly states at all, more like geographical areas in the grip of one or another war lord, subject to much mutual raiding and highly vulnerable to attack from outside. One could easily be led to conclude that there was no such thing as a Welsh or Irish nation in political terms. Obviously the Welsh were not English, as English-men were able to recognise well enough: 'As you well know, Welshmen are Welshmen', wrote a weary official of Edward I in 1296.[2] The Welsh and the Irish in the early medieval period had certainly not developed an English sort of state-linked nation and they were to pay for that failure very heavily. Nevertheless, their national identity was not, therefore, to be deemed nonexistent nor even entirely unpolitical. Early medieval government and political identity were quite as much a matter of law and custom as of anything that a named ruler might be or do, and both Wales and Ireland had developed an extensive vernacular law recognised as authoritative throughout the land. Wales was politically one to the very real extent that it had one law, the law of Hywel Dda, and Ireland was similarly unified by Brehon law.

Each was, moreover, entirely conscious of its distinct identity separate from that of foreigners of whatever kind. The Welsh identified themselves and their land as *Cymry*, 'Compatriots', a nicely horizontalist term and one which goes back at least as far as the seventh century. For long it was used parallel to their still earlier self-definition, *Brytaniaid*. *Brytaniaid* related to their origin, the surviving remnant of Roman Britain. Memory of that far past remained the principal founding myth of the Welsh. They had in fact few other myths, royal or religious, which were not clearly localised. To be British and Roman too was enough. But from the twelfth century that name was displaced in current use by that of Cymry, an expression of contemporary fact rather than of remote antiquity.

The Irish distinction between themselves and foreigners was no less clear but it was combined with an ability little by little to absorb the foreigner within the national community, Vikings in the past, Anglo-Normans in the future. Where Welsh Christian identity was grounded above all in a sense of the heritage of Roman Britain renewed by a wave of monks in the sixth century, none of whom had much more than local significance, that of the Irish was dominated by a single figure, St Patrick, whose fifth-century mission, surviving writings and extended myth have provided a foundation charter for national unity in a way achieved by no other single religious figure in these islands. Ireland was, furthermore, greatly helped to attain the consciousness of being a single society by its geography, both as not too large an island and as one rather easily passable in all directions, even if it lacked the amenity of Roman roads. In consequence it early attained a sense of cultural unity which has continually eluded its larger sister-isle.

Language, law, literature, a sense of historic identity, a particular kind of culture sustained by the orders of bards, jurists and monks, that surely is sufficient to show that Wales and Ireland were by the mid-eleventh century well past the dividing line between ethnicity and nation, far as they were from achieving, or even seeking, a nation-state.[3] When the Lord Rhys of Deheubarth held his famous assembly of poets and musicians at Cardigan in 1176, where the men of Gwynedd carried off all the poetry prizes, he was doing something very Welsh, but also something significantly national. It reminds one of that other great assembly of bards and scholars held at Christmas 1351 in Ui' Mhaine, in Connaught – an exciting moment in the

Irish Gaelic revival of the fourteenth century. This was to demonstrate a different way of imagining a nation. It was something which
the English could not conceivably have done.

In almost all of this Scotland could not be more different and
anyone wanting to define roads to nationhood and the role of
ethnicity therein could hardly do better than ponder the contrast
between Scotland and Wales. A Committee of the Church of
Scotland reporting in 1923 upon Irish Immigration, seen as a
dangerous intrusion into Scottish life and tradition, concluded that
'God placed the people of this world in families, and history, which
is the narrative of His providence, tells that when kingdoms are
divided against themselves they cannot stand. Those nations which
were homogeneous in race were the most prosperous and were
entrusted by the Almighty with the highest tasks.'[4] The point of
recalling here this particularly absurd statement is that of all the
peoples of our islands the Scots have been by far the least 'homogeneous in race'.[5] In the mid-eleventh century there was already a
King of Scotland – Macbeth (1040–1057) or Malcolm Canmore
(1057–1093) – but he ruled over what had been four quite distinct
ethnicities, with their own languages and laws: the Picts in the
north-east, the Scots in the north-west, the British of Strathclyde
and the Angles south of the Forth in Lothian. They were not one
nation, hardly one state. A precarious kingship held them together.

This hybrid kingdom of 'Scotia' had begun north of the Forth
with a uniting of Picts and Scots. It went on to draw into it the
southern peoples who might just as well have formed a state instead
with the northern English of Northumbria and Cumbria. The
Pictish and British languages disappeared, leaving by the fourteenth
century a bipartite kingdom of Gaelic highlanders and English-
speaking lowlanders. In each of the four countries in these islands
there has been a divide of some sort between Celt and Saxon but
only in Scotland did it go down the very middle of society. What is
amazing about Scotland's nationhood is that it ever happened.
Unlike Wales or Ireland Scotland's nation did not, then, derive from
a single ethnicity or language group. Indeed it has never been quite
clear which ethnicity, if any, should be regarded as constituting its
core. The early kingdom was Gaelic; quite quickly, however, it
became heavily anglicised, a process beginning under the influence
of Malcolm's English queen, the able and devout Margaret. The hub

of power shifted from the Gaelic to the Saxon side. Royal administration, borough life and church government were all modelled
upon an English prototype and English took over too as the language
of the court. Here as in England, if less strikingly, a nation-wide
network of dioceses effectively precedes any comparable royal
administrative presence.

While Englishmen in Wales and Ireland remained essentially
intruders in a society whose language was alien to them, in Scotland
they were quickly incorporated within the community, due largely
to the fact that the south-east was already English-speaking. By the
twelfth century Scotland was far more of a state than Wales or
Ireland but still far less of a nation. What turned it into a nation over
the following centuries were two things: on the one hand the
struggle against domination by the King of England, on the other
the slow impact of state formation of an English sort within a clearly
defined territory. The two go together. It was because Scotland was
so like England that it could resist England successfully. But the
territorial factor is no less important. Sharing a land and a king
created a nation. Scotland, even better than England or France,
represents the triumph of territoriality over ethnicity in the construction of nationhood, quite the opposite to the narrow homogeneity
of a single ethnicity so foolishly appealed to by the Church of
Scotland Committee in the 1920s. Yet it is also sadly true that the
post-Reformation dominant Protestant establishment of Scotland
increasingly feared and belittled the ethnicity of the Highlands, just
as Englishmen long regarded the Welsh and the Irish as barbarians.
In practice, Scotland veered steadily towards being a mono-ethnic
state with a colonial Gaelic fringe just as England veered towards
being a mono-ethnic state with a colonial Welsh fringe.

For Wales, Ireland and Scotland alike, the impact of English
invaders, spearheaded by Normans, decisively altered national consciousness from the late eleventh to the fourteenth century. R.R.
Davies, in his splendid Wiles Lectures of six years ago, analysed the
effect of that domination and conquest superbly well, demonstrating
the rise in feelings that can appropriately be called nationalist in the
resistance of all three peoples, as expressed in such things as the
Declaration of Arbroath or the last assertions of defiance coming out
of Gwynedd in the 1270s, the final years of 'serious struggle for
Welsh independence'.[6] The life or death of what the Welsh did not

hesitate to call 'nostra nacio' was seen to be at stake. Such was the bitterness over English oppression that it could be claimed that the people of Wales as a whole 'preferred to die rather than to live'.[7] Quite comparable expressions could be heard in Ireland. The fate of the three countries, however, was different. Scotland, with greater resources and considerable territorial depth to fall back upon, threw out the invaders and immensely strengthened its own sense of nationhood in the process. Wales succumbed and Welshmen were reduced for two hundred years to a state of severe discrimination within their own country. Their national consciousness slowly declined in consequence. Acceptance of being an English dependency had become gloomily inevitable. Ireland stood midway. It could not throw out the English as Scotland had done but equally the English showed themselves to lack the resources or willpower to control most of the country. They were, moreover, quietly hibernianised. By the close of the Middle Ages the English invasion might appear to have had relatively little effect, so that when we reach the sixteenth century the political status of Ireland still lies in the balance as that of Scotland and Wales do not.

Henry VIII's unification of Wales with England after 1536 provided it at last with shires and parliamentary representation, but was intended as the abolition of Wales. Welsh law was simply abolished. Henry's intention, moreover, was that no person or persons 'that use the Welsh speech shall have or enjoy any manner of office or fees within this realm'.[8] The 'sinister usages and customs' of Wales were all to disappear. The new sovereign state of the Reformation had decreed that there was no room for significant ethnic deviation within a single nation.

Yet it did not work out quite like that under the impact of the Protestant revolution in religion. Religion had very little to do with nationalisms or nation-formation in the later centuries of the Middle Ages in any of these countries but with the sixteenth century it inevitably came centre-stage once more in several different ways, as we have already seen in regard to England. Rather curiously the Bible and the Reformation commitment to the language of the people may actually have saved Welsh nationhood, despite the intentions of Henry VIII. So few Welsh people understood English that it was clearly useless to try and convert Wales to Protestantism with an English Bible or Book of Common Prayer. The parliamentary decision to provide instead Welsh versions of both in 1563 was of momentous importance for the future of the Welsh language. Prepared by Bishop Richard Davies of St David's and William Salesbury, a Welsh New Testament and Prayer Book appeared already in 1567 and a complete Bible, the work of Bishop Morgan of St Asaph, in 1588. With the loss of Welsh law the language absolutely needed a new literary base and in the Bible it received it magnificently. The sale from 1630 of the *Beibl Bach*, the 'little Bible', at five shillings a copy for ordinary householders, ensured that it would be widely spread. The effect was to Protestantise Wales but also to rejuvenate Welsh national consciousness and ensure that it would not quietly fade away in the Cornish manner.

In Scotland the decision went the other way. Writers of the early Scottish renaissance, like Gavin Douglas, had wanted Scots to be recognised as a language of its own, distinct from English as Dutch had become from German. It was the decision of John Knox and the Scottish reformers not to produce a Scottish translation of the Bible, but simply to reprint the English Geneva version, which more than anything else ensured this would not happen. The language of Scotland would be English, with no more than dialectic differences. By the time James VI of Scotland had become James I of England it was agreed that the two countries had a common language. The effect of this on the relationship between the two in encouraging the feeling that as they shared a single language they could be merged into a single nation was considerable. It is true that the conflicts of the seventeenth century would ensure that there remained a sharp ecclesiastical difference between the two countries, a difference especially over bishops towards whom most Scots Protestants felt intense dislike. It would not, then, be true to say that religion made for unity and only secular institutions, including the law, continued to assert difference. Nevertheless, at the lay level the two countries were united by their common Protestantism, a shared Bible, and hatred of the Pope. Linda Colley is right to stress the importance of the religious factor in the development of a common British identity, something to be seen particularly clearly in settlement overseas.

To settlement in Ireland and America we must now turn. It is here that the new English Protestant nationalism appears at its purest, here too that the Reformation decisively alters the relationship between the English and the Irish and by so doing provides us with a

classical scenario for the relationship between religion and nationalism. Let us consider America first, both because it is less problematic
in itself and because it helps provide an additional context for the
elucidation of what happened in Ireland.

Settlement in America came a little after the major settlements in
Ireland and it was self-propelled in a way the latter were not. But
both represent the expansionism of a nation which none the less felt
itself under threat. The coexistence within a nation of intense
defensiveness and aggressiveness normally produces nationalism in its
most virulent and self-righteous form. The New England settlers
were out to create exactly what that name implies, a New England,
absolutely English but purified of the dregs of an old England they
had chosen to leave. 'New' meant fully Protestant, fully biblical,
purged of all episcopalian and papist corruptions, the true Israel of
God which Foxe had already shown England to be but which at
home remained somehow still imperfectly achieved. When John
Cotton preached at Gravesend in June 1630 to the passengers of the
Winthrop fleet from II Samuel 7.10, 'I will appoint a place for my
people Israel and wil plant it, that they may dwelle in a place of their
owne',[9] he was undoubtedly in a way suggesting that only true
Protestants constituted God's people but the Protestantness and the
Englishness seemed finally inseparable in divine providence as they
were in the minds of the settlers. 'It be the people that makes the
Land English, not the Land the People', declared Richard Eburne in
his 1624 *A Plaine Path-way to Plantations*, while Sir William Vaughan
remarked two years later in his *Golden Fleece* that 'God had reserved
Newfoundland for us Britains, as the next land beyond Ireland'.[10]

In sociological terms, the New England migration was a distinctly
national one. Most people paid their own way; whole families went
together; almost all ranks of society were represented; there was even
a reasonable sex balance. The initiative was neither governmental
nor capitalist. On the contrary, there was a strong sense of horizontality, of the determination to carry into a geographically new land
an already established national and religious identity. That new land
Cotton Mather, writing his *Magnalia Christi Americana* at the end of
the century, a genuine church history of New England, even a sort
of continuation of John Foxe, could describe as a 'horrible wilderness'.[11] The New Englanders were God's peculiar people, led
'meerly for their being well-willers unto the Reformation' into the

wilderness, which turned little by little in consequence into 'English America'.[12] In the 1720s the General Council of Massachusetts could still declare emphatically that 'they were as much Englishmen as those in England, and thought they had a right to all the privileges that the people of England had'.[13]

Most other colonies were not as religiously constructed as Massachusetts. Powerful as the early New England Protestant ideology was, it is well known how quickly, even in the lifetime of Cotton Mather, the American mind was being secularised. A powerful residue of Protestant identity nevertheless remained almost irremovable for generations more. Secularisation did not remove, rather it diffused, the sense of America's unique calling, 'a city set on a hill'. Moreover, the Protestant nationalism which was, on the one hand, an English export, could, on the other, become quite easily the spiritual fuelling of Anti-Englishness. New England had always been both an extension and a critique of Old England. Anglican plans pushed particularly by Archbishop Secker (d. 1768) to establish an American bishopric were certainly one of the factors which produced the alienation behind the War of Independence[14] and the British decision to protect the Catholic Church in Canada, guaranteed by the Quebec Act of 1774, was another. Never had there been 'such a bare-faced attempt against the success of the Protestant religion', thundered the *Pennsylvania Packet* in advance.[15] The establishment of the Inquisition was likely to follow and it was surmised that the 'seat of the supreme head of the Catholic Church might well be translated from Rome to London'.[16] That, doubtless, was an idiosyncratically ironical comment. Nevertheless, the huge excitement with which 'Pope Day', 5 November, was celebrated in many places in New England in 1774 formed a significant part of the emotional raising of the temperature preparatory to the decisive split from Britain eighteen months later. Britain could now be demonised as Egypt, and Washington hailed as the new Moses. But once France entered the war on the American side, Washington in a famous instruction asked his men to refrain from celebrating 'Pope's Day' in order not to upset French Catholic susceptibilities, and once the war was over both anti-popery and anti-episcopacy quickly subsided. In March 1785 the *Boston Gazette* could report almost as a joke the passing of the surface issues that had generated the war: 'TWO WONDERS OF THE WORLD — a Stamp Act in Boston and a Bishop in

Connecticut'.[17] Samuel Seabury had been appointed the first Episcopal bishop in the United States.

The most decisive of horizontalist experiences behind American identity as a whole had never, however, been a religious but a linguistic one: Americans spoke and wrote, in so extremely uniform a way, the English language. They spoke it, in fact, better than did the people of England because they had all been to school, had extremely little dialectical divergence from colony to colony and they really did possess a Bible in every home. It had been crucial for the maintenance of Englishness that they did not change the language and, despite large numbers of German and other immigrants, they introduced only a handful of new words into their speech in the course of the eighteenth century. Remarkably few books were written or printed in America, despite the standards of its education, before the nineteenth century. The London book market remained absolutely dominant. In nothing was it made clearer that Americans wanted to stay English. 'I hope with you', Benjamin Franklin assured David Hume, 'that we shall always in America make the best English of this island our standard, and I believe it will be so. I assure you it often gives me pleasure to reflect, how greatly the audience (if I may so term it) of a good English writer will, in another century or two, be increased by the increase of English people in our colonies.'[18]

There was, however, one group of English-speaking inhabitants of America to which none of this applied: the Black people. They did not go to school. They were, with few exceptions, illiterate. They certainly did not speak English with a proper purity; indeed any writing about them tended until much later to make play with their linguistic confusion. But, as they were not part of the nation as established at Independence, being excluded from its essential freedoms, this merely reinforced the cruciality of language for the horizontal unity of whites.

Yet, once independent, Americans were faced with a linguistic quandary: how to be culturally and psychologically American when the core of their identity was emphatically English. If the English language had for so long ensured their Englishness, how could they cease to be English and be genuinely American if they continued to speak in the same way? What made them different, they claimed, was precisely that they had achieved a national appropriation of

English far beyond that of the English themselves, divided by class and dialect and half-illiterate as they were. Linguistically, then, their very Englishness had made them American! The people of the United States, Fenimore Cooper insisted in 1828, 'with the exception of a few of German and French descent, speak as a body, an incomparably better English than the people of the mother country . . . In fine, we speak our language, as a nation, better than any other people speak their language.'[19] Our language. It was the great lexicographer, Noah Webster, with his spellers and dictionary, who set himself to provide it. His *Spelling Book* (the only American book to sell 100,000,000 copies) and his 1828 *American Dictionary of the English Language*, with their quite deliberate assertion of precise linguistic differentia from England, are crucial to our wider theme. While Americans have never got themselves as far, psychologically, as to assert consistently that they speak American, not English, Webster's markers of differentiation in spelling and pronunciation, religiously adhered to ever since (once the 'war of the dictionaries' had been won), were sufficient to ensure a necessary linguistic distinction underpinning the separation of nations.

The political argument itself had not been dissimilar with its insistent appeal to 'English liberties'. It was actually because they were English, members of a long-established political nation, that they had to follow the course which made of them Americans. Initially, like all settlers in a hostile land, they needed the protection of the mother country. In 1700 they were still only a quarter-million strong. There was a long frontier to defend and the French in Quebec. A diminution in explicit loyalty would have been madness. By the middle of the century they were two million. Philadelphia was already a larger town than any in Britain other than London, and the colonies were bristling with new universities. The fall of Quebec removed the one remaining threat and the gaucheness of George III's ministers simply clarified the underlying contradictions. 'American Englishmen' were inherently denied the primary 'liberty' of English Englishmen – representation in the parliament that exercised sovereignty over them. Yet they knew themselves to be actually more English than the English. As Greenfeld has put it, 'If the English were God's own people, the American English were the elect of the elect.'[20] Moreover by the late eighteenth century they no longer needed to put up with such a grave deprivation of their rights as propertied Englishmen. It is fascinating to see how Edmund Burke in his speech in the House of Commons in March 1775 on 'conciliation with the American colonies' both recognised the problem and failed quite to draw the inevitable conclusion. 'Are not the people of America as much Englishmen as the Welsh?' he demanded.[21] 'How can their lack of representation be justified, for that is the characteristic mark and seal of British freedom?' 'An Englishman', he insisted, 'is the unfittest person on earth to argue another Englishman into slavery.'[22] Burke was, of course, an Irish Englishman appealing, as he thought, for the rights of American Englishmen. Even he, however, recognised that it was impracticable to elect Americans to parliament.

It was not, however, just a matter of impracticality in terms of travel. What had happened was that the principle of territoriality was little by little triumphing over that of ethnicity. In the long term Richard Eburne was mistaken in claiming that the land does not make the people. For the early settlers America was only a 'horrible wilderness', but then it became a matter of providence that the discovery of America had coincided with the Reformation and the expansion of England, God's Israel. America was discovered to be a value in itself. Englishmen became 'American English' and then just Americans. By the mid-eighteenth century the single word 'America' was being used, particularly in England, to cover the thirteen distinct colonies. A new unity was recognised even before it was claimed. Elie Kedourie, in his diatribe against nationalism, wrote that 'on nationalist logic, the separate existence of Britain and America' is a 'monstrosity of nature'.[23] That is only true if nationalist logic is limited to a narrow conception of ethnicity, but of course it is not. As late as 1766, an American, Francis Hopkinson, could still express a general opinion when he insisted that 'we in America are in all respects Englishmen, notwithstanding that the Atlantic rolls her waves between us . . .'[24] but in the end territoriality generally triumphs and just as it unites ethnicities in some cases, such as Scotland, so it divides them in others, such as the emergence of America. This was made a little easier by the large number of new Americans, immigrants from other European countries; but they were almost always people who lacked the political tradition native to their seventeenth-century predecessors and in consequence had almost no impact on America's political identity. Through the

Declaration of Independence, in the words of Abraham Lincoln, 'our fathers brought forth upon this continent a new nation'.[25] In some ways this seems a questionable assertion, questionable at least in that if its national consciousness was already a reality in 1776 (despite the quarter of the population still looking back as loyalists to their 'former' national identity) it was precisely because the attitudes, law, mythology and local institutions appropriate to a nation had long been in place, being no other than the attitudes, law and local government proper to the English nation. What American Englishmen had lacked was both representation in a parliament claiming sovereignty and any formal bond between the different colonies. The creation of the requisite institutions was not so difficult once their necessity had become obvious. The land had enforced distinctiveness; territory had prevailed over ethnicity to demonstrate that, *pace* Burke, the Welsh could be more English than the Americans; and what happened was not a 'monstrosity of nature' but a fine example of the reshaping of nations and even of ethnicity and culture beneath the pervasive control of time and territory.

Lincoln's assertion, crucial as it was to his position in 1863 at Gettysburg, is questionable also on the issue as to whether, once the American English ceased to be English, they really were a single nation. What other than Englishness clearly made of the inhabitants of Virginia and Massachusetts a single nation? There was unquestionably an unexplained ambiguity in the very words 'United States'. Richard Henry Lee's original resolution in 1776 asserted that 'these United Colonies are, and of right ought to be, free and independent States'.[26] State or states? Nation or nations? That really was what the Civil War was to be all about. The immediate circumstances of the War of Independence generated a single political will. But could that endure once the threat of reconquest was removed? Was it sufficient to forge not a confederacy of opportunism but a nation? If the South had won in the Civil War (as it could have done) the judgement of history would probably have been that there never had been one American nation and today there would be three, not two, English-speaking nations inhabiting North America.

Protestantism survived across the nineteenth century as an underlying fact central to American identity, yet because it was unthreatened it receded in its power to control the collective imagination. Its public *persona* was secularised to the point of extinction, leaving nothing more than a self-satisfied sense of 'manifest destiny', like the smile of the Cheshire Cat. When we turn to Ireland we see something similar beginning to happen at times in the eighteenth and nineteenth centuries, but it never really happens. Instead the religio-national fervours of the seventeenth century engendered in England and exported to America and Ireland continue only in Ireland as a major force in the shaping of public life. Why has this been so?

In Ireland in 1600 there were two nations but maybe not much more than one nationalism, English nationalism. The English were undoubtedly a nation themselves and they did not cease to be English once settled in Ireland any more than they did in America. That the Irish were also a distinct nation was clear to Englishmen at the time[27] and it should be clear to us too, as I have already sufficiently argued. That the English were moved by a pretty powerful nationalism tied to the defence and extension of the English nation-state should also now be obvious. There was, however, no comparable Irish nationalism and that is not surprising because there was nothing even remotely like an Irish nation-state for it to relate to. Irishmen had long accepted an English lordship or kingship as a fact of life together with a great deal of local feuding both inter-Irish and Irish–English. It took a lot of oppression in such circumstances to produce even a little nationalism. Nationalism as a collective condition of the mind is in point of fact a characteristically English thing, going as it does with an English sort of state, not a Gaelic sort. The earnest endeavour to find nationalism in pre-modern Ireland can easily turn into an anachronistic piece of Anglicisation, though the worse the Irish were treated the more like nationalists they naturally became.

A 'two nations' account of late sixteenth-century Ireland is, nevertheless, a serious over-simplification, given the existence of the 'Old English'. It is their role throughout the crucial century in which modern Irish society was decisively shaped that complicates the story and has, even now, been very inadequately recognised. By 1600 they had been settled in the Pale and in and around other towns, mostly of the south-east, for three hundred years or more. They thought of themselves as English, controlled the pretty ineffectual Irish parliament, sent their sons to study law in London at the Inns of Court and were almost entirely bilingual. Many of them must have spoken more Gaelic than English. They were in every way highly hibernia-nised and recognised as such by the English of England. They were 'English by blood': English to the Irish but Irish to the English – a fairly regular condition for long-established settlers anywhere in the world. Of course many of them had not been English in the first place but Danes, Normans or Flemish, and there had since been a large measure of Irish intermingling too.

Probably the most crucial factor in the religious history of Reformation Ireland was that, by and large, the Old English stuck to Catholicism and became in due course both a recipient and a producer of Counter-Reformation clergy. Their loyalty to the English Crown did not carry them into the English church of Elizabeth and therefore made them increasingly unreliable subjects in the eyes of her government and of the new English Protestant nationalism represented by waves of Englishmen (and then Scots-men) being settled in Ireland from the last years of the Queen's reign. The war with Spain, the threat of a Spanish invasion of England and the manifest collapse of any sort of English state control of most of Ireland had produced a new determination on the part of government to subdue the island definitively. That determination seems to date from the 1570s when Francis Walsingham – an anti-Catholic nationalist of the most unyielding sort – came to take the lead in formulating Irish policy.

To subdue Ireland in a context of war with Spain and of the growing pressures of both the Counter-Reformation and Protestant nationalism could only be done reliably by Protestants. Though in the past the crown had always largely relied upon the presence of the Old English to see its policies through, their religion now made them inherently unreliable. Why did they not follow the new religion of the English? The fact that they did not might be thought to suggest how qualified their Englishness had become, and yet one can as well ask the same question of Lancashire or of Richmondshire, Swaledale and Nidderdale in Yorkshire, areas which still had what may well have been a Catholic majority in the 1590s.[28] Only enormous government pressure could push Protestantism forward in such places. English Catholics, whether in England or in Ireland, went on refusing to see national loyalty in religious terms. The religious effectiveness of the Counter-Reformation now appears far greater than that of the Reformers in places where ordinary people remained attached to their traditional beliefs and practices. In English Ireland local government remained too much in the control of Catholics, parliament included, for the sort of squeezing of recusants which was just possible in Lancashire to work. Moreover for Counter-Reformation priests trained on the continent, the Old English in their towns were an easier primary target than the pure Irish. They were in consequence coming to represent a genuinely Counter-Reformation form of Christianity.

As England reconquered and reordered Ireland from the reign of Elizabeth to that of William of Orange, the Old English were in consequence dispossessed of control of parliament and most of their economic position by the new English settlers and driven into an ever closer union of shared religion and oppression with the Irish. It is, I believe, precisely the role of the Old English within the conflict between the New English and the Irish which best explains how across the catastrophic course of seventeenth-century history a new form of Irish identity developed, sprouting a kind of consciousness which may most appropriately be described as nationalism. I would like to illustrate what was happening by considering three literary figures. The first is Edmund Spenser.

Spenser represents the poetic quintessence of Elizabethan nationalism in a way that Shakespeare certainly does not. In *The Faerie Queene* we are offered a synthesis of Bible, nationalist history and a wealth of medieval imagery.[29] In the multiple allegories whose complexity almost defies the modern reader, faith, morality and politics come marvellously together through the interplay of three, variously named, sliding personages. First comes the Redcrosse Knight who is, of course, St George, England's patron, but whose role is also played by Arthur, Britain's primordial emperor and medieval hero of chivalry; Redcrosse is furthermore an image of England itself, of the redeemed Christian and, perhaps, even of Christ. Secondly there is his lady, Gloriana, Queene of Fairy Land, also named Astraea, Mercilla and Una. She is the one true church, universal, pre-papist, resurrected in the Church of England, Elizabeth herself. Finally, there is her rival, Duessa, Lucifera or Radigund, the other woman, at times appearing almost equally beautiful but utterly dangerous; she is the Papacy, Babylon, Anti-Christ, Mary Queen of Scots. Across a range of allegory and the mutation of names Spenser merges contemporary history with spiritual war of an apocalyptic sort, a subtle insinuation of Foxe's history of the church in which Protestantism brings holiness and even a sort of pastoral paradise.

The strategy of *The Faerie Queene* is not a narrowly puritan one. Far from rejecting England's medieval past as irremediably polluted by false religion, it reclaims huge chunks of myth, imagery and knightly virtue, to put at the service of Protestant nationalism. It is throughout the celebration of the providential union of England and true religion under the sovereignty of Elizabeth. It is thus a work of reconciliation between old Englishness and new Englishness, a closing of ranks between the 'Merrie England' which Catholics claimed had been lost with the Reformation and the Protestant gospel. Too many critics have succumbed to the temptation to read 'sweet Spenser' non-politically, even non-theologically, wallowing instead in a vast maze of allegory of the moral life. Universalist as *The Faerie Queene* may be, it is so only across an embedding of the general within a highly particularist and militant context. Its first three books were published in 1590, shortly after the defeat of the Armada and four years after the execution of Mary Stuart, an act it is intent on justifying. But the point that matters for us here still more is that it was written in Munster, where Spenser was in government service, at the sharp end of the nationalist war and it has absolutely to be read in that context. It was the work of a man who had begun his literary career by translating into English a piece of apocalyptic anti-Catholic propaganda written by a Dutch Calvinist and who went on to write *A View of the Present State of Ireland*, which he completed in 1596, the same year that the other three books of *The Faerie Queene* were printed. *A View* is written as a dialogue providing an intelligent, well-informed but utterly uncompromising denunciation of the 'licentious barbarism' of the Irish together with a more veiled but very consistent critique of the Elizabethan state for not being sufficiently ruthless in regard to their suppression and, in particular, for still maintaining the use of common law. Its real purpose was less to expose the lack of civilisation of the Irish than to berate both the Old English for succumbing to, and even supporting, the Irish, and the Queen's government for being pussyfooted in response. For Spenser the only solution was 'the sworde'.[30] Three years later, having fled the Munster Rising and left his burnt-out home, he returned a refugee to London. Just before he died he composed a further 'Brief Note on Ireland' which was still less restrained. While not actually appealing for genocide – 'that were to bloudie a course: and yet there continuall rebelliouse deedes deserve little better'[31] – his advice as to how 'to subdue Ireland throughly' sounded hardly less than genocidal: 'Great force must be the instrument but famine must be the means for till Ireland be famished it cannot be subdued . . . There can be no conformitie of government whereis no conformitie of religion . . . There can be no sounde agreement betwene twoe equall contraries viz: the English and Irish.'[32]

The point of quoting Spenser is that through his poetry he had made himself a leading ideologist of English nationalism while being at the same time the man on the spot. There is no evidence of any internal shift in conviction between writing *The Faerie Queene* and writing *A View* or *A Brief Note* or to imagine that any real contrast is to be found between them, despite the 'sweetness' of the one, the harshness of the other. Both equally represent the mind of an out-and-out English Protestant nationalist. While his views were not shared by all the settlers, particularly in his own Munster where the leading figure, Richard Boyle, the Earl of Cork, was far more of a pragmatist, and were somewhat more extreme than those of the government in London, which is why *The View* remained unprinted for forty years, there is no reason to think that they were not widely characteristic of the New English in Ireland. Effectively Spenser's views were acted upon by Mountjoy and, still more, by Cromwell. They do not represent a marginal eccentricity and the consequences still remain. To quote the rhetoric of Winston Churchill, a politician whose judgement oscillated throughout his life between statesmanship and English nationalism, commenting upon Cromwell's work in Ireland,

> By an uncompleted process of terror, by an iniquitous land settlement, by the virtual proscription of the Catholic religion, by the bloody deeds already described, he cut new gulfs between the nations and the creeds. 'Hell or Connaught' were the terms he thrust upon the native inhabitants, and they for their part, across three hundred years, have used as their keenest expression of hatred 'The curse of Cromwell on you' . . . Upon all of us there still lies 'the curse of Cromwell'.[33]

Despite Spenser's extremely low view of the religious qualities of

Irish Catholics, he admitted in a remarkable passage that for zeal and courage their priests educated abroad far outstripped the Protestant clergy. It was, he wrote, 'great wonder to see the odds which is betwene the zeale of the popishe priestes and the ministers of the gosple for they spare not to come out of Spaine from Rome and from Reymnes by longe toile and dangerous travell hither wheare they knowe perill of deathe awaite them and no Rewarde or Riches is to be found'.[34] Those words may be used to introduce my second example, Geoffrey Keating.

Keating was born around 1580 in County Tipperary of a particularly Gaelicised Old English family. He had attended a bardic school as well as learning Latin and was ordained in Ireland before going for further study to France in 1603. He returned in 1610 and remained in Munster until his death thirty-five years later. A scholar, poet and preacher of distinction, he wrote works in Gaelic on the Mass, the rosary and death of a typically Counter-Reformation kind before composing his great work on early Irish history, the *Foras Feasa ar Éirinn*. Keating has been hailed as 'the Herodotus of Ireland'. He pursued the manuscripts and the oral traditions already threatened by the growing collapse of Gaelic society but he put them together with a new orderliness, characteristic of his Old English background and continental training. The aim of *Foras Feasa ar Éirinn* was, moreover, a highly strategic one, and not dissimilar to Geoffrey of Monmouth's *Historia Britonnum*. On the one hand it created a unified history within the framework of a list of kings of Ireland, instead of continuing the old pattern of a series of annals; on the other hand, by showing that Irish history was also one of a series of arrivals of new groups who became integrated into the national story, he was able to place the Old English inside, instead of outside, the Irish story line. It was then essentially a reconciliatory book between Old Irish and the Old English who were now at last becoming a sort of New Irish. Just as Spenser's *The Faerie Queene* can be seen as an attempt to reconcile English medieval national spirit with post-Reformation nationalism as the battle between Protestantism and Counter-Reformation Catholicism hotted up, so was Keating's *Foras Feasa ar Éirinn* negotiating the union of the Old English with the Gaelic tradition to consolidate a common front against the attacks of the Protestant New English. Where Spenser and all the English-language historians found barbarism, Keating defended the civility. He did it very well and his book was widely popular. It was circulated widely in manuscript and was, in part, printed in English and yet in Irish it was never printed before the twentieth century.[35]

That brings us to a point we can pursue further by considering the Irish Bible. Elizabeth provided money at the start of her reign for the printing of it but there was remarkably little enthusiasm to translate the scriptures in Gaelic. At last in 1602 the New Testament appeared. Thirty years later William Bedell, the extraordinarily ecumenical Bishop of Kilmore, appealed for the Old Testament to be translated too.[36] With the help of a team of translators the work was completed by 1640 but it was not printed until 1685. The original edition of the New Testament was extremely small and it was not reprinted until 1681. The two appeared together for the first time in 1690. All this activity from 1681 on was chiefly due to Robert Boyle, the scientist, a son of the Earl of Cork. But Robert Boyle had moved from Munster to London and his prolonged concern to see a Gaelic Bible, for use in Scotland at least as much as Ireland, did not represent the normal Protestant attitude to Gaelic. It is striking how Dublin-born Archbishop Ussher, despite his Old English background and extensive scholarship, consistently opposed Bedell's plans for an Irish-language Bible. In this Bedell, while fully in line with Protestant insistence that the Bible should be available in every vernacular, was quite out of line with most English Protestants in Ireland. Far from wanting to convert the Irish through their own language, they believed that the language was a basic part of the problem. Protestantism and English must go together. From the sixteenth to the eighteenth century there were few Protestant clergy or laity who did not agree with Dean Swift that 'it would be a noble achievement to abolish the Irish language' or Bishop Woodward of Cloyne that 'if it be asked, why the clergy do not learn the Irish language, I answer, that it should be the object of government rather to take measures to bring it into entire disuse'.[37]

It is only too clear that, despite exceptions, the Church of Ireland was far too committed to the Anglicisation of Ireland to be faithful to its own Protestant principles. Only in the nineteenth century, when the people were anyway abandoning Gaelic by leaps and bounds, did the Church of Ireland become seriously interested in the language. Its committed Englishness had hitherto been in reality a saving grace for Irish Catholicism. But what about the Catholic side? What was its role in the language battle and what was its responsibility for the nation's effective abandonment of Gaelic by the mid-nineteenth century? It appears to me that that is a question absolutely central to Irish identity but one which does seem to have been too long evaded. Why indeed did the Irish people abandon Gaelic?

The answer seems to me to be clear enough. It is twofold. There was next to no printed Gaelic literature and the Catholic clergy abandoned the language before the laity. If the former had not done so, the latter would not have. The attitude of the clergy to Gaelic is, of course, more complex than that might suggest. In the seventeenth century with the ruin of the traditional Irish order, the near disappearance of aristocracy, jurists and bards, the role of the clergy, both the seculars and the religious, the Franciscans particularly, became overwhelmingly important. The fate of the nation was largely in their hands. As Irish seminaries and religious houses multiplied on the continent, training priests in a new Counter-Reformation manner, there was a very great effort, especially in Louvain, to save the Gaelic literary tradition. The historical value of that effort was immeasurable. Nevertheless what is clear is how little was actually ever printed and how limited were the more popular works produced in Irish. It is only too significant that Keating's great history never was, until this century. In an age of print a national language will not survive under pressure, if its national leaders are choosing not to use it. Of course the seminaries trained men to know both English and Gaelic for pastoral purposes, but understandably enough the Catholic clerical culture, first on the continent and then in Ireland, became an English-language one. When Maynooth was opened in 1795, there was no question but that English was its principal language. If English was good enough for the clergy, it was good enough for the laity too. There seems to me little doubt that if Irish scholars abroad in the seventeenth century had produced an Irish Bible and a mass of printed Irish Catholic literature – as the English exiles at Douai did in English – then Irish would have remained the language of Ireland.

Why did they not do so, despite their undoubted loyalty to the Gaelic tradition and desire to preserve it? The answer to that question lies under three heads – people, policy and circumstances. Let us consider the people first.

There does not seem much doubt that in the early seventeenth century when Ireland and the Irish church faced the greatest threat to their existence, the role of the so-called 'Old English' was decisive in shaping the response. They were Gaelic speakers, unattracted by the ways of the 'New English' and now, at last, when the Old Ireland was about to tumble to pieces, realising that they were fully part of it. Their being so made all the difference. Their disputes with the Old Irish could still remain sharp enough yet it was they by and large who provided the early base for the clergy of the Counter-Reformation; they from whom so many of the first leaders of that clergy came, they who in consequence largely shaped the colleges and priories of the church overseas. Archbishop Lombard, Bishop Rothe, the Franciscan, Luke Wadding, and Keating himself were all Old English. Both Lombard and Wadding exercised a great deal of influence on the continent, while Rothe as Vicar-General of Armagh and Bishop of Ossory virtually led the Irish church for many years. Such men, like Archbishop Oliver Plunkett in the next generation, were wholly committed to the survival and effectiveness of Irish Catholicism but they could still put up the backs of the Old Irish by the way they went about things. They were keener on 'civilitie' than on Gaelicness.

While the Old English were inevitably small in number compared with the pure Irish, circumstances favoured the maximisation of their influence over the developing ethos of the clergy. There seemed much advantage on the continent in using English rather than Irish, but there was also in time a political advantage at home. The Anglicisation of the country was going on and if the Catholic Church could use English effectively, then it was in a way stealing Protestantism's clothes. The conversion of the Catholic clergy to a systematic use of English implied for them the primacy of the interest of religion over language – even if it naturally appealed to the Old English mindset – whereas the failure of the Protestant clergy to follow the Bedell line and learn Gaelic implied for them the primacy of national, English, interest over religious principle, because a failure to use Gaelic was betrayal of a most central principle of the Reformation.

The impact of the Old English on the New Ireland was not merely a clerical one. They were townsmen attuned by past tradition – their long control of parliament, their multitude of common-law lawyers trained in London – to play the English game as the pure Irish were not. In consequence, in the post-Cromwellian situation, the experience of the Old English type of leadership remained valid in a way that the Old Irish type did not. Their differentiation as a group disappeared but not the sense of identity of individual family groups and urban communities in Dublin, Waterford and elsewhere. Many nineteenth-century Irish Catholics prided themselves, if not too publicly, on being of Old English stock. Just as the new Irish church, geared increasingly to the use of English, could hardly have come into existence with the quick effectiveness it did if it had not been able to draw upon the Old English clergy, so the new Irish nationalism would draw some of its character from Old English lay experience, just as it would draw some of its inspiration and leadership from the creative minority of New English who came to put Ireland before England, from Swift to Parnell. I cannot help thinking that this is an under-researched theme, perhaps because it is an uncongenial one both for Gaelic nationalists and for revisionists! If medieval Scottish nationalism had in a way been a branch of English nationalism turned against the main tree, so to some extent was the new Irish nationalism. Each grew in part out of the injection by English minorities of a nation-state view of politics into a Celtic nation.

It seems strange that Irish nationhood suffered so little from the abandonment of its strongest redoubt, the language, and it was only possible because Gaelic had in a very real way been replaced by an alternative principle, that of Catholicism. The fact that the threat to national identity in the seventeenth century was so clearly a Protestant one, and that Protestantism went necessarily with the dominance of England, inevitably identified Catholicism with Irish resistance to loss of national identity. Moreover the fact that the Old English had finally sided against England helped to demonstrate that the speaking of English was no longer in principle a threat to the nation. When Protestants in the nineteenth or twentieth century have protested against the Catholic-nationalist identity the only answer which could historically be given is that they had themselves made it inevitable and, indeed, continued to do so by stressing their Englishness or Britishness. While individual 'new English' like Parnell could jump the dividing line, yet remain Protestants, it seems almost impossible to imagine that as a group they could have done so, willingly abandoning the sense of being primarily British in the Victorian age when Britain was the most powerful country in the world, and with it their ascendancy.

Could the Catholic Irish too in the nineteenth century conceivably have forgone Irish nationalism in favour of being primarily British in a united kingdom and empire where Protestantism mattered less and less and where they now had the vote? Could they have behaved in fact like the Scots or the Welsh who were content to channel their national distinctiveness into the ecclesiastical rather than the political arena? The English Catholics, after all, had no difficulty in being patriotically British in a still nominally Protestant state, and the general advantage to the Catholic Church of having forty or fifty Catholic Irish MPs at Westminster was huge. Nothing is impossible with time and there can be no doubt that many Irish Catholics were happy and loyal enough within the British state. Some rose to very high positions in parts of the empire. There seem, however, to be at least four reasons why in general this was not possible. First, the alienating experience of Ireland at British hands had been vastly more painful than that of Scotland or Wales, at least in recent centuries. The memory could not be overcome in a few decades. Second, while the Protestant ethos of British power had notably diminished, it was still far too obvious in Ireland for the Catholic majority to acquiesce in it to the extent that the tiny minority of English Catholics across the Irish Sea could comfortably do. Thirdly, the fact that Ireland had had a parliament of sorts until 1800 meant that there was a plausible alternative to incorporation within Britain as for Wales at least there was not. Dublin was too obviously a capital – and indeed remained such with its Lord Lieutenant and all the ritual of Dublin Castle – for it not to keep the nationalist option more than open. But fourthly, and finally, Ireland had out of the agony of the seventeenth century refined its ancient national identity in something of a new form, but one no less powerful than its old, purely Gaelic, one. Nationalisms once conjured up just don't go away when basically unsatisfied, and yet still seemingly attainable in aim. If there had been no nationalist spirit in Ireland, maybe its people, Catholics included, could have been as satisfied with a British identity as were the Scots or the Welsh in the heyday of the British Empire. But such an 'if' requires the absurdity of forgetting the whole history of Ireland prior to 1829, and how the role of religion in all of that, first Protestantism and then Catholicism, had been absolutely decisive. It shaped the lines which have still not gone away and much as church leaders may wish to affirm that the conflicts of today are not about religion and are not between religious people, the fact remains that without the impact of religion they would be totally incomprehensible.

If I contemplate Irish history across the *longue durée*, I can see no even moderately plausible alternative to what one may fairly call a nationalist interpretation. Roy Foster, hardly a nationalist historian, has summarised early seventeenth-century developments with the words 'What was happening to the government of Ireland was "Anglicisation" . . . in the sense of governing Ireland with English priorities and in English interests. Part of this strategy meant Protestantisation.'[38] One must, of course, in a history of details point to ups and downs, twists and turns, within a long process but the point of the *longue durée* is that Foster's words summarise fairly enough not twenty but three hundred and fifty years of Irish history. It is striking, for instance, how the arrival of Evangelicalism from the mid-eighteenth century merely reinforced an already ancient Anglo-Protestant determination to beat down Irishness. Elsewhere, and in its very origins, Evangelicalism was an anti-establishment religious movement but not here. Its very 'lack of denominational and doctrinal homogeneity'[39] in Ireland actually seems to have made it the easier for Evangelicalism to reconsolidate a conviction that, regardless of the niceties of church or doctrine, Protestants must stand together – whether Episcopalian, Presbyterian or Methodist – to ensure that Ireland remained both British and Protestant. Thus Methodists, despite their relatively low social class and contempt for the Church of England at home, were gripped in regard to Ireland – as Professor Hempton has shown[40] – by an ill-informed paranoia in their opposition to Catholic Emancipation. The point is that popular Protestantism, in whatever new form of religious enthusiasm it appeared, shared exactly the same political objectives as older, drier and more establishment forms. While Catholic political attitudes varied greatly in Ireland over the centuries, what strikes one is the sheer stability of the Protestant political position from the late sixteenth to the late twentieth century. As the genuinely religious views of the Protestant and post-Protestant community have altered as much as anyone else's over this period, it is hard not to conclude that such stability must derive chiefly from a political ideology, that of British nationalism, an ideology seen as a matter of self-protection by a minority community. Richard Sheridan's late eighteenth-century definition of 'Protestant Ascendancy' was unambiguous:

> A Protestant king, to whom only being Protestant we owed allegiance; a Protestant house of peers composed of Protestant Lords Spiritual, in Protestant succession, of Protestant Lords Temporal, with Protestant inheritance, and a Protestant House of Commons elected and deputed by Protestant constituents: in short a Protestant legislature, a Protestant judicial [sic] and a Protestant executive in all and each of their varieties, degrees and gradations.[41]

Extreme as such a formulation sounds, it is not significantly different from the ideology of the Stormont Ulster statelet and Dr Paisley, yet in essence both in the eighteenth and the twentieth century it is nothing more than an anachronistic survival of English nationalism in its seventeenth-century guise.

Large-scale settlement in a foreign land is bound to go one of three ways in terms of nationhood. The first and most natural is that of assimilation into the existing population, while contributing something new to its cultural and political texture; in this case, despite some inevitable tension, both sides come to accept the primacy of the principle of territoriality over that of ethnicity. This is what happened with the Normans in England and with the Old English, eventually, in Ireland. Whether the immigrant minority come as conquerors or not may make relatively little difference across a few generations.

The second possibility is that of the virtual elimination of the existing population; in which case the immigrants establish what becomes quickly enough a new nation or ethnicity, detached from its home base though in some continuity with it, but entirely discontinuous from the communities hitherto in the country. This is what happened with the English settlers in America, what has happened more recently in Australia, and – a thousand years earlier – what happened in the eastern parts of the country that then became known as England. It is what the New English would at times like to have happened in Ireland, and even half pretended had happened, as in an amazing assertion in William Mollyneux's famous pamphlet, *The Case of Ireland's being Bound by Acts of*

Parliament in England Stated, the first unfurling of a Protestant Ireland's nationalist flag. But the plausibility of the nationalism was dependent upon swallowing this assertion in all its implausibility: 'The great Body of the present People of Ireland are the Proginy of the English and Britains (Britons), that from time to time have come over into this kingdom, and there remains but a mere handful of the Ancient Irish at this day, I may say, not one in a thousand.'[42] If Spencer's hint had been adopted and genocide carried out, then the New English in Ireland might have become the Irish Nation just as the New English in America became the American Nation. It was the obstinate refusal of the Old Irish to die out which made that inherently impossible, though for a century after the Battle of the Boyne native quiescence made it possible almost to pretend that it had happened and for Protestants to evolve towards an anti-English patriotism in consequence.

The third possibility is that the settlers fail to eliminate the existing inhabitants as a coherent community but also refuse to be assimilated with them. This is what actually happened in Ireland, just as it happened until recently with the white population in South Africa, or the French in Algeria. Such a settlement clings on to its originating identity with an essentially uncertain status in regard to the land it now occupies. This is only likely to happen if there is some great factor, real or perceived, racial or religious, preventing assimilation. If the immigrant community is content to be an apolitical one, their settlement may be peacefully accepted but in which case it has become an ethnicity rather than a nation. If, however, it claims a fully political identity, it must force the grounding of national identity back from territoriality to 'ethnicity' not only for itself but also for its hosts and by so doing create a situation in which conflict is bound to be endemic.

When one considers the Irish case and the unchanging commitment of the mass of the New English to a fusion of Britishness and Protestantism, one cannot but reflect on the one moment when it seemed almost possible for the conflict to be overcome through recognition that they had acquired an irrevocable Irish national identity which could only be in essence an Irish identity shared with the Catholic majority, that they were in consequence one nation and must develop as such through a parliamentary reform involving Catholic Emancipation. I am thinking, of course, of the late eighteenth century, the age of Grattan, when the leadership within the British settlement in Ireland appears to have developed in a way not so different from that of the Americans with whom they sympathised a great deal in the struggle of the 1770s. If Emancipation had arrived in the spirit of Grattan's famous 'Independence' speech of 1780 or the relief bill of 1795 and parliament had remained in Dublin, the two nations would surely have become one. While the Catholics would have gained enormously in the long run, Protestant interests would have been protected by their huge ascendancy in terms of landownership and wealth. Territoriality and common sense, not religious ethnicity, would have prevailed. That, surely, was Grattan's aim. It was defeated by anti-Catholic prejudice both in London and in Dublin, the fear of ordinary Protestants of losing ascendancy, their basic sense of being British more than Irish, as well as the general disturbance of mind produced by the revolution in France. It may be that a certain territorialisation of Irish consciousness was subsequently assisted, at least for many middle-class Protestants in the south, precisely by the security produced by the Union and direct dependence upon Westminster. But for most Protestants Irishness remained a sub-identity of a rather non-political sort, natural enough within the Victorian Empire and somewhat similar to the way the Scots and the Welsh felt. But for Catholics it could not be a sub-identity. In consequence nineteenth-century Ireland presents some appearance of national fusion, but one without substantial reality. The reality could only come through a collective escape from the mirage of linguistic, religious or ethnic principles for the definition of national identity in favour of the territorial. To counter Englishness with the revival of Gaelic was understandable enough but it was not realistic and could only be divisive by the late nineteenth century. The Catholic clergy had made the definitive decision in regard to Ireland's language a century and a half before. Neither Protestant British nor Catholic Gaelic identities could, in national terms, be other than destructive. It seems to me that Grattan, Parnell and their like arrived at the very same conclusion that the Old English had come to a good deal earlier. Minorities and majorities must be united by acceptance of a common Irishness definable only in territorial terms: we are here because we are here.

A structural analysis of what used to be called the Irish Question can only be done, I am suggesting, in terms of an understanding of the dynamics of nationhood and nationalism wider than Ireland itself. It is striking how general books on nationalism tend to give Ireland a miss.[43] It is striking too how almost every British analysis of Irish history and even today those described as 'revisionist' get off to a false start by near avoidance of the all-pervasive reality of English nationalism. It is only if one begins from this, I have been arguing, that Irish history becomes intelligible, but sound analysis further requires recognition of the enormous difference between imagining a nation in territorial terms and doing so in ethnic-religious terms, as well as of the decisive significance for Irish nationhood of the fate of the Gaelic language and responsibility for its collapse, together with the implications for the wider nature of Irishness of the history of the Old English. It is certainly striking how the role of the Old English is highlighted in modern Irish historiography, such as Roy Foster's *Modern Ireland*, up to the 'patriot' parliament of 1689, but from then they are never mentioned again. Their political role in seventeenth-century history was certainly an important one but their social, religious and educational role both then and afterwards though more invisible may also have been more lastingly significant. They pointed the path which their successors, the 'New English', would need some day to follow. For an understanding of Irish nationhood and a resolution of the perennial conflict resulting from the English domination of Ireland, the example of Geoffrey Keating remains of the most central importance.

CHAPTER FOUR

Western Europe

In this chapter we will consider, though far more briefly, the shaping of nationhood and nationalism among the principal peoples of western Europe in order both to provide a context and necessary comparison for England and to define the linkage between pre-1780 and post-1780 – to adopt Hobsbawm's date-line – within the long history of our subject. This will at the same time help provide an outline of the principal alternative European approaches to the political structuring of nationality.

The impact of English nationhood was felt both westward and eastward. Westward we have explored the effect of its direct export into Scotland, Ireland and America, and the very different ways in which this export was received in the diverse circumstances of these three countries. Eastward there was no direct export except to sixteenth-century Holland, but elsewhere its impact was in the course of time even more powerful. England's model, to some extent revamped in America, became in the late eighteenth century the example of the world's only seemingly thoroughly successful political-social system: stronger, more powerful, more expansive, more capable of harnessing the energies of its people at home, of building up colonies overseas, of transforming its own economy into new industrial directions than any of its possible rivals. Compared with a decadent Spain, Germany and Italy divided into a multitude of states, mostly very unprogressive, France betrayed into defeat after defeat by its autocratic bonds, Britain's advance from the relative insignificance of a century earlier to become the master model of modernity, political, economic and intellectual, was strikingly obvious. It was, it could be argued, the long extent of Anglo-French wars from the age of Louis XIV to that of Louis XVI which disillusioned Frenchmen with their own system and revealed to them, through the eyes of Voltaire, Montesquieu and others, the inherent superiority of England's way of doing things, the superiority of a national over a dynastic state.

Yet England was no less France's primary enemy, the country which had driven her out of India, conquered Quebec, and prevented her again and again from advancing her frontier significantly eastward. If the comparison between the two systems could produce admiration for England in Voltaire, in most people it simply compounded the vast resentment, an Anglophobia which delighted to do England down by supporting the American colonies in the War of Independence. Yet deep down the American victory proved to be just a further channel for the advance of ideas derived from an English source into continental minds.

France in the mid-eighteenth century was by no means a nation to the degree that England had become, despite centralised government, its language and its literature, its famous history. Why was this so? The very word 'nation' was not a particularly significant term in French vocabulary at the beginning of the eighteenth century, yet it was an all-significant term by its end. Once both word and model had been appropriated, England could be denounced, not unreasonably, for not being faithful to its own ideas, for possessing only a half-liberty.[1] When the Revolution came, it would ensure in all its extreme insistence upon freshly discovered principles that France seized all England's clothes and surpassed England, at the purely verbal level, a hundred times. France would from now on be not just a nation but in its own eyes 'La Grande Nation', the new and final model of all that a nation should be, yet it was only, it seems, in the 1750s that the idea of nationhood had really taken hold of the French imagination, both the word and the concept.

Nevertheless, one must insist that this could not have happened with such speed and conviction if the basic requirements for a nation in waiting had not been there since the later Middle Ages. It is true that the literary development of the French language in the high Middle Ages was not so much as a national but as an international and court language for a large part of northern Europe, England included, Latin's first replacement for the laity. The very width of its use could impede its nation-constructing role. It is also true that the 'Franks' glorified in the *Chanson de Roland* and the *Gesta Dei per*

Francos and seen from Carolingian times as God's New Israel were certainly not just the French. It was the First Crusade which really established a wide currency for the term 'Franks' as including the whole knighthood of western Europe. This version of God's New Israel consisted of the newly Christianised peoples of northern Europe as a whole, but particularly in their resistance to Muslim advances and in responding to the call of Crusade. When Baldwin, the first king of the Crusader state of Jerusalem died, he was mourned as a new Joshua[2] – Baldwin from Lorraine was hardly a Frenchman. Nevertheless with time the claim to be the New Israel became increasingly restricted to the kingdom of France, from which the largest group of Crusaders had come.

The claim, articulated more and more explicitly from the thirteenth century on, that the French crown and kingdom were uniquely Catholic and Christian, derived, then, from a kind of focused universalism, rather than from a straight claim that the French were the chosen of the Lord. But the result was the same. The kingdom of France, fortified by the canonisation of Louis IX, had seized the ideological space left half vacant by the discrediting of the Empire. The French king, it was now constantly repeated, was the *Rex Christianissimus* (a title at first used, sparingly, for other kings as well) and his kingdom one 'chosen by the Lord and blessed above all other kingdoms of the world', as Philip the Fair's minister, Nogaret, insisted.[3] Yet it was Nogaret who stormed the Papal Palace at Anagni, arresting and insulting Boniface VIII. A few years later Clement V, a Frenchman who had so far succumbed to French domination of the church as to establish papal residence at Avignon, confirmed this view of things: 'The kingdom of France, as a peculiar people chosen by the Lord to carry out the orders of Heaven, is distinguished by marks of special honour and grace.'[4] This claim to be a 'peculiar people' did not remain merely royal or ecclesiastical; rather was it mediated by the clergy to the people as a whole providing one of the most enduring roots of French nationhood and nationalism, but its justifying grounding remained a royal one. A century later, a peasant girl from Champagne could have no doubt that 'all those who fight against the holy kingdom of France fight against the Lord Jesus'.[5] The words, a recent commentator has remarked, 'may have been uniquely hers, but the sentiments they expressed were not'. Joan was simply breathing new life into existing

'French political assumptions'.[6] Her popular impact in stirring up an anti-English French national spirit should not be underestimated. She certainly provides one of the finest working examplars for a fusion of religion and nationalism. If in her own life it was an essentially defensive nationalism, the later usage of the myth of Joan has gone far beyond that – which is what generally happens in religious–nationalist fusions. What begins defensively ends offensively.

While the French monarchy ruled over plenty of non-French-speaking areas – so much so that the multiple languages of the French kingdom could be cited as a proof of France's superiority over little England with only its one tongue[7] – it was, nevertheless, true that the development of the French state and monarchy by the close of the Middle Ages would be inconceivable without the existence of a strong French-speaking society at its heart in the Île de France but one spreading out into towns throughout the kingdom, a French-speaking society whose political and cultural identity was being established through the development of its own characteristic literature. In France as in England, national identity owed almost as much to its writers, Montaigne, Rabelais or Ronsard, as to its kings. The early modern French state had, moreover, plenty of other institutions which were, at least potentially, nation-building: universities, *parlements*, the States General itself, even though its extra-monarchical political structures were undoubtedly far weaker than those of England in any power they possessed. Joan of Arc's France possessed an identity which even a peasant girl could share. When, a hundred and fifty years later, Henri IV converted from Protestantism to Catholicism in 1589 and ascended the throne, he could appeal to his people, 'We are all French and fellow-citizens of the same country.'[8] National identity was seen as binding together Catholics and Protestants even after years of religious wars and numerous atrocities. I find it absurd to refuse to recognise the essentials of a nation in fifteenth- or sixteenth-century France. Yet Henri IV's detente strategy, defined in the Edict of Nantes, was decidedly risky.[9] The unity of the French nation depended upon the mystique of its monarchy in a way that of England never did, and the monarchy's mystique was an intensely Catholic one. In consequence French late medieval national unity owed more to religion than did the English. The Edict of Nantes could only make lasting sense in a

more secularised and constitutionalised state. The option of absolutism led back to a reaffirmation of the unity of the religious, the royal
and the national, epitomised by the Edict's revocation. The institutional undergirding of the nation was to recede rather than mature
under the impact of a monarchical absolutism which effectively
eroded every genuinely national institution other than itself and the
church.

One should not, nevertheless, underestimate the continued na-
tion-sustaining role of institutions like the *parlements*, of Paris itself
with its university and, above all, of the church. Thus it would be an
act of sheer blindness not to recognise the significance from this
point of view of the City of Paris, the largest town anywhere in
Christendom, a town open like London to the whole country of
which it was the capital. If the kings moved from Paris to Versailles,
the move not only represented withdrawal into the splendour and
isolation of the monarchy as shaped by Louis XIV, it also left Paris
free to get on all the more with the business of just being itself, the
true heart of civil society for the French community and one of
immense variety and vitality. To focus one's picture of France in the
century before the Revolution, as people very easily do, upon
Versailles, where an English-type nation was indeed wholly negated,
and to forget about Paris where it was on the contrary very much
alive, is to make an understanding of what happened next almost
impossible.

Yet the role of the church was possibly still more important
because of its uniquely extensive pastoral and educational network.
Its effective organisational separation from Rome, decreed by the
monarchy, had made of it something exceedingly national in ethos
and administration, dominated by the spirit of Gallicanism. The
seventeenth century was a time of great spiritual vitality for French
Catholicism. It was the likes of Francis of Sales, Vincent de Paul and
Jean-Jacques Olier, of countless Lazarists, Sulpicians and Maurists,
quite as much as Pascal, Bossuet and Fénelon – or Racine and
Molière – who shaped French national consciousness in the seventeenth century by vastly improving the learning, zeal and profession-
alism of the clergy through institutions like St Sulpice which were
totally French and, in its case, based in Paris. They did so particularly
through the large-scale provision in French of religious literature,
works like the 1702 *Catéchisme du diocèse de Québec*, a book

recognised as hugely influential for the shaping of the French Canadian identity. It may seem appallingly revisionist to suggest that it could have been Gallicanism together with such things as catechisms and the Port-Royal translation of the Bible (1667–95), acclaimed as a huge literary success, as well as the greatly increased use of French in services in the eighteenth century (for instance, the regular reading of the epistle and gospel in French immediately after their Latin reading in Mass) and the generally altered attitude of Catholicism towards encouraging the laity to read the scriptures in the vernacular, which actually prepared the ground for nationalism and the Revolution. It is not surprising that it seems to have been a priest, the Abbé Coyer, who in the 1750s really set the ball of national discourse rolling in France and that many of the early thinkers of the Revolution were priests like Talleyrand, Sieyes and Grégoire. The role of the church in developing the French nation in the seventeenth and eighteenth centuries is not something which theorists and historians of nationalism have much considered, but its avoidance may be just another unfortunate consequence of the underlying modernist hypothesis behind studies of the subject.

The moment at which the modern French nation came into self-conscious existence can be far better placed in the 1760s than the 1780s; and its decisive cultural symbolisation lay in the triumph of Gallicanism with the expulsion of the internal enemy, the Jesuits, in 1764. At the same time the fires of nationalism were being stoked by the loss of empire in both America and India to the external enemy, the British. It is hardly surprising that in 1765 the *Comédie Française* presented Pierre de Belloy's patriotic play, the *Siège de Calais*, to huge popular acclaim.

When in 1766 Louis XV declared to the *parlements* that it was false to pretend that they represented 'the organ of the Nation, the protector of the Nation's liberty, interests and rights' and that, on the contrary, 'the rights and interests of the Nation, which some would make a body separate from the monarch, are necessarily joined with mine and rest only in my hands',[10] he was upholding a doctrine of the monarchy central to the development of France as it had never been to the development of England. But it was by then a fundamentally implausible and increasingly discredited position, outwardly pervasive as the mystique of monarchy still remained. The use of the word 'nation' might be somewhat new but the reality was that the nation had existed for centuries in a semi-conscious state, even if stifled by the requirements of absolutism. Now that the monarchy was manifestly failing to deliver the goods, the nation was re-asserting the necessity of expressing itself through other institutions. However unpleasant it was to take anything from the national enemy, it was rather obvious that the English state model was working incomparably better than the French and that at its heart lay recognition of the nation's priority to its government. Twenty-five years after that reassertion by Louis XV of the monarchy's monopoly over nationhood, the Revolution enforced, with a remorseless logic all its own, not only 'fraternity', but 'equality' and 'liberty' as necessary qualities of a model of nationhood, far more sharp-edged and threatening than the solid, conservative-looking and still rather aristocratically led English example.

The fact remains, however, that, place oneself at Hobsbawm's entry date of 1780, England was ever so much more of a nation-state than France and it is worth listing the principal structural reasons why that was so. Undoubtedly, the primary reason was the central organ of government of the two. For France it was an absolute monarchy and its rule remained profoundly dynastic in a way that England's had not been for centuries. Since 1660 the monarchy in England had existed, if not quite on sufferance, nevertheless only upon condition that it accepted the will of the nation as expressed through Parliament. That had been made clear once more with the expulsion of James II in 1688 and, yet again, when the Elector of Hanover was selected as king. It was so little a dynastic state that the Hanoverian dynasty had been chosen to suit its needs rather as one might choose the right kind of washing powder off a supermarket shelf. The central political structure of France stressed verticality, the central structure of England horizontality, the sovereignty of a parliament elected by people from every part of the country. What the monarchy was to France – 'L'état, c'est moi' – parliament was to England.

Secondly, England was a remarkably unified country. It had had relatively little change to its borders since the late tenth century; while France had changed its borders enormously, many large areas, like Franche-Comté and Lorraine, having only recently been incorporated into the kingdom. England's shires, established since the early eleventh century, were a wholly different thing from the divisions of France into huge, largely autonomous, provinces, like Brittany, Burgundy, Provence and Lorraine, which, if they were reduced to central control from the time of Richelieu and Mazarin, retained enormous diversity in law and custom. The *Départements* of the Revolution would, indeed, be not unlike English shires.

Again, the French were not united by language at all to the extent that ordinary English people were. Cornwall and Wales were England's only linguistic islands and Wales was, in consequence, never integrated into the nation effectively. But France was full of comparable cases which were then as now seen as simply part of France but have only been linguistically integrated in the nineteenth or even the twentieth century. As Eugen Weber has demonstrated so effectively in *Peasants into Frenchmen*, a very high proportion of French people hardly spoke French even in the late nineteenth century. Breton, Basque, Flemish, German, Provençal and a medley of patois, most of them far more distinct from French than were the dialects of the shires from London English, completely divided the common people of France in terms of linguistic and cultural community. In the eighteenth century the foreign traveller was struck by the linguistic unity of England but by the diversity of France, as of Italy or Germany. Get into the countryside a hundred miles from Paris and it could be impossible to make yourself understood in French. French remained an international language, a language of culture and diplomacy spoken by the upper class across half of Europe; English was a national language spoken by the English.

A chief reason for the difference in relationship of the two languages to ordinary people was a religious and ecclesiastical one. The impact of the French Church upon the language of the common people was severely limited by the continued liturgical use of Latin. We have already considered the massive influence of the Bible, especially the Protestant Bible, in the vernacular. There were various printed Bibles in French by the seventeenth century but the Bible was not to be found as the one book in every respectable home as the English Bible, whether Geneva or King James, was present and read in any English home. Not even in the home of every French *curé*. On the contrary, he was expected to read his Bible in Latin, if he read it at all. Latin was the language of his theological studies, of his breviary and of his missal. Perhaps it is in the contrast between the impact of the Latin missal and the English Book of Common Prayer that the root of the difference between the national development of the two languages should be sought – in orality grounded upon text. In every English church the Book of Common Prayer with its fine Cranmerian style was to be heard being read out every week of the year. It and the English Bible, chapters of which were read as well each Sunday, shaped the spoken language of the nation from the sixteenth century on. In a French Catholic church there was little similar. Everything official was in Latin and most of what was unofficial could well be in a patois. As suggested above, only in the eighteenth century was this beginning to change. In neither country was there any rival for popular education to the services of the established church before the nineteenth century.

France, then, lacked the firm geographical delineation which England acquired so early. Despite unification by royal power, it also lacked the administrative unity of England, a uniformity in courts and taxes. It lacked the linguistic unity of England and the very consciousness of having at a popular level a genuinely national language. It was the Revolution which set itself to create that consciousness – 'The Unity of the Republic demands unity of speech', abolishing 'the diversity of primitive idioms' in favour of 'the language of the Declaration of Rights' but, despite the eloquence of such appeals by men like the Abbé Grégoire,[11] it did not succeed in that endeavour in the south, east, far north or far west for more than a hundred years. As late as 1864 a government report on the *État de l'instruction primaire* could admit that, throughout the south of France, 'Despite all efforts the French language spreads itself only with difficulty.' In the revealing words of the Marseillais historian François Mazuy, 'French is for us a language imposed by right of conquest.'[12] That again equates half of France with Wales or Ireland. Turning Oc into France was like making Ireland English. The French finally succeeded in the endeavour, the English did not, but the comparison demonstrates the difference between the national unity of what we think of as France today and that of England.

Finally, France lacked a unifying political institution comparable to parliament or, to put it more precisely, comparable to the House of Commons, an elected body representing the shires and towns of the country and meeting on a regular basis.

Arthur Young, travelling in France in July 1789, just as the

Revolution was beginning, was struck by the absence of newspapers in the provinces: 'The backwardness of France is beyond credibility in everything that pertains to intelligence', and, after remarking that there are men every day 'puffing themselves off for the First Nation in Europe', went on to comment that 'the universal circulation of intelligence which in England transmits the least vibration of feeling or alarm, with electric sensibility, from one end of the kingdom to another, and which unites in bonds of connection men of similar interests and situations, has no existence in France.'[13] One can see why. Almost everything which made of England a nation – and Young's observation is a rather good description of what it is to be a working nation – was still absent in France.

France was, to conclude, even in the fifteenth and sixteenth centuries, less clearly a nation, self-awarely united in a horizontal manner by shared language and institutions, than England and since then it had fallen back considerably under the weight of royal absolutism while England had, on the contrary, dotted its parliamentary Is and crossed its Protestant Ts, to become even more of one. The failure of French absolutism to deliver military victory or colonial expansion opened the way in the late eighteenth century for a violent explosion at once of democratic 'liberty' and nationalist 'fraternity', intended by its enthusiastic supporters to outdo anything that had been achieved in England and to produce a new model of the nation. In point of fact the 'nationalising' of the French in the more remote parts had still hardly begun a century later.[14] Creating nationhood is easier said than done. The nationalism of the Revolution was all the same so abrasive and so communicative that historians have been able to convince themselves that nationalism itself only began at that time. It certainly did not, as we have seen, and even for France it remains vital to recognise that the nation had had existence of a not inconsiderable sort well before late eighteenth-century nationalism and that it was precisely because it had long survived, despite profound institutional frustration, swallowed up for a while in 'La Gloire' of the monarchy, that it was able, with rather little further intellectual grounding – far less theoretical stimulation than German nationalism received a generation later – to burst upon the world.

Turn now to Germany, another too largely misunderstood case. The sudden eruption of nationalist sentiment among the German intelligentsia in the first decades of the nineteenth century is not in question, nor the impact of the French Revolution itself, followed by the Napoleonic treatment of Germany, in producing this. The new French national model had been proved to work very potently, and in a way extremely humiliating for Germans. Just as the English had humiliated the French, so had the French humiliated the Germans. Their country had been shown up in all its political insignificance and, led by its intellectuals, Germany suddenly began to rediscover the vision of its own nationhood. I say 'rediscover' deliberately because, here again, a history of nations and nationalism which would begin in the late eighteenth century, dismissing the predetermining factors of ethnicity, language and past political history, can make very little sense of this sudden eruption of German nationalism. 'The development of German national consciousness was singularly rapid', writes Liah Greenfeld, 'One cannot speak of it before 1806; by 1815 it had come of age . . . This development, from birth to maturity, in other nations took a century.'[15] Is that really credible? Huge as the leap forward in that decade undoubtedly was, 'German national consciousness' had far from 'come of age' in 1815 and was only possible at all because a sense of German nationhood was already very deeply present, even if apparently somnolent. Why, after all, was it Germanness which was activated by resentment against the French and not Prussianness or Austrianness or whatever? They, after all, were the states which the French had crushed so devastatingly. The Austrian and Prussian armies were defeated at Austerlitz and Jena but it was Germany which took affront, though it would be more than another fifty years before nationalism really took root among the large majority of ordinary people and as a consequence rather than a cause of the Prussian 'reunification' of the country.

To explain why French imperialism at the start of the nineteenth century was able to set in motion a specifically German national consciousness it is, once more, essential to return to a far earlier stage in nation-formation, the Middle Ages, when the German nation possessed for centuries political consciousness as a single entity, even though it failed again and again to achieve a stable political structure to hold that entity together. Susan Reynolds has, quite rightly, derided 'the belief that the German nation was doomed to wait in the anteroom of history until the modern nationalist movement summoned it forth in the nineteenth century'.[16] The 'Regnum Teutonicum' existed in its own right as a community of law, custom, language and kingship well before it became identified with the Holy Roman Empire in the fourteenth century so that the two were officially redefined as the 'Holy Roman Empire of the German People', a geographically somewhat vague reality located between the Rhine and the Oder. That title was certainly not without meaning, but it was deeply ambiguous. The Empire remained in principle the central and highest political institution within western Christendom, something essentially more than national. Its attachment to Germany reflected the wealth and potential power of its people and their centrality to Europe, but it also blocked Germany's ability to develop nationally or dynastically. It was not a dynastic but an elective empire. The seven electors of the emperor, three bishops and four lay princes, were not mere ciphers; nor were the great imperial assemblies such as the Diets of Worms of 1495 and 1521, the Diet of Regensburg of 1532 or the 1555 Diet of Augsburg mere reflections of an imperial court. They represented a genuine, if embryonic and ineffectual, political structure for a culturally self-conscious nation which was still trying to be more than a nation. While they disastrously failed to counter the centrifugal pressures of a state which lacked even a capital, they did demonstrate over several centuries that the German nation saw itself as a political entity. The memory of that understanding was dimmed but never wholly lost. However, the hardening of the divide between Catholics and Protestants, the practical monopoly by the Habsburgs of the imperial throne and the limitation of their power-base to Austria and non-German lands to the south-east ensured that in practice any political dimension to the existence of the German nation, beyond a basic community of law, simply disappeared.

With the rupture of both political and religious bonds, only the underlying linguistic bond remained present and in consequence assumed an overriding importance. The literary development of German in the Middle Ages had paralleled the economic importance of this part of Europe. The invention of printing itself reflected the culture and needs of great cities like Mainz, Cologne, Augsburg and Nuremberg. If Gutenberg's Latin Bible was printed about 1455, a complete German Bible followed only ten years later, making use of a translation dating from the previous century. Here as everywhere extensive circulation of written texts standardised both the language and the identity of the people employing the language, even if they also employed many oral dialects as well. It is significant that the only German-speaking group to opt out of the German nation, before the mid-twentieth century opt-out of Austria, was the Swiss who had begun to form their own state before the development of printing and remained unaffected by the whole subsequent evolution of Germanness. Yet a long uncertainty about the distinct national identity of the Swiss owes a great deal to the lack of hard political structure for the German nation prior to the nineteenth century. While being German was so much a matter of sharing in a linguistic and cultural community, how could people who were German speakers opt out of being German?

The 1466 German Bible had gone through fourteen editions by 1518, after which the baton was taken over by Luther's more contemporary version based, moreover, not on the Vulgate but on the original languages. His Bible and his numerous other works, mostly immensely popular, did more than anything else to establish a literary German which was then regularly communicated to the whole population of Protestant Germany, not only through Bible reading in the home but also as everywhere else in the Protestant world through the Sunday service. Added to this was the role of the universities, which continued to uphold a basic sense of collective identity, particularly through their law faculties. Despite the absence of any significant political unity for almost three centuries, the identity of Germanness was ensured in fundamentally national terms in this way, but it was one felt in consequence at popular level a good deal more by Protestants than by Catholics.

If the idea of Germanness as a continuing reality could hardly be grounded in political facts – as it could in England or France – or even in terms of a clearly delimited territory (for the borders of the German-speaking community were extremely confused and there was much intermingling particularly with Slavs) then it had little more than language left, language imagined as a legacy of ethnic origins. An idea of nation dependent on language seems necessarily to push the claim back beyond language to an assumed genetic identity, the identity in this case of the *Volk*. One's ethnic identity becomes primary but manifested through linguistic identity. The German predicament – consciousness of nationhood, absence of a state, strength of German as a literary language – made the particular form which German nationalism would take almost inevitable, the nationalism of *jus sanguinis*, the most dangerous of all nationalism's forms. A combination of high prestige and ineffectiveness in the medieval empire held the German political nation in thrall, leaving the task of national identification to language and literature. The initial nineteenth-century explosion of anti-French resentment had necessarily to be a cultural one. There was, in a sense, an inevitability in the whole process and yet the entire history both of nationalism and of Europe underwent in consequence a subtle, intensely dangerous, shift whereby the territorially imagined nationalisms of England, France and America became instead the ethnically–linguistically imagined nationalism of Germany. It would soon serve as model to many others. It was certainly the nineteenth century which produced German nationalism, but it could only do so – one must once more insist – out of the half-submerged reality of a medieval nation.

Why did German nationalism need to appeal so strongly to a single ethnic origin and the idea of ethnic purity to defend Germanness? Why was the community of language not enough? Language-speaking is, after all, a fact of sorts within contemporary experience while ethnic origins in the remote past are inevitably in large part a myth. Yet the very factuality of language-speaking is in a way its Achilles' heel. On the one hand oral German was particularly diverse – inevitably, given the very wide expanse of German-speaking areas. On the other, people can learn a language and they do. A nation so defined is blissfully open to newcomers in a way that a bristly national spirit, a little unsure of its precise identity, is unlikely to tolerate. A principle of national unity which is so inclusivist may be all very well if you have the matrix of a strong state but the very vagueness of the German nation in hard fact, disunited politically and spread across huge tracts of central and eastern Europe, may have all the more impressed the need for a mythical principle of unity which laid down a hard frontier of separation, if only an imaginary one. This was no merely theoretical issue. There were so many Jews in Germany and they spoke German; even Yiddish was a form of German. A nationalism grounded explicitly on language must include them within the nation – and on French principles they were unquestionably to be included. The French could do it because they had the unity of the state; Germans, without the political bonding, jibbed at it. There were too many Jews – far more than in France – and too much long-standing hostility, including Luther's particular hatred for them. A national identity based on blood could conveniently exclude them.

Germans could, moreover, appeal to their ethnic purity rather more plausibly than the French and the English. They had within historic memory no obvious binarity with which to cope. France and Britain had been within the Roman Empire as the lands east of the Rhine had not. This already involved, for peoples conscious of their arrival within their present countries as newcomers between the fifth and seventh centuries, a dual foundation charter. France's origins are both Gallic and Frank, England's British, Anglo-Saxon, Danish and Norman – its national myths include elements from all these sources – but Germans could claim that there was no such mongrel mixing in their ancestry, no multiple mythology. There were German tribes in Germany when Julius Caesar was conquering Gaul and invading Britain. Germans and no one else.

It was possible to think so simplistically about German ethnicity because Germany had held quite tenaciously to the generic name given to a considerable number of related tribes while the English and French were identified instead with the names of specific German tribes – Angles and Franks. In consequence any shift from one group to another was eliminated linguistically and an impression of unchangeable identity remained dominant. East of the Rhine narrower names like 'East Franks', Saxons or Bavarians never for long seemed to provide a principal political identity. Ethnic unity could in consequence provide an underlying basis for German consciousness denied to England and France. Yet in historical reality all three had the character of a nation by the later Middle Ages for much the same basic reasons – the fusing together of smaller ethnic groups through a literary language enhanced by some measure of national state formation. Only the measure varied. But while political unity and territorial integrity became firmer in France and England, for Germany they simply fell away, leaving the language, one might say, to cope on its own, fortified by the mythology of ethnic unity.

The threat from an internal enemy is as potent as the external and its countering is almost inevitably more destructively autarchic. It is, to a very large degree, in terms of 'the other', one's closest perceived threat, that one defines oneself. In this at least Germany and Spain have been much alike, each's nationalism intent in consequence in discovering an internal enemy that threatened its ethnic purity and each at its most extreme set upon pursuing the road of ethnic cleansing. It may seem strange that Spain needed to take this road. Its Christian kingdoms had won their long struggle with the Moors, and by the late fifteenth century it was not far off the unity of a self-contained geographical peninsula, a powerfully centralised government, the excitement of a shared imperial enterprise and a developed vernacular literature. Why did one need ethnic purity too? Here as in England consciousness of national identity preceded political unity. Because the conquest of the Moorish kingdoms achieved in the thirteenth century came to be seen both as a national war of liberation and as a crusade, there was a special holiness, a special Christianness and Catholicism, in Spain's very existence. Spain had found its own special way to be a peculiar people.[17] That holiness and therefore national identity too seemed inherently threatened by the survival of Muslim or Jew in the kingdom and especially by secret Jews or Muslims, huge numbers of double-faced people existing in the nationalist and Catholic imagination as only pretending to be Spanish and Christian. Their expulsion appeared as the consummation of the struggle for Spanish identity. The Spanish Catholic Church was more wholly controlled by the monarchy than any other part of west European Catholicism. It was controlled through the Inquisition, which became in its hands an extraordinarily efficient instrument for the defence at once of religious and national purity, conceived as a single reality, doctrine upon the one hand, 'purezza de sangwe' on the other. Spanish identity came thus to be defined in the narrowest, yet also the most extended, of terms, both racial and religious. The mass expulsion of Jews and Muslims in 1493, followed by the Inquisition's pursuit for two centuries of pollution brought about through 'New Christians', wrote ethnic cleansing into the very constitution of Spanishness but it also reinforced the sense of the latter as something in principle shared horizontally by the whole community.

In both Spain and Germany the endemic antisemitism of the Christian tradition provided additional support for a type of nationalism which was not shaped primarily by this but by its own

inherent, particularist, logic. Christian antisemitism was not significantly worse in Germany or Spain than in Poland or France. Both
Catholic and Lutheran antisemitism were in the end subsidiary
factors only, and in both Spain and Germany it was the race, more
than the religion, of the Jews that guaranteed their persecution.
Nothing, after all, could change their race, though religious
conversion might mask it across a couple of generations and, of
course, often did. It was that which threatened Iberian or German
purity.

At this point German and Iberian nationalisms part course. German nationalism was shaped relatively little by religion except in the
ways that every European nationalism was shaped by an underlying
biblical vision of the world and the impact of the vernacular Bible
which affected German Protestants so much more than German
Catholics and, in consequence, encouraged in the former a greater
commitment to Germanness. Apart from this, the country's division
between Catholic and Protestant, and its remoteness from the front
line with Islam, removed from it the principal religious factors
discoverable elsewhere in the construction of a national identity.
Only the otherness of the Jews remained as a pole for the shaping of
one's own consciousness. Spanish nationhood, on the contrary, was
shaped by its position on the frontier with Islam. Here religion was
more continually decisive than for any other in western Europe,
decisive through the character of the medieval wars which initially
established it, decisive through the activity of the Inquisition in
ensuring its continuance, decisive in the highly and narrowly
religious ideal which became nationally normative. Spanishness and
Catholicism, the Catholicism of Isabella, 'La Catolica', seemed for
centuries inseparable and only a very agonised modern history would
tear them, partially, apart.

If there is no clear geographical unit and no successful central
state, what is a half-self-conscious nation, sharing a common
language and literature, to turn to in justification of its claim to exist
and, indeed, to be recognised as a uniquely important segment of
humanity? The answer seems necessarily to lie in a return to some
myth of ethnic origin, a myth basically available in the self-history of
almost every group. The sense of nationhood of most peoples
distances itself from that myth because it is not needed any more and
too gravely oversimplifies subsequent history. But it is almost always

mass of local ethnicities, many of them of a fairly unstable sort. Take Britain of the sixth to the eighth century. There are Scots and Picts and Britons, there are kingdoms in Strathclyde and Cumbria, Powys, Gwynedd, Cornwall; there are incoming Angles, Saxons and Jutes who then form a medley of other kingdoms – Kent and East Anglia, Lindsay, Northumbria, Mercia, the West Saxon. Later they are joined by Danes of various sorts and Normans. That is surely not a complete list. The continent is much the same. While there is a king of Kent and one of Lindsay, there are others of Soissons, Metz and Paris. Brittany, Burgundy and Bavaria all look at one time or another like independent politico-ethnic entities, yet none of them quite makes it into the national league. Some of these names quickly disappear, one or two survive indefinitely but it would, of course, be absurd to argue for any special continuity of identity between, say, sixth-century Angles and the English of today, to the exclusion of all the other lines of ethnic, cultural and political descent. Picts and Jutes early disappear from the nomenclature but that does not necessarily make the contribution of their descendants less important. Little by little the development of one or two literary languages and large state formations diminish the complexity and fluidity of the map. As this happens a sense of something which we can properly call nationality and which medieval writers often did refer to as one of 'nations' emerged firmly and steadily. That is the second stage.

By the fifteenth century most of the main nations of western Europe can be seen to exist. People regularly spoke of them as such. They are precisely the same nations produced by nationalisms from the late eighteenth century on, according to the theorists of modernism. The correlation is so close that it would be absurd to regard it as accidental. Germans, French, English, Spaniards, Italians, Danes, Dutch, even small peoples like the Scots – they are all firmly in place well before 1500. While the criterion was certainly not a primarily political one, but far more that of a people with a literary language of its own, it does seem to have been recognised that a nation should in some form or other have a government corresponding to its particular culture. As the Frenchman Claude Seyssel remarked in the early sixteenth century, 'All nations and reasonable men prefer to be governed by men of their own country and nation – who know their habits, laws and customs and share the same language and lifestyle as them – rather than by strangers.'[19] Custom and language shape the nation but government should follow suit. That seems the right way round, then and now.

Undoubtedly there were many peoples in Europe who continued to fall between rather than within such nations. They were still, essentially, the smaller ethnicities which had covered the whole continent six centuries earlier, even though in many of them there was now some degree of writing in their own vernaculars. Mostly small in size and in less economically developed areas, they were nevertheless being forced inside the circle of the nation closest to them. Brittany, Wales, Navarre and many others were neither fully distinct nor fully integrated. Some would survive to assert their own nationhood even if the likelihood of this must have seemed small at the time. Cornwall was fully integrated into England despite its different language, but Wales never would be. Surprisingly perhaps, some of the German-speaking groups in the foothills of the Alps were little by little differentiating themselves from Germany, despite a common language, and turning themselves into a Swiss nation. In this case a unique political and military experience proved of itself decisive. Just as English nationhood came to owe a lot to the long bow, so Swiss nationhood owed still more to the pike. In each case the combination of war with a rather democratic, common-man way of waging it proved extremely important in the business of nation-building. But I doubt whether many a fifteenth-century European observer would have included the Swiss in his list of nations.

To the north-west the Dutch are another interesting case. Their claim to be a distinct political nation is not so obvious and yet the Dutch do seem to have been accorded nation-status by the late Middle Ages. They had come adrift of the German hinterland, with a recognisably distinct language and a social history of their own: the building of the huge sea dykes, beginning on a large scale in the thirteenth century, proved as remarkably nation-building for the Dutch as the use of the bow and the pike proved so for English and Swiss. In each case it was the shared public responsibility of common people for activity decisively important for the state which proved nation-making. But the possession of a distinct written language mattered still more. The appearance in 1522 of a first printed Dutch New Testament, based on the Vulgate, following on a range of scriptural translations all across the later Middle Ages, may be the best proof that the Dutch were by then within the nation category despite the absence of any clearly corresponding state. They seem to have been recognised by others to be so. The national distinction between what is now Belgium and what is now the Netherlands did, however, come later, the division being dependent upon the politics and religion of the sixteenth century. The national divisions of twentieth-century western Europe are not precisely and irreversibly present in the fifteenth, but they are there for some 80 per cent, as they were not in the eighth.

Austria is worthy of special consideration, especially against Renan's famous question, 'Why is Holland a nation, while Hanover and the Grand Duchy of Parma are not?'[20] If not Hanover, why Austria? Austria was in point of fact just another bit of Germany and, traditionally, in the same constitutional position – their two rulers were both Electors. Vienna might well have been claimed as Germany's natural capital. Yet, little by little, Austria became distanced from Germany, tied too closely to Slav societies to provide a specifically German leadership, a situation upon which Prussia successfully seized. Austria was no longer to be the leader of Germany, but was it not still a part – by language, culture, ethnicity? On the principle of German nationhood, still not repudiated, the answer could only be in the affirmative. Probably very few Austrians in the 1930s really disagreed with the *Anschluss*, whether or not they cared for Hitler. It would seem that only in the last fifty years have the Austrians really become a nation of their own. By being so, they undermine the key determinant of German nationhood, as indeed do the Swiss. If one asks why Austria is a nation but Bavaria or Hanover is not, there is no ethnic, linguistic or religious reason. The vagaries of history, state formation and community consciousness have simply, and belatedly, made it so.

The case of Italy is also exceptional. An Italian national identity was recognised in the fifteenth century, yet its hardening had been held back precisely by the leading role Italy had taken in the culture, church life and economic development of previous centuries. Italian was for long less of a language recognised as a national tongue distinct from Latin than those north of the Alps. Indeed, Italian dialects were so diverse that the literary development of the Italian of Tuscany had little general impact, and that development was itself retarded by the anxiety of Renaissance scholars to stick to Latin.

Again, the very prosperity of individual Italian cities, in this like German ones, had given them an independence which inhibited effective nation-forming developments. But, most important of all, there was the papacy, firmly ensconced back in Rome after a painful fourteenth-century period in France – painful particularly for Italy. Rome was the obvious capital of Italy but it was also, even more obviously, the city of the Pope and the papacy could never be a merely Italian matter. Even in the nineteenth century Italian nationalism would be profoundly embarrassed about how it should relate to the Popes. In the fifteenth the political, international and religious importance of the papacy was such that it placed the construction of Italian nationhood in a category all its own.

Let us conclude this discussion of the late medieval nation with some remarks of two witnesses of that time. The first is one of the most cultured, well-travelled and brilliant of fifteenth-century Europeans, Enea Silvio Piccolomini, who became Pope as Pius II in 1458. A novelist, a trusted civil servant of the Emperor of Germany and, for a while, even Bishop of Trieste, Enea was a Tuscan who was also, pre-eminently, a European. Writing in 1458, just before papal election, he was replying to German grievances against both the Roman See and the Italians who manned it. No, Enea replied, you may blame the Italians but not the papacy itself. Italians, he admits, are money-grubbers but they aren't alone in being so: 'You will never find a people who easily permit money to be taken out of their region. It is a common disease and spread equally over all provinces. For just as the Germans hate the Italians for this reason, so the Hungarians hate the Germans . . . The Poles have the same grievance, so do the Danes and the Swedes.'[21] Our second witness is an anonymous late fourteenth-century Englishman defending the translation of the scriptures into the vernacular to help people who are not learned but, equally, are not illiterate. For the ordinary literate, he argues, there should be 'bookis of her moder tongue, to Frensche men bokis of Frensche, to Ytaliens bokis of Latyne corrupte, to Duche men bokis Duche, to Englische men bokis of Englische'.[22] One could multiply such quotations almost indefinitely. Admittedly, some of the nations mentioned then did not quite make it later – Lombards or Catalonians, for example. Yet such groups had already gone so far along the road of nationhood that five centuries later their claim to be such can still be seriously resurrected.

Medieval historians seem to me increasingly agreed that in the fourteenth and fifteenth centuries national identities in western Europe had stabilised in a form, for the most part, that we take for granted still today and texts like the remarkable 1320 Scottish Declaration of Arbroath make it clear that such national identities were expected to be a matter of government as well as of language and custom.

There remained, nevertheless, no very clear sense of just how the bond between nation and state – 'gens' or 'natio' and 'regnum' – was to be seen. It could be asserted emphatically in a struggle for liberation from foreign rule of the sort that engendered the Declaration of Arbroath or it could be recognised more philosophically by a writer like Claude Seyssel. Where England was far ahead of any rival already in the fourteenth century was in regard to developing structures of government which actually facilitated an on-going experience of being a nation-state. States existed of all sorts, shaped at the personal level of the prince by feudal and dynastic criteria which paid scant attention to anything very national. Yet this mattered less than we might think because societies were all ruled to such a large extent by their own accumulated law and custom rather than by kings or princes. The axiom of the thirteenth-century English lawyer Henry Bracton, 'rex non debet esse sub homine, sed sub Deo et lege', provides a clue to medieval government everywhere. Even kings were meant to be ruled by the law. Law and custom, rather than the person of the prince, defined the kingdom and the nation with it. In consequence, as Susan Reynolds has insisted, the medieval idea of the 'community of the realm' closely resembles the modern idea of the 'permanent and objectively real nation'.[23] If Henry II was at once King of England and Duke of Normandy, that did not in any way equate the law of Normandy with that of England. The prince was, at least in theory, under the law of every province he had obtained dynastically or feudally. Each, then, was ruled in a way proper to itself. But in England the law, the administrative structure of the realm, and the whole pattern of government had been for centuries developing on lines which tended to produce a far closer integration of state and nation. If England is Europe's first-born nation, it is not that it was ahead – as Greenfeld thinks – by the sixteenth century but by the tenth and still more by the fourteenth. There were plenty of recognisable nations in western Europe by the fourteenth century but only one nation-state and that was England.

While on the continent in the sixteenth and seventeenth centuries the main leading countries all moved strongly towards absolutist forms of government which effectively diminished the bond between nation and state by insisting that legitimacy depended upon dynastic correctness not the consent of the governed, in England that tendency was successfully resisted and the model of a parliamentary nation-state advanced all the more while proving its potency externally at the same time. Hence the gap between England on the one hand and France, Germany or Spain on the other was far greater in the mid-eighteenth century than in the fourteenth.

The third stage in the development of nationhood, misleadingly regarded by modernists as its total history, was that beginning in the late eighteenth century, when the collapse of the French monarchy, the cultural standard-bearer of a view of the state as legitimatised by something other than its subjects, opened the floodgates to revolutionary movements which were also nationalist. If the people legitimised the state, they must have an identity, a collective unity which precedes the state. They must, in other words, be a nation and states must then be nation-states. The revolutionary movements of the nineteenth century, except in so far as they were socialist or Marxist, were almost of necessity nationalist. The British-American model underlying everything was a parliamentary model in which the authority of an elected body was supreme, and supreme because in theory at least it represented the nation that elected it. For the *ancien régime* the people in a state were simply subjects, an aggregate of the population of provinces ruled by that state. They needed no other principle of unity. For the new world of constitutional government, the very nature of government and of state legitimacy required an organic unity of its citizens which is what being a nation signifies.

The great French effort to turn the rural inhabitants of Brittany, Alsace, Provence and the rest into Frenchmen was the inevitable consequence. Basically it was for France a feasible enterprise because of the size and centrality of the Old French, the inhabitants of an enlarged Île de France, within what had become the kingdom of France. An existing state was convertible into a nation, even if it took over a century to do it. Russia could conceivably do the same, incorporating its Slav neighbours who shared not only a linguistic but also the same religious tradition. It is noticeable how different it was to try to incorporate Catholic Poles or Armenians from incorporating Ukrainians, most of whom were Orthodox Christians. The Russian enterprise was, then, comparable with the French, in that an enlarged, more self-conscious nation was compatible with the shape of a pre-national state, though in this case, of course, the state was still defining itself in dynastic and partially pre-national terms. It is one of the threads greatly complicating a history of nationalism and the nation in the modern era – though one rather little considered by its analysts – that while the original thrust into nationalism was an anti-dynastic and democratic one, nevertheless, once the nationalist bandwagon was rolling, it could largely drop its democratic shaping and refashion itself in places behind a 'national' dynasty or populist movement. This could indeed be almost required where, having defined itself in ethnic terms, a nationalism had effectively to exclude large sections of the population of an area from full citizenship. While a territorial nationalism can consistently live with 'democracy' (or the semi-democracy more characteristic of liberal regimes in the nineteenth century), ethnic nationalism could seldom do so, given the mixed ethnic character of most of Europe and, indeed, of the world.

Outside France and Russia, nineteenth-century nationalism came up against the hard fact that the state system of the *ancien régime* was simply not convertible into one of nation-states. It had, on the contrary, to be dissolved. A united Italy and a largely united Germany were the main successors in nationalist terms. Otherwise the great dissolvent of the First World War was needed to give nationalist doctrine, now publicly upheld by President Wilson and the Versailles peace settlement, a chance to prove itself. Nationalism then came up against a second hard fact – that the peoples of much of Europe were in reality not divided along the neat lines presupposed by a viable ethnic nationalism, but were, on the contrary, almost inextricably mixed together. They had, hitherto, never experienced, nor needed to experience, the ethnic cleansing Spain had for centuries imposed upon itself. The imposition of a nationalist logic, taken for granted in the era of Versailles, by western liberal pundits could only lead on to case after case of ethnic cleansing from the Jews of Poland via the Germans of the Sudetenland to the Muslims of Bosnia.

The model of the nation-state which had appeared so fruitful, and even so liberal, in Britain, when 'pirated' across time and place, had been turned into a model of state and society both barren and intolerant. In the meantime the older model of political Europe, that of the Holy Roman Empire, a more or less confederate union of very diverse communities, had been wholly discredited and inevitably so, given that its final standard-bearer was as unimaginative as the Habsburg dynasty. In the old Europe, still clinging tenuously enough to the ideal of continuity with ancient Rome, entities like Bavaria, Croatia, Cologne or Venice did not have to prove themselves in national terms. They prospered through participating in a series of communities: local in terms of immediate government, national in terms of language and literary culture, but something much wider in terms of effective defence and a sense of intellectual community. Like most political systems, sooner or later, it decayed irretrievably, and it was somewhat inevitable if in many ways disastrous that a twisted version of the English model should come to replace it. There is a sad appropriateness in the coincidence in 1802 of some of Wordsworth's finest sonnets – on the one side 'On the Extinction of the Venetian Republic', on the other the five deeply nationalist poems entitled 'England, 1802'. Venice, 'eldest child of liberty', had decayed until 'her long life hath reach'd its final day', while England where men still 'speak the tongue, that Shakespeare spoke; the faith and morals hold, which Milton held', remains 'a bulwark for the cause of men', the model of the future.

Inevitable as the nationalisation of Italy, Germany and eastern Europe could appear a hundred years ago, it cannot be the end of the story. Few people in Venice or Cologne can look back with enormous pride on their brief century of nation-statehood. It seems unsurprising that the Holy Roman Empire has now been resurrected in the European Community and resurrected because it is so obviously necessary and preferable to what has immediately preceded it. It is fitting that Jacques Santer, a Luxembourger, should be President of its Commission at the time that it is becoming an irreversible political structure replacing the dominance of nation-states, because Luxembourg represents almost the only significant survivor from the pre-national era. No one in their senses could regard Luxembourg as a nation any more than Rutland is a nation. Its existence has made no theoretical sense in an era of nation-states but it managed to survive, happily linking a political order central to medieval Europe with that which is now emerging.

Luxembourg is in fact just part of what constitutes Europe's true heartland – the lands along and west of the Rhine, from Strasbourg to Aachen and Maastricht, lands which both the German and the French nations have claimed as their own, but which have obstinately refused to be fully incorporated into either, partly perhaps because of their sturdy but fairly ecumenical Catholicism. Instead of being the football kicked back and forth by opposing nationalisms, they are now the natural home to a supra-national European community, something to which they belong across a very long history. Luxembourg was the birthplace of Robert Schuman, the French statesman responsible for the Schuman Plan out of which the European Union has evolved. It is worthy of note that almost everyone who has been really influential in the creating of the EU has been a socially minded Catholic from Schuman and Adenauer to Delors and Santer. Not only institutionally but intellectually it represents a resurgence of the central European Christian tradition as against the nationalisms which supplanted it from the later Middle Ages.

If it is wholly understandable that Luxembourg, Strasbourg or Brussels should welcome the EC, it is easy to see too why the gut reaction of English people should be so largely hostile. No national tradition was so clearly outside the Empire as that of medieval England, and yet if England was never within the Empire and could not, like France, look back even on a shared inheritance of Charlemagne, it was actually politically subject to the papacy to which it paid an annual tribute for a century after King John's submission in 1213. While England may well have benefited from that relationship, nationalist hostility to its memory – pretty obvious for long even in historians of the pre-Powicke era – is in post-Reformation terms understandable enough. But its long acceptance does suggest that it would be a mistake so to interpret English identity as to make it necessarily exclude any room for a European political belonging.

In the *longue durée* of European history there has been a constant jostling between two great principles of political and cultural identity: the more universalist and the national. Both derive in part from aspects of Christianity, as we will see further in chapter 8. Both attained a certain stability of form in the High Middle Ages, when the major literary languages of the continent became firmly established, generating recognisable national communities around them. To some extent those languages, especially German and French, were at first used universalistically, in a role comparable to that of Latin. Europeanness did not easily expire. However, both the main universalist institutions – papacy and empire – went into a long retreat as national identities grew more and more decisive. By the fifteenth century Europe's nations were almost entirely fixed and recognised to be such, though very few could possibly be said to be also nation-states. When the English model was marketed as a conspicuous success towards the end of the eighteenth century and the old dynastic and local institutions from the Holy Roman Empire to Venice lost their last appeal, the nationalist movements that arose to fill the gap and modernise the political order took out of the cupboard the 'nations' that had actually already been there for centuries. But not everyone had such a nation. Besides the nations there were numerous other ethnicities. Some of them were indeed absorbable in the expansion of existing nations. Others refused to be, or had survived as a series of small regional communities, characterised more by religion than by anything else, beneath Ottoman rule. If the new nationalisms revived some nations, they invented others, but they invented them on the model of the old ones. The process of moving from ethnicity to nationhood can take place in any age and if it happened for some peoples in the fourth, the tenth or the twelfth century, and for others in the sixteenth, it could happen just as decisively in the nineteenth or twentieth. In the first half of the twentieth century, the world's public doctrine became nationalism enshrined in the League of Nations and the United Nations. Every state has been presumed to be a nation, so everyone has been encouraged to do their political thinking in nationalist terms. Ethnic cleansing has all too frequently been the result. To get away from that will require a very long march.

CHAPTER FIVE

The South Slavs

It may seem strange to place a discussion of ex-Yugoslavia between western Europe and Africa, but it is not without its point. We are once more seeking to explain the relationship between ethnicity, nationhood and nationalism in the light of territoriality, language, literature and religion through examination of a much disputed group of examples. The group consists of the South Slavs apart from Bulgaria and Macedonia, that is to say the inhabitants of Slovenia, Croatia, Herzegovina (formerly Hum), Bosnia, Montenegro and Serbia. Are they so many nations? If so, when, why and how did they become so? H. Kohn, in his standard (though now quite dated) work of fifty years ago, *The Idea of Nationalism*, had this to say of their early nineteenth-century state: 'The southern Slavs, divided according to historical regions rather than ethnographic principles, without a uniform language and spelling, were no more than ethnographic raw material out of which nationalities could grow.'[1] Against that let us place a document published in London in May 1915 entitled a 'Jugoslav Manifesto to the British Nation'. It was an appeal to Britain to recognise that Serbia's war with Austria-Hungary was one of emancipation intended to free and unite 'the Jugoslav nation'. The Serbs, Croats and Slovenes inhabiting Serbia, Montenegro, Croatia-Slavonia-Dalmatia, Bosnia, Herzegovina, Carniola and much else 'form a single nation, alike by identity of language, by the unanswerable laws of geography and by national consciousness'.[2] It is remarkable that this Manifesto was published in London just a month after a Secret Treaty of London signed by Britain, France, Russia and Italy offered to give Italy most of the Dalmatian coast in return for a declaration of war against Germany and Austria. In that context and under the threat of being handed over from Austrian to

Italian rule it may seem less surprising that most of the signatories to this Manifesto were in fact fairly nationally minded Croats led by Ante Trumbic, President of the Croat National Party in Dalmatia and former Mayor of Split. Yet in retrospect the Manifesto remains striking enough because an assertion that these various Slav peoples were really only one nation is so diametrically opposed to most views held today, particularly by Croats. In practice such an appeal was almost bound to lead to the creation of a greater Serbia and it is not surprising that the book from which I have taken this quotation was written by an attaché to the Serbian Legation in London who insisted elsewhere that 'the Serbians are the most representative of the Balkan Slavs' and that the Jugo-Slavs as a whole 'were looking to Serbia to lead them toward independence as Piedmont had led the other Italian States in 1860'.[3]

The greatest British experts on the Balkans at the time were inclined to agree. Thus, much as R.W. Seton-Watson disliked the government of Serbia and preferred that of Austria, he was convinced, nevertheless, that Southern Slav political unity must come. 'As surely as Germany and Italy have won their liberty and unity, so surely will it be won by the Croato-Serb race', he declared, adding 'That a Southern Slav should prefer to call himself Croat rather than Serb, or Serb rather than Croat, ought to be a matter with which the state or society are in no way concerned. The larger Southern Slav patriotism should include and transcend the sense of racial individuality.'[4] Again, for Harold Temperley, 'The kingdom of Serbia has held up the same kind of hope and example of unity to the Southern Slavs that the Kingdom of Piedmont did . . . The spiritual unity of the Jugo-Slav race has already been achieved.'[5] Eighty years ago that view won the battle in the international forum: Croat, Serb and Slovene were to be regarded as no more than ethnicities within a single Southern Slav nation. Yugoslavia was invented at Versailles in consequence. Hugh Seton-Watson, R.W.'s son, was the leading British authority on the subject a generation later. In his *Nationalism – Old and New*, published in 1965, he wrote, nevertheless, very differently from his father: 'The conflict between Serbs and Croats in modern times has been a conflict not about religion but about nationality. Serbs and Croats are not two religious groups but two nations.'[6] Thirty years later Yugoslavia is no more and it is now generally accepted that Croats, Slovenes, Serbs and perhaps even

Bosnians are separate nations, that the Yugoslav idea, dominant among the enlightened at the start of this century and upheld as we have seen not only by Serbs but by British academics and even some Croats, was but a mirage. Is it possible that Kohn's view is right after all and that the mirage of the Southern Slav nation was actually only possible because so short a time before all the people concerned were 'no more than ethnographic raw material' or, alternatively, that there were two or three nations firmly in existence all along? The aim of our discussion must be to disengage and evaluate the factors constructive of ethnicity and nationhood among the South Slavs in order to decide who was the more correct: Seton-Watson *père* or Seton-Watson *fils*.

Waves of Slavs coming from the east settled in the Balkans across several centuries, mingling with the existing inhabitants, Vlachs, Illyrians, Greeks in the south, Germans in the north-west. In some areas they were incorporated into existing peoples so that many modern Greeks are Slav in ethnic origin as are many modern Germans. But through the central areas of the Balkans it was the language and cultural identity of the Slav incomers that prevailed, incorporating earlier inhabitants within it. Of the history of the migrations and settlements we know rather little. What is certain is that the Slavs had no strong central leadership to hold them together; instead as they settled in different areas divided for the most part by a mountainous terrain and great distances, they came to be differentiated above all by the shaping facts of local and regional geography as well as by the varying cultural and religious influences to which they were subjected in consequence. Western Slavs came under Latin, German and Italian influence, Eastern Slavs under Greek influence. Yet, in ecclesiastical terms, that contrast should not for the early centuries be overstressed.

The first mass conversions to Christianity among the Slavs seem to have come around the ninth century, and inevitably meant entry into one or another ecclesiastical tradition. It could result in effective incorporation within a Greek or Germanic world. Yet it also produced a whole new tradition of Christianity resulting above all from the activity of the brothers Constantine (later renamed Cyril) and Methodius, aristocratic Greek priests who were sent from Constantinople to Moravia with the task of teaching religion not in German or Latin but in the vernacular. They translated the liturgy and some of the scriptures into Slavonic and invented a new alphabet, Glagolitic, with which to write it. Encountering the hostility of the German bishops, the brothers went to Rome where Cyril died and Methodius was consecrated archbishop. What is striking is the way this dual sponsorship, Constantinopolitan and Roman, enabled the 'Old Church Slavonic' of the Cyrilian liturgy to be diffused throughout the Slav peoples from the Croats in the west to Russia in the east and so provide a common literary and liturgical bond linking people whose ecclesiastical allegiance would subsequently be divided between the Latin and Greek churches. While the spoken languages of the Slav peoples would inevitably diverge over the centuries, that divergence was held back by a shared commitment to the old Slavonic liturgy, even though it would come to be written differently in west and east. Cyril's own Glagolitic alphabet became restricted to the Croats who used it concurrently with the Latin, while those within the Orthodox church adopted a modification which, though produced long after his lifetime, came, confusingly, to be called 'Cyrillic'. The use of Cyrillic has come, nevertheless, to have an immense cultural and political impact, ring-fencing Russians, Bulgars and Serbs from both western Slavs like Poles and Croats and anyone else making use of the Latin alphabet.

At this point it seems still far from certain what national form the various groups of southern Slavs would take. Would there develop a single Slav nation, just as Angles, Saxons and Jutes were becoming one at the same time in Britain? If we look three or four centuries on, we find the rise and decline of various unstable kingdoms, produced by the temporary ascendancy of one or another local ruler. Thus we know of a Croat kingdom from the time of Tomislav of Knin in the tenth century, a Serb kingdom flourishing in the thirteenth and fourteenth centuries, a Bosnian kingdom in the fourteenth and fifteenth. Each appears to have had a core area enlarged fairly temporarily by military success to include territory which, at some other time, belonged to a different state. It is worth for a moment pausing to consider the names of such kingdoms. The common name of 'Slav' was clearly widely used: Slovenia, Slovakia and Slavonia are all simply ways of saying a land of Slavs, names comparable with Germany. Serb and Croat, on the other hand, refer to more specific tribes, already occasionally mentioned at the time of the migrations. Bosnia is different again, being a specifically territorial name taken from that of a local river and thus comparable to Northumbria, the Rhineland or indeed Montenegro. There is little significance in this diversity of name type. It is something common throughout Europe. The entities represented by the names were not as such very different from one another.

It is not to be imagined that there is any clear genetic division separating the population of any of these areas. Everywhere it consists in reality of a mixture of pre-Slav groups, Vlach, Illyrian or Albanian, and the descendants of one or another Slav migration. But throughout the last millennium the population map was never static, one intermingling or migration, voluntary or enforced, being followed quickly by another. Even the spoken language did not divide according to the lines of the present states because, while there was a range of dialects within the one language which we may call today with some temerity Serbo-Croato-Bosnian, the lines between them did not coincide with those divisions, the majority of Croats, Serbs and Bosnians all speaking the dialect called Štokavian, while the north-western Croats spoke either Kajkavian around Zagreb or Čakavian in Istria and parts of the Dalmatian coast. The Croats, as we know them today, were then significantly divided in terms of spoken language, the Kajkavian-speakers being quite close to Slovene. Such linguistic divisions of dialect were mainly an expression of territorial contiguity, but they help to underline the absence of clear markers in national identity.

Populations were not dense, the economy was far from advanced even in medieval terms, both doubtless held back by the extremely mountainous character of much of the area, and all the groups to which we have referred had developed considerable internal divisions of their own by the close of the Middle Ages. The Croat group as we know it now was divided politically into three – Croatia proper, together with Slavonia, Venetian-ruled Dalmatia and the independent republic of Ragusa (Dubrovnik). The Serbian group was divided between the old Serbian heartland south of Belgrade around Novi Pazar (much of it now repopulated by Albanians), and a western branch which became Montenegro. A later northern branch beyond the Danube in Vojvodina derived from the migration of refugees fleeing the Ottomans for Austrian protection. Again, the Bosnian group was divided between its old northern core around Jajce and what became Herzegovina (Hum) in the south. Nothing in the ups and downs of the medieval history of these peoples would seem quite adequate either to prevent them from becoming eventually a single nation-state, as was the case with England or Germany, or to make them so. Yet both religion and political history were steadily increasing the divergences.

It was not the fault of the Slavs that they had settled on what became the frontier area dividing two increasingly different forms of Christianity, the Latin and the Greek, between which by the later Middle Ages there would be deep hostility. It was inevitable that the Bulgars should give their allegiance to Constantinople and no less inevitable that the Slovenes (eventually incorporated into medieval Austria) and the Croats, so close to Venice, would become part of the Latin Church. In between it was less obvious. Even the Serbs in the early thirteenth century were quite close to choosing the Latin option. Bosnia seems basically Latin, if so cut off in its mountains as to have produced a strange rural church of its own, but there were also well-established Orthodox monasteries within Herzegovina. Throughout these lands as elsewhere in Europe a people's developing cultural and political identity in the early centuries of its Christianity very largely depended upon the way it was shaped by the church but no other churchman in the Balkans was half as influential in doing so as St Sava, Serbia's first archbishop (1219–35), the son of one ruler and brother of another.[7] It was St Sava, previously a monk on Mount Athos, who stabilised Serbia's Christian conversion, established bishoprics and monasteries, commissioned the translation of books from the Greek into Serbian, and, above all, provided Serbia's normative pattern of a particularly close integration of church and state. The very fact that the Byzantine Empire was falling apart meant that a new Christian kingdom entering into this tradition would be able to receive rather little from outside. Sava had been on Mount Athos when in 1204 the Latin army had seized Constantinople. When, next year, Mount Athos was placed under the authority of a Catholic bishop, Sava was one of the many monks to leave at once, returning to Serbia to become Abbot of the Studenica monastery. It may have been his experience of alienation from Latins at that time which ensured that Serbia would become a bastion of Orthodoxy with a particular suspicion of Latin Christianity.

Croatia's Christian history was bound to be different. Close to

Italy, to Austria and to Hungary, it shared quite easily in the religious and cultural evolution of central Europe; it developed a learning and a literature of its own, but in accepting the King of Hungary, and then the Emperor in Vienna, as its sovereign, it lost much of the fierce independence which Poland, its closest Slav parallel, retained into the eighteenth century. The pressure of Hungary upon the Slav peoples to its south was, however, little in comparison with the pressure from the Ottoman Turks in and after the fourteenth century. Their conquest of most of the Balkan peninsula meant that it became in religious terms a double frontier zone – not only one between Latin and Orthodox but between Christian and Muslim as well. For the next five hundred years all the South Slavs were either subjects of the Ottoman Empire, subjects of Vienna, or footballs kicked to and fro across the military frontier.

Bosnia fared the best. It had had two centuries of existence as a kingdom before it fell, after a lengthy resistance, to the Ottoman armies in the late fifteenth century. Its last king, Stephen Tomasevic, was beheaded after the fall of Kljuc in 1463 but Bosnia's territorial identity was retained, its administrative unity even enhanced. As a political province of the Ottoman Empire with frontiers recognisably close to those of the kingdom it used to be, Bosnia appears as actually the most stable and well organised of all the entities within the Ottoman Balkans, its identity remaining clearly territorial rather than ethnic or religious.

The long-term fate of the Serbs was different. To understand what happened we can best focus upon the Battle of Kosovo in 1389, its antecedents, its actual character, its consequences and, finally, the myths surrounding it.[8] All this needs a deal of untangling but the effort to do so is absolutely worthwhile, as an analysis of one of the most potent of all symbols of religious nationalism.

The brief fourteenth-century Serbian Empire of Dusan fell rapidly to pieces after his death in 1355. It had been made possible by his own ability and the weakness of what survived of the Byzantine Empire, but it had no effective undergirding, and it was replaced by a loose grouping of nobles led, thirty years later, by Prince Lazar. As the power of Serbia declined, that of the kingdom of Bosnia grew. While the 1380s probably represented something of a brief recovery for Serbia, King Turtko of Bosnia was at the time a ruler of greater significance than anyone in Serbia.

When in 1389 an Ottoman army led by Sultan Murat advanced into this part of the Balkans, it was met by a joint Bosnian–Serb army, the former sent by Turtko and led by Vlatko Vukovic, the latter led by Prince Lazar in person and his son-in-law, Vuk Brankovic. The battle of Kosovo, fought on 28 June, was somewhat indecisive but for some it actually looked like a Christian victory; while both Murat and Lazar were killed in or after the battle, the invading Ottoman army rapidly withdrew. Certainly in the eyes of Turtko it represented a victory which he announced triumphantly to friends in the west. The city of Florence replied four months later, 'Fortunate is the Bosnian Kingdom to which it was given to fight such a glorious battle and, with Christ's right hand, to score such a victory.'[9]

Very little was changed within Serbia by the battle, but the body of Lazar, the only Serbian ruler to die in battle, was buried in the memorial monastery of Ravanica and around him grew up a body of poetry, characteristic of monastic hagiography. It is noteworthy that this early poetry showed almost no interest in Kosovo itself. Vuk Brankovic survived the battle and was one of Serbia's principal rulers in the following years.

Divided as Serbia was, it stood little chance of long resisting Ottoman pressure. Brankovic and Lazar's widow, Milica, in fact led the Serbs to accept a client relationship to the Turks. In the following decades they were normally to be found fighting as auxiliaries upon the Ottoman side while Bosnia, for instance, was still firmly resisting their advance. Serbia however soon ceased to be a recognisable political entity and the preservation of its identity was thrown back upon the institutional leadership of the Orthodox Church. For two hundred years, from the late fifteenth to the late seventeenth century, this actually produced something of a Serb–Ottoman, Orthodox–Muslim, alliance. Once Constantinople had fallen and the supreme patriarchate had become effectively a prisoner within the Ottoman Empire, the latter naturally privileged Orthodox against Catholic Christians. It is in consequence only in the sixteenth century that one sees, for instance, an expansion of Orthodoxy into most parts of hitherto Catholic Bosnia.[10] For the Ottomans, Catholics were under suspicion as their enemies – Hungary, Austria, Venice and the Pope – were all Catholics, while the Orthodox could better be trusted. It is in this context that one sees the Grand Vizier, Mehmet Sokolovic, restoring the Serbian Patriarchate in 1557. Sokolovic himself was a Serb and the Patriarchate was then held by various members of his family. This Serb–Ottoman entente only really broke down after the Austrian–Turkish war of 1689 when many Serbs rose in revolt to support an Austrian invasion and then, led by their Patriarch, fled northwards to resettle within the Habsburg Empire in the territory now known as Vojvodina. From that point the Serb collective consciousness exercised a fierce amnesia in regard to much that had happened from the fourteenth to the seventeenth century, rewriting their role from one of Ottoman auxiliary to one of a perennial victimhood – summed up in the epic of Kosovo and its guarantee, through the identification of Lazar with Christ, in a final resurrection of the empire of Dusan with whom Lazar was now intimately linked.

And so to the epic itself, embodied in a mass of popular poetry.[11] Its chief elements lie in the Christlikeness of Lazar, symbol of Serbdom, who has a vision before the battle and chooses the heavenly over the earthly kingdom, the betrayal by Vuk Brankovic, and the heroic death of Milos, the old knight who had been falsely accused of treachery but who then goes to the Turkish camp, gains access to the Sultan and plunges his dagger into Murat's body. As already noted, the earliest form of the epic was no more than a depicting of the dead prince Lazar as a saint. A separate poem of the death of Murat at the hands of Milos may be almost as old. Vuk's treachery would seem to have developed later and the rounding of the three into a single epic of national catastrophe later still, perhaps towards the late seventeenth century. Moreover, it was just one of many such Serbian epics, others of which celebrated Muslim heroes or 'Prince Marko', a Christian who fought on the Turkish side. It seems only in the nineteenth century that its status was transformed to make of it the supreme national epic. Paintings of Lazar's 'Last Supper' now depicted him in imitation of Jesus with Brankovic, the Judas, representing those Serbs who had defected to Islam. By the late nineteenth century the 'cult of the 1389 battle' was believed to have inspired the Serbian people for centuries. It was certainly the perfect myth to enthuse the new nationalism. The fifth centenary, in 1889, was fervently celebrated and even in Zagreb the newspaper *Obzor* could pay its tribute, despite Austrian attempts to stifle any expression of support for Serbia:

Whenever the Serbs rose up to lead whatever part of their people to freedom, they always appeared with the wreath of Kosovo around their heads to say in unison: This, O people, is what we are, what we want, and what we can do. And we Croatians, brothers by blood and by desire with the Serbs, today sing: Praise to the eternal Kosovo heroes.[12]

In far-off Britain too in 1916, an address by R.W. Seton-Watson on 'Serbia: Yesterday, Today and Tomorrow' was read out in thousands of schools, stressing 'how completely the story of Kosovo is bound up with the daily life of the Serbian nation'.[13] If this, historically fallacious, epic fuelled nineteenth-century Serb nationalism and the creation at Versailles of a Serb-dominated Yugoslavia, its resurrection in the 1980s by the Orthodox Church and President Milosevic with his fiery June 1989 speech at Kosovo fuelled the refurbishment of that nationalism and its violent anti-Muslim direction. That very virulence may, sadly, be a reaction to the reality of history in which Orthodox Serbs were for centuries the principal Balkan Christian co-operators with the Turkish Empire.

Croatia's fate was different again. While legally it remained a distinct kingdom, it was in practice little more than a province of the conglomerate Habsburg Empire, a province ruled in the nineteenth century ever more irritatingly from Budapest. Yet it had retained its medieval institutions, the Sabor or Diet above all. Moreover from the sixteenth century Venetian-ruled Dalmatia and the independent Republic of Ragusa (Dubrovnik) produced a considerable written literature in Štokavian. Where in the thirteenth century Croatians, Bosnians and Serbians – though it is a little anachronistic even to describe them as such – were not far apart in circumstance and might well at a favourable moment have been united easily enough into one kingdom, as were the peoples of Burgundy, Champagne and the Île de France, by the end of the eighteenth century their histories, religion and culture had grown so diversely that no magic wand would prove sufficiently powerful to turn them into a single nation. They were clearly a great deal more than Kohn's 'ethnographic raw material' but they were very far from being a single nation.

It was, nevertheless, almost inevitable that many intelligent people should see that as the reasonable way forward. They disliked being ruled by Turks in Constantinople, Magyars in Budapest or Germans in Vienna. Here were a multitude of Slav ethnicities. Surely if they stood together they could become a state of their own and as only Serbia, at least after 1830, was virtually independent, it was natural that Slav nationalists of any background should think in terms of a South Slav nation, a Yugoslavia based federally on an enlarged Serbia. The great Croat Catholic Bishop Strossmayer, founder of the University of Zagreb and one of the leading inopportunists at the first Vatican Council in 1870, was such a person. So, of course, were the more astute politicians in Belgrade such as Ilija Garasanin, Prime Minister through most of the 1850s and 1860s. A strenuous advocate of South Slav unity, he meant by it in reality not a Yugoslavia at all, but the creation of an ethnically cleansed Greater Serbia, the re-creation of the brief fourteenth-century empire of Dusan. Yet as we have seen even many Croats were prepared for a time to believe in some such plan. While there were indeed Croat nationalist intellectuals in the nineteenth century led by Ante Starcevic for whom the Croat identity was absolutely primary and for whom the Serbs were 'really' Croats who had turned Orthodox, there were others more sympathetic to a 'Yugoslav Idea' in more ecumenical terms. Some understandably admired Serbia's achievement as an independent state. They were willing to say with Ante Kovacic that 'the greatest harm that has befallen the Croats and Serbs is that we are too much a name and too little a nation',[14] or that 'Croatdom is the potential and Serbdom the kinetic energy of our people. Croatdom is reflection, Serbdom is action.'[15] In the naive dawn of modern ethnic nationalism, Serbia could represent a Slav purity defined in essentially East European and Orthodox terms, yet superficially attractive even for many Young Croats, repelled by German and Hungarian dominance within the Habsburg Empire.

The First World War, by allying Britain and France with Serbia against Austria-Hungary, Germany and Turkey, appeared to provide the Slavs with their great opportunity. The collapse of the empires that had dominated the Balkans for centuries left a vacuum requiring the construction of a new state system and the providential moment for South Slav unity seemed to have arrived. Was it, however, to be a 'nation-state', an enlarged Serbia – and the age of Versailles represented the high point of belief in the appropriateness of such things – or, rather, a 'federal state of nations', a Yugoslavia? Which of these groups, if any, could really be called a nation?

One obvious answer to that question was 'Only Serbia'. That

Serbia was a nation, indeed a nation-state, there could by 1920 be little question. Poor as it was economically and educationally, addicted as it was to assassinating its rulers, absurd and dangerous as its ambitions could appear to both Austrians and Turks, its character of a nation-state, dominated indeed by an intensely single-minded nationalism, seems absolutely clear. Its nationhood derived from the memory of the medieval kingdom, from the leadership of the national church which had maintained a practical identity between Serbdom and Orthodoxy, from a tradition of oppression and struggle for freedom whose meaning had been communicated to everyone through the *pjesme*, the epic poetry at the heart of its popular culture. The enormous, and deeply nationalist, influence of such oral poetry is indeed evidence of how dangerous it is to follow too closely the Benedict Anderson line that a nation is unimaginable before the coming of mass print-capitalism.

Finally, the Serbian understanding of its own nationhood derived increasingly in the late nineteenth century from its language, Štokavian, as refurbished by Vuk Karadzic. In the course of the first half of the nineteenth century, Vuk, working mostly from Vienna, produced a remarkable series of books, dictionaries, a translation of the New Testament and numerous collections of folk stories. For Karadzic Štokavian equalled Serb and anyone who spoke it as far as Dubrovnik, whether they knew it or not, was in consequence a Serb just as for Starcevic they were all Croats. The Štokavian–Serb equivalence was not Vuk's invention. Typical of German concepts of ethno-linguistics, it had been developed by the early German school of Slavonic studies, such as August von Schlözer (1735–1809). Following an ethno-linguistic criterion of nationality, Croats were to be defined as those speaking Čakavian or Kajkavian and Serbs as those speaking Štokavian, regardless of what their actual community consciousness might be.[16] A similar approach was used to prove Alsace German at just the same time. As the great French historian, Fustel de Coulanges, wrote to the great German historian, Mommsen, in October 1870, 'It is possible that Alsace is German by race and by language but it is French by nationality and by its sense of fatherland.'[17] So might a Croat have written to Karadzic about Dubrovnik and no less correctly.

Karadzic's literary upgrading of current peasant speech threatened the status of Old Church Slavonic and was bitterly opposed in consequence by church authorities which for years prevented both his Dictionary and his New Testament from entering Serbia. In due course, however, he won his linguistic battle, contributing enormously thereby to the long term aggressiveness of Serb nationalism and in a way reinforcing the Orthodox Church's own national role. He provided, we may say, a second principle of national self-identity. While the first had been membership of the Serb Orthodox Church, the second was the reinterpretation of Štokavian as essentially a Serb language. The first made for internal intolerance, the second appeared to give a sort of scientific justification for a claim to all the lands where Štokavian was spoken, including Bosnia and half of Croatia, the Greater Serbia of Garasanin.[18] It is remarkable how largely that claim has been taken seriously by western scholars and politicians and how much, in consequence, it has affected the world's judgement on the acceptability of the aims of Serbian nationalism. Thus, a history of the Serbs published by Oxford University Press in 1918 asserted that the Croats of Croatia spoke 'the Serbian language'.[19] Its author also described Bosnia and Herzegovina as 'Serbian lands'. A year before, Leon Dominian in his massive *The Frontiers of Language and Nationality in Europe* spoke of 'the westernmost Serbs who are also known as Croats',[20] and declared that 'By its geography, no less than racially, Bosnia is an integral part of Serbia',[21] while H.A.L. Fisher in his extremely influential *History of Europe* described Croatians as 'Serb in speech and Serb in race'.[22] With such apparent academic support for the claims of Serb nationalism, it seems hardly surprising that Thorvald Stoltenberg, co-chairman of the Steering Committee of the International Conference on Former Yugoslavia and Special Representative of the UN Secretary-General, could declare in May 1995, 'Ethnic war? I don't think so. The whole lot of them are Serbs. The Serbs who call themselves that are obviously Serbs. So are the Muslims. They are in fact Serbs who converted to Islam. And a great number of those who have the appearance of Croats, who present themselves as Croats, are in fact also Serbs.'[23] Thus entirely fallacious ethno-nationalist theories of the mid-nineteenth century were still shaping the mind of putatively neutral representatives of the international community a hundred and fifty years later.

Nineteenth-century Croatian nationhood has all the same to be evaluated rather more hesitantly, with a measure of ambiguity. For many centuries the people we call Croats were divided politically three ways: Croatia in the narrow sense (the area around Zagreb) and Slavonia were effectively a single province of the Habsburg Empire, represented within the Hungarian Diet in Budapest; Dalmatia was ruled by Venice; Ragusa, or Dubrovnik, was an independent state. Only for four brief illusory years under Napoleon were they, and parts of Slovenia too, united politically. The Congress of Vienna handed all these lands to the Habsburg monarchy but they were not united administratively because Dalmatia was given to Austria while Croatia and Slavonia remained in and under Hungary. Nor, as we have seen, were they one linguistically. Dubrovnik and most of Dalmatia spoke and wrote Štokavian, Zagreb Kajkavian, a language far closer to Slovene, Istria and the rest of Dalmatia Čakavian. Moreover these were not merely oral dialects, for both Štokavian and Kajkavian had come to boast a considerable printed literature. While the claim of Karadzic that all Štokavian speakers were in reality Serbs was absurd, the language division undoubtedly put a question mark against the reality of any Croat national unity. Indeed, as nineteenth-century Croat nationalism got under way it recognised the problem and strove to overcome it by seeking the general adoption of Štokavian.

Let us turn now to the dimension of religion. While Croatia, Slavonia and Dalmatia all shared Catholic Christianity (with many Bosnians and almost all Slovenes), this was less significant for them as a mark of identity in narrowly national terms than was Orthodoxy for Serbia because it was also the religion of their rulers, Hungary, Austria and Venice. Indeed as hostility to Hungary grew in the nineteenth century, the Catholic Church could be seen at times in almost hostile terms. Nevertheless Catholicism as mediated specifically through the survival of the Glagolitic rite in Dalmatia and its attendant literature may be judged as having had an absolutely decisive and irreversible effect upon the distinct national shaping of the Croats. It is true that it was not used around Zagreb or in Slavonia, nevertheless Croatdom was provided with a literary benchmark centuries before the emergence of any wider Štokavian literature by the continuous religious use of Glagolitic. Croats alone in the Catholic Church in the West had been permitted to keep a vernacular liturgy which set them firmly apart from other Latin Catholics and ensured the retention of a unique identity. It is clear from the number of fourteenth- and fifteenth-century manuscript missals and breviaries in Glagolitic which have survived and from their regular printing with papal approval in the sixteenth, seventeenth, eighteenth and nineteenth centuries that Glagolitic continued to provide a religious and cultural criterion of identity of which they were very proud.[24] It meant that whereas Catholic priests in Italy, France or Germany read the office in Latin, Dalmatian Croat priests read it in the vernacular. With an entire vernacular psalter, the liturgy could have the same kind of nationalising effect that the vernacular Bible had in Protestant countries, and it was in fact supplemented by a new Protestant translation of the New Testament into Croat, printed in both Glagolitic and Cyrillic in Germany in the 1560s. In its own way, Glagolitic represents yet another example of the decisiveness for nation formation of the growth of biblical and religious literature in the vernacular during the Middle Ages and after, a vernacular alphabet adding powerfully to the particularising effect of a vernacular language.

The Croats along the Dalmatian Coast had participated the most extensively, through their regular Italian contacts, in the culture of western Europe and were far from having experienced the intense isolation and intellectual poverty of Serbia. They enjoyed the theatre, masques and poetry. They had not needed, and had not experienced, the call of nationalism in the same way. They had, one may say, better things to do. Maybe it was the brief political unity they were given by the Napoleonic administration, the elimination of Dubrovnik's historic statehood, and subsequent dissatisfaction both with the divide-and-rule policies of Vienna and with subordination to an increasingly nationalist Hungary which turned them to think more nationalistically themselves. They also felt the impact of an increasingly nationalist Italy, their neighbour to the west. In these circumstances, the absence of a clear and undivided Croat national consciousness is unsurprising. On the one hand the difference in political and cultural experience between, say, Dubrovnik in the south-west and Vukovar in the north-east had been enormous; on the other hand, for many people the attraction of a South Slav state based on an already existing Serbia was at least initially seductive – so much better than rule by Germans, Magyars or Italians. Commitment to a separate Croat nation-state was still, at least on the surface, in a condition of flux.

Slovenia was far less of a nation, with only the most remote history of its own to look back to, prior to its long social and political incorporation into Austria. A brief flowering of Slovene literature in the sixteenth century under Protestant influence included an entire Slovene Bible completed in 1584, but Slovenia remained Catholic and this beginning of vernacular literature had a very limited impact until the mid-eighteenth century. Here as elsewhere it was the development of a literary language out of an oral vernacular which led the way to a Slovene sense of national identity. Nevertheless, the very heterogeneity of the Habsburg Empire incorporating as it did, not too intolerantly, many different Slav nations and ethnicities – Czech, Slovak, Polish, Slovene and Croat – offered a model of political life very different from that of the nation-state but arguably no less attractive, especially for smaller groups with no powerful national history of their own to look back to in yearning. Slovenes could be happier within such an empire than Poles. They were too small a group to think much of forming a state of their own and while some Slovenes inevitably responded to a 'Yugoslav' ideal when it became popular elsewhere by the late nineteenth century, for most people union with Serbs – from whom they were significantly different in language as well as in religion – remained less attractive than belonging to the Habsburg Empire.[25]

Bosnia was even less nation-minded. It was a quality naturally alien to its Muslim leadership in a relatively favoured province of the Ottoman Empire. Moreover, in the course of the nineteenth century whatever there was of a traditional sense of Bosnianness was under-mined, in regard to the Christian half of the population, by the advance first of Serb nationalism and then of a new Croat–Catholic identification. The near invisibility of Bosnia as a specific identity of a more than geographical kind is one of the most remarkable characteristics of almost all pre-1992 literature relating to Yugoslavia. The absence even of a category of 'Bosniaks' among the 'nations' in the Yugoslav constitution is itself extraordinary. Every other 'state' had its corresponding 'nation'. Bosnia did not. And yet Muslims, Catholics and Orthodox in Bosnia shared ethnicity, language and dialect. Bosnian Christians had not in fact for the most part been either Serbs or Croats. They, like the Muslims, were descendants of the inhabitants of pre-Ottoman Bosnia. In the nineteenth century their identity was eroded under the growing pressure of nationalism in neighbouring lands. Bosnian Orthodox as members of the Serb Orthodox Church, the central pillar of a revived Serb kingdom, were drawn by their shared religious identity into a national one. In due course for Catholics it was the same and Bosnian Catholics who had lived for centuries in places like Sarajevo and Banja Luka, survivors of medieval Catholic Bosnia, came to think of themselves instead as being Croats. Their Catholic identity refocused their social identity, a process strongly encouraged by the first Archbishop of Sarajevo, Mgr Stadler, in the 1890s, and rendered more credible by the undoubted closeness in culture and religion between Bosnia and Croatia in the Middle Ages. For years before 1992 both Serb and Croat nationalist intellectuals consistently deconstructed Bosnia, denying it any existence in the world of a Greater Serbia and a Greater Croatia other than as an expression of 'Turk' aggression against Slavs.[26] The inevitable consequence is that insofar as Bosnia survives, its 'Croat' and 'Serb' citizens will find themselves deconstructed unless they can somehow recognise that they share a single Bosnian nationhood, made up of diverse ethnicities derived from nothing else except different religious traditions. Even so stout a defender of an integral Bosnia as the present Archbishop of Sarajevo, Cardinal Puljic, does not escape this when the editorial to his moving book, *Suffering with Hope*, hails him as 'a son of the Croatian nation'.[27] There can, alas, be little future for Bosnian Catholics if they still see themselves nationally not as Bosnians but as Croats. As Ivan Lovrenovic, one of the most perceptive of Bosnian 'Croat' writers, has recently written, 'they will disappear without ever really understanding what has happened to them',[28] just one more set of victims to nationhood conceived in terms not of territoriality but of a pseudo-ethnicity. The very pluralism of culture and religion which Bosnia had in its fairly simple way managed to achieve within a territorial state has been used to undermine its specific identity.

The existence or elimination of Bosnia and its nationhood provides so enlightening an example of the issues involved in national construction that it is useful to explore the central problem of its identity still more precisely. If its long-established mix of population actually corresponded better with that of Yugoslavia as a whole than any other Yugoslav state, the correspondence was with a federal Yugoslavia, not a 'Greater Serbia' Yugoslavia. Once the former was effectively abandoned, Bosnia became of all parts of the country the most vulnerable, yet vulnerable precisely because of implicit contradictions within the constitution Tito had left to Yugoslavia. On the one side Yugoslavia was a federation of six states and two autonomous areas (Kosovo and Vojvodina) but on the other it recognised a specific number of nations or ethnicities, each parallel to a state or autonomous area, but of which Bosnians were not one, though from 1974 'Muslim' was recognised as a national category, thus in some way creating a distinct 'Muslim' 'nation' where none had existed and which in the paper terms where alone it had reality could include Muslims anywhere in Yugoslavia wholly unrelated to Bosnia.

By the dual recognition of 'state' and 'nation' the Yugoslav constitution, whether wittingly or not, played straight into the hands of Serb and Croat nationalists. The Serb nationalist could claim possession of the Sandjak (or, more dubiously, Kosovo) as part of the 'state' of Serbia, despite lack of a Serb majority in either, but claim too the Croatian Krajina or eastern Herzegovina on the contra-dictory principle that they were occupied by members of the Serb 'nation'. Croat nationalists did quite the same, claiming the Serb-majority Krajina on territorial grounds of being within the Croatian 'state' but western Herzegovina on grounds of the population there being 'Croats'. Each thus played both the ethnic and the territorial card when it suited them to do so. If Yugoslavia was to be divided, an ethnic delineation of states could not work without enormous suffering given the intermingling of the population map, and it further lacked any justification within political or administrative history. The territorial delineation could work (and in due course is likely to do so) but, again, with huge suffering and cultural loss caused by the simultaneous playing up of ethnic categories – of treating, for instance, Krajina 'Serbs' as less fully citizens of Croatia than 'Croats'.

But for Bosnia the effects of all this were immensely more disastrous than for its neighbours. As Bosnia had not been permitted by the Yugoslav constitution a parallel 'Bosnian' category of nation-ality but only a 'Muslim' one, inherently bound to exclude its citizens of Christian background, it was placed to fall an inevitable victim through constitutional ambiguity to the nationalism of its neighbours. As Bosnia had no 'nation' of its own, its existence could be claimed as 'artificial', a consequence of Ottoman rule and religious conversion, while Croatia and Serbia were claimed as 'natural'. The very recognition of a Muslim 'nation' actually added to the deconstruction of legitimate identity for a specifically Muslim 'nation' neither had existed nor could exist. What had existed was a territorial identity inclusive of all religious traditions, but it was an identity rendered almost invisible both by the claims of the nationalism of its neighbours and by the consequent confusion within the Yugoslav constitution.

The final entity we need to refer to is Montenegro. Here, undoubtedly, we are on the Serb side of the cultural and religious frontier. Just as the separation between Slovenes and Croats could look relatively small, given both were predominantly Catholic, so could that between Serbs and Montenegrans, both being Orthodox. Indeed the gap was even smaller. Croats were differentiated from Slovenes by their tradition of Glagolitic, Slovenes from Croats by long integration as an inferior class within a dominantly German society. Serbs and Montenegrans were divided by no more than territory and political history in which the latter, under a succession of Prince Bishops, had retained a lone independent state within their mountain fastness, whereas the Serbs had for long lost any political identity but were none the less largely led by their bishops. While it is quite uncertain whether Serbs and Montenegrans will continue to form a single federal state, and Montenegran resentment of enforced Serbianisation can be profound, it is clear that only between these two entities was fusion ever likely to be feasible if the Yugoslav state was conceived on dominantly Serb lines. While the reason for that was undoubtedly in part religious, we need at once to remind ourselves that Orthodoxy alone cannot for any length of time paper over other factors of division, as conflict between Serbs and Bulgars – the next South Slav people to the east – has repeatedly made clear. Moreover even in terms of religion Montenegran Orthodoxy has resisted, and still resists, incorporation within a Serb church.

What sort of state was Yugoslavia, then, to be? The profoundly contradictory answers given to that question in 1918 provide ample explanation for the frequently tragic sequence of events across the next seventy years and suggest how disastrous some models of nation and nationalism can prove. It is a case study of how not to construct a nation from a mix of closely related ethnicities and proto-nations. Inter-war Yugoslavia was constructed as a Greater Serbia just as the heirs of Karadzic and Garasanin were determined it should be. Serbia was the only part which entered it as already politically independent. Its royal family, its capital, its army became those of the new state and, with nearly 40 per cent of the population Serbs, its ability to dominate the whole and in doing so to alienate everyone else and generate counter-nationalisms was immense. Given the existing nationalist identity of Serbia and its 'Greater Serbia' ambition, it was next to inevitable that Serb leaders should look on Yugoslavia from the start, not as some sort of federal union of peoples in a larger whole as its original title 'the Kingdom of Serbs, Croats and Slovenes' was meant to imply (while still conveniently forgetting about Bosnia, Macedonia, the Hungarians of Vojvodina and the Albanians of Kosovo), but as a simple enlargement of Serbdom. 'Serbia does not want to drown in Yugoslavia but to have Yugoslavia drown in her', Nikola Pasic, the Serbian Prime Minister, admitted disingenuously.[29] The comparison between Serbia and Piedmont regularly pressed in these years was fundamentally flawed because Piedmont was far too provincial a part of Italy to dominate and alienate the rest of a once united country. Serbia, on the other hand, was a country already gripped by an obsessive nationalism, basically of a Germanic sort, bent on the 'ethnic cleansing' of a 'Greater Serbia' long before the 1990s. Ethnic cleansing had been written into Serb nationalism from the early nineteenth century.[30] 'Greater Serbianism' was in fact a close cousin to what in Germany became Nazi 'National Socialism'. In each case extreme ethnic nationalism led finally to genocide. It was impossible that a Serbia dominated by a nationalism of this sort could conceivably provide the core of a far larger union of disparate peoples. Even a genuine union of Serbs, Croats and Slovenes simply ignored the identities of Bosnia and Macedonia, let alone the million Albanians, Hungarians and others who did not even speak a Slav language, while the aggressively Christian identity of the Serb leadership of the new state hardly boded well for the future of more than a million Muslims. If Yugoslavia was ever to survive, it needed a cosmopolitan tolerance of diversity comparable to that of the Habsburg Empire at its best. In practice the 'Greater Serbia' view of Belgrade almost wholly determined the character of inter-war Yugoslavia, annihilating any likelihood that either a single nation, or some other form of harmonious political society, would emerge, and providing the ideal stimulant for an alienated Croat nationalism to jump on the Fascist bandwagon in the Second World War and take a horrible revenge on its Serb fellow citizens.

Just as French nationalism stimulated German, German nationalism Hungarian and Hungarian South Slav, so now Serb nationalism could only stimulate Croat and Slovene nationalism, with a final production of Bosnian Muslim nationalism engineered as a child born out of due time by the pressures of both Serb and Croat nationalism. Already thirty years ago Hugh Seton-Watson summed up the heart of the problem succinctly enough:

> In Yugoslavia the official doctrine was Yugoslav nationalism. This was supposed to comprise, and to transform into a higher quality, the nationalism of Serbs, Croats and Slovenes. But in practice it was interpreted as Serbian nationalism write large. Slovenes and Croats were considered to be bad Yugoslavs if they continued to be Slovene and Croat nationalists, but Serbs were never accused of this when they continued to be Serbian nationalists.[31]

For a while Tito diffused the strains beneath the lid of a centralised Communist Party while actually allowing the federal dimension of the state to grow steadily stronger, but beneath the lid little had changed in the beguiling power of Serb and Croat nationalisms or in the Serb grip upon both the army and the central organs of the state in Belgrade. With Tito's death, the collapse of Communism and the deliberately fomented resurgence of Serbian nationalism by President Milosevic, symbolised by his grandiose celebration of the 600th anniversary of the battle of Kosovo in the summer of 1989, the end of Yugoslavia became inevitable. Yet that does not mean that it had been inevitable all along. Here as elsewhere one must firmly resist the primordialism which holds that the 'national' divisions of today have been irrevocably determined by ethnicities of a thousand years ago. If the ideals of Strossmayer, Trumbic and even Tito had been held as well by Serbs of influence, a new sort of nation might genuinely have been formed across the generations and the ethnic diversities contained much as English, Scottish and Welsh identities have been for long contained within Britain. It is to be remembered that between the censuses of 1971 and 1981 the number of people describing themselves, not as Croat, Serb or whatever, but as 'Yugoslav by nationality' increased by no fewer than 943,000. Even someone so convinced of the 'centuries-long' existence of a number of 'different nations' within what became Yugoslavia as Branka Magas has also recognised that it 'was once a far-from-artificial state . . . a country that was not fated to disintegrate . . . There was more to Yugoslavia than its name.'[32]

But the enterprise of Yugoslavia did not succeed, and, in retrospect, given the presence of two aggressive nationalisms, temporarily somnolent but never extinguished, the deep differences shaped across many centuries in religion and culture, together with extreme democratic immaturity, that may be judged hardly surprising. The aim of this case study of what, eighty years ago, used to be called the 'South Slav Question' has been to throw light on the formation of nationhood and nationalism in a fourfold way. First, to argue the case, not for primordialism, but for a late medieval or early modern gelling of national identities, at least in regard to Serbs and Croats, comparable with what was happening elsewhere in Europe, a gelling produced by a mix of religion, literature and political history which – once it has happened – is hard indeed to alter. This point is made against scholars and politicians in the West who have so often implied either that the Southern Slavs remained into modern times 'no more than ethnographic raw material' or that they were all 'Serbs really'.

Secondly, I have argued that such ethnically conceived and medievally constructed national identities were far from universal in the region. They were also potentially destructive of other more territorially based societies such as the Bosnian, whose identity lacked both the one-to-one relationship with a religious tradition, so important for Serbia and Croatia, and also the pressurising produced by nineteenth-century intellectual nationalism, something inherently foreign to the ethos of Bosnia's Muslim leadership.

Thirdly, I have tried to suggest that the complex mix of nations, ethnic units, religious and territorial demarcations characteristic of the area could be satisfactorily contained neither by a single nation-state centred upon Serbdom nor by a multitude of separate nation-states, given that so many of the peoples involved were inextricably intermixed while some could not reasonably be described as nations, but rather by a tolerant federation based on territoriality rather than ethnicity, something not too unlike the Habsburg and Ottoman Empires themselves.

Fourthly, and finally, I have stressed that what made Yugoslavia unrealisable was the particular character of Greater Serbian nationalism, its narrowly ethno-religious construction, huge territorial ambitions and long addiction to ethnic cleansing. No nationalism has ever made better use of a mythology which has turned history on its head and got the world to believe in it: first, in regard to the Battle of Kosovo and the early Turk–Serb relationship; second, in regard to the 'Serb' identity of Croats and Bosnians; but, third, also in regard to twentieth-century history, especially the Second World War, in which a myth of Serbs in the 1940s as Anti-Fascist protectors of Jews, contrasted with Croats and Muslims as Fascist co-operators, has been sedulously spread and widely accepted in the West, wholly in defiance of the facts,[33] but as providing a subtle justification of Serb aggression in the 1990s.

At its most accepting Yugoslavia represented its people's best hope, a territorial state able to protect the interests of the smaller groups – the Kosovo Albanians, the Krajina Serbs, the Vojvodina Hungarians, the Sandjak Muslims – while waiting for a stronger common national identity to emerge. From this point of view it represented the kind of state from which a Nigerian or Ugandan nation may one day emerge. What made that impossible was precisely the recognition by nationalists preoccupied with the maintenance of the older national identities, Serb and Croat, that such an emergence would indeed create a new and different kind of nation, a territorial nation, something which must not be allowed to happen.

We should note, finally, the very considerable part religion has played in the horrible dénouement of this story.[34] Quite apart from the extent to which it has across history determined the 'ethnic' character of Serb and Croat, it has been used by both in the 1990s to inflame and justify aggressive nationalism. This has been particularly systematic in the Serbian case. They portrayed the seizure of power in Kosovo and the attack on Bosnia as little less than a crusade against Muslims, the long-awaited revenge for 1389, and wherever they gained control in Bosnia they destroyed every mosque and every Muslim tombstone, while hastily building Orthodox churches to replace them. On the Croat-Catholic side, there has been nothing quite as systematic or as blessed by ecclesiastical authorities. Indeed, several Catholic bishops have strongly condemned such behaviour. Nevertheless in Herzegovina the Croat anti-Islamic crusade has been little milder than the Serb. It is clear that the nationalist whipping up of religious antagonisms in a country where they had long been notably absent has been done mostly by politicians who had hitherto shown no great commitment to religion. Unfortunately they believed, quite correctly, that it would be easier to persuade ordinary people to murder or expel their neighbours, plunder their possessions and destroy their tombstones if it could be made to appear that all this was part of a great religious revival, a crusade to fulfil the vision of Kosovo and to expel once and for all 'Turks' and Muslim 'Fundamentalists' in order, as Radovan Karadzic frequently insisted, to fulfil God's will for the 'national rebirth' of the Serbs.

CHAPTER SIX

Some African case studies

When one turns to Africa the problems of interpretation seem, if anything, almost more acute and relatively little in any modern school of discourse actually helps to resolve them. The words 'nation' and 'nationalism' have been used so indiscriminately since the 1950s that an analysis of African realities in terms which tally with those used elsewhere is exceedingly difficult. But the difficulty has been further compounded by a fashionable school of current academic theory of an Hobsbawmian sort, represented in particular by a collection of essays entitled *The Creation of Tribalism in Southern Africa.*[1] This school wants to de-tribalise or de-ethnicise pre-colonial Africa, that is to say it is bent on claiming that Europeans, missionaries in particular but colonial officials and early anthropologists as well, invented tribes because it was convenient to them to do so. The very effort to put oral vernaculars into writing, to provide an administrative network or to dissect African society for the purposes of study, created identities which did not until then exist. Ethnic identity is something essentially modern.

It should be clear from the entire argument of this book that I am unlikely to want to play down the social impact of the introduction of writing and the translation of biblical texts into a range of vernaculars. Unquestionably, as we will see, this could significantly alter and extend identities, even occasionally it could be said to have created new ones. Nevertheless this way of interpreting things can easily be carried a great deal too far and it does not seem altogether surprising that, while purportedly anti-colonial in its critical edge, it is very much a South African academic view of the impact of the West upon Africa because – like so much of traditional white South African culture – its thrust is to deny any significant identity to pre-colonial Africa. Every identity must be found to have been somehow given by Europeans, even ethnic identity. Africa, like the Balkans, is to be reduced to the level of 'raw ethnographic material'. It was surprising to find Terence Ranger, who has spent his academic life defending African initiative, appearing to succumb to a theory which wished to deny Africans even the ability to provide themselves with the sort of ethnic identity which every people possesses in Europe and to leave them with identities 'invented' for them in colonial times by Europeans. Fortunately he is too good an Africanist not quickly to have recognised how shallow and anti-African such a view really is, an odd mix of Marxism and white racism, and in a recent essay, 'The Invention of Tradition Revisited: The Case of Colonial Africa',[2] has largely repudiated the claim that African ethnicities were a colonial 'invention'.

The truth is very different. African communities had an inherent sense of identity, sometimes wider, sometimes narrower, whereby insiders were distinguished from outsiders, and that sense of identity was very closely linked with language use. Very seldom, *pace* Marxists, did it have its origin in relations of inequality. As John Lonsdale has stressed in his defence of 'moral ethnicity' as something very different from tribalism, but a universal reality in pre-colonial times, 'transactions with members of other ethnic groups were relatively equal'.[3] Undoubtedly ethnicity was in most places a very flexible identity — as unwritten identities tend to be — alterable quickly enough under pressure of migration, war, conquest, the interchange of words and customs with territorially close neighbours. The added impact of missionaries and colonial officials fitted within that framework. That it affected identities quite quickly and considerably, both through administrative labelling and by privileging and stabilising certain forms of speech characteristic of one place while disregarding other varieties, is unquestionable. Nevertheless 'tribal' or 'ethnic' diversities were as such in no way an imposition upon Africa of western interpreters: it would be totally absurd and unhistorical, for example, to suggest that the difference between Baganda, Basoga and Banyoro in Uganda, to take quite deliberately three peoples culturally close together, was invented by western outsiders or was something of which they themselves were hitherto unaware.[4] 'Ethnicity' was a universal fact of life in pre-colonial Africa but not a hard unchangeable ethnicity, a pattern of primordial peoples, as westerners tended to imagine it, far back as many distinctions between closely related peoples did undoubtedly go. The distinction between Nuer and Dinka, for instance, must have existed for many centuries, given the relationship between their two languages, close as the two peoples in many ways remain.

The existence of nations is another matter. While chapter 7 further examines the meaning of ethnicity, often with Africa in mind, our purpose here is to focus rather upon the idea of the nation and to ask how far and in what circumstances 'nation' and 'nationalism' are terms genuinely appropriate for the understanding of African history. The discussion will relate largely to two things: the impact of vernacular literacy from the nineteenth century, particularly as a tool for biblical knowledge, and the construction of independent 'nation-states' during the past fifty years. It will however begin with the Ethiopian example, precisely because it completely predates any modern western impact. We will also sympathetically consider the claim of some other African peoples to a significant degree of nationhood prior to the coming of literacy. Besides Ethiopia, three ethnicities, the Ronga, Baganda and Yoruba, will be used to help elucidate these issues, together with a further range of post-Independence states, including especially Tanzania and Zimbabwe.

The Ethiopian case seems in some ways unAfrican. Here is a state with a continuous history of 1,500 years, with a literature, including the Bible, in its own ancient vernacular, Ge'ez, and an extraordinarily strong and enduring sense of its own identity, political, religious and literary. If there is one people in history to have been shaped in its own self-consciousness by the Bible, it is the Ethiopian, with their extraordinary early medieval myth of origin, recorded in the Kebra Nagast, that the Mosaic Ark of the Covenant was carried from Jerusalem to Ethiopia, by Menelik I, son of Solomon, to constitute their nation as the new Israel. It is a myth which probably goes back at least to the sixth century.[5] In consequence the whole Hebraic model of land, people, monarchy and religion could here be reproduced. There is no reason to think that this was merely the outlook of a small ruling class. It was rather something permeating the Amharic people and the huge number of their monks, clergy and lay musicians. Liturgy and music were at a popular level the continuous constructors of Ethiopian identity.[6] The social horizontality of this consciousness, achieved largely through liturgy, rather than some mere vertical acceptance of royal authority, is demonstrated powerfully by the series of popular rebellions against the emperor Susenyos in the seventeenth century when he attempted to change the Christian identity of Ethiopia by following the instructions of Jesuit missionaries and accepting Roman authority. He was finally compelled to abdicate by pressure from below of a genuinely nationalist sort. Yet he had been one of the most powerful and long-ruled of Ethiopian emperors. It is hard to deny that the basic characteristics of a nation were present in Ethiopia – though not, of course, in the non-Amharic peoples who were conquered by it unless and until they were assimilated into its religious and linguistic unity. Becoming a Christian meant becoming Amharic.

Here was an entirely rural people about as far removed from the Enlightenment as conceivable. Its national identity, both in continuous tradition and in the horizontal mass participation of the present through the rites and music of the Orthodox Church, was made possible only by its own vernacular literature, and the considerable growth in that literature from the fourteenth century onward, almost entirely religious as it was, continually reinforced this identity. If Ethiopia passes the test, and I believe it does, it passes it because it had for centuries possessed something which no sub-Saharan African people could lay claim to. On one side that must make it hard to react positively to any other African claim to nationhood: on the other it says something of enormous significance to Europe and to the theorists of nationalism. The specific root of nationalism does not lie in the circumstances of post-Enlightenment modernity. On the contrary. It lies rather in the impact of the Bible, of vernacular literature and of the two combined in creating a politically stable ethnicity, effectively 'imagined' by its members across a unique mythology.

Throughout nineteenth- and twentieth-century Africa, we may discern the beginnings of something similar. The nineteenth-century Protestant missionary was, above all, a Bible man, bent upon its translation into the local language. For that he had first to write grammars and dictionaries. The literary impact of the missionary was immense, in dozens of different languages, but in translating into a language he was often to a considerable extent creating the language, and, with it, a defined ethnicity as well. It is not, with very few exceptions indeed, that he wanted to do so or thought he was doing so. He was in fact simply learning as well as he could from a very limited number of people the language they spoke in its specific local form of that precise time. If he had settled thirty miles away, he would inevitably have learnt it rather differently but the form he adopted then became normative for all over a far wider area who learnt to read and write through this particular missionary's texts.

The flexibility and fluidity of a purely oral language gave way to something far more definite. People who spoke a little differently might, for a while, find this particular way of expressing things a trifle odd but once texts were printed in one form, they would not easily be printed in another only a little different, so while spoken language might continue to vary from place to place, the published scriptures quickly began to establish a new kind of language community and to affect spoken forms as well. What happened in nineteenth-century Africa was very like what had happened in Europe so many centuries earlier. Only it happened much more quickly but it also happened with very many more literary forms. Nineteenth-century missionaries were desperately anxious to bring the scriptures to everyone in their own maternal speech; in this they were backed by the resources of the Bible Societies and they were in a hurry.

Whereas in Europe major translated texts were established in a single form of a group of closely linked vernaculars and in consequence over a long period of time drew people together into a single language group despite a diversity of spoken dialects, in Africa and elsewhere the modern missionary ideal of multiplying translations to suit everyone at once has often had a very different social effect. Patrick Harries[7] has analysed the way this happened in regard to the Thonga and Ronga of southern Africa, two closely related 'languages' within the vast Bantu family. As a case study it is quite illuminating, though the facts he considers can easily be misinterpreted. Swiss missionaries from the Canton of Vaud began to evangelise the people in the Spelonken of eastern Transvaal in the 1870s. They had previously worked with the Paris Missionary Society in Basutoland and when they moved to the Transvaal they brought three African evangelists with them, so it was in Sesotho that they first began to preach, assisted by a Sesotho Bible, grammar and vocabulary.

Their assumption was that Sesotho and the local language they called Thonga were essentially one. They quickly realised, however, that this would not work. The two were far too different. The missionary desire for linguistic unity had to submit to the diversity on the ground. Bible translation, grammar and dictionary would have to be begun again. Though in the Spelonken they soon found they were dealing with an extremely mixed population, they felt that, this time round, linguistic unity could be maintained. Despite a number of varied dialects, Thonga was seen as essentially one language spoken by people all the way between the Spelonken and the Indian Ocean.

When part of the mission moved to the coast near Lourenço Marques, they therefore recognised in the local 'Ronga' just another Thonga dialect. Henri Berthoud, the mission's most gifted linguist, believed that the unity of Thonga could delineate the entire area of the Swiss Mission. Henri Junod, the mission's no less outstanding ethnographer, working on the coast and not, like Berthoud, in the Spelonken, did not at first disagree. For Junod, 'the language of a nation' was the best guide to the manifestation of its mind. Through developing its literary form it was possible at once both to grapple with its past – and Junod soon began to do that with a book of Ronga songs and stories – and to shape its Christian future. As he did so, however, he became convinced that the Ronga could not be evangelised through Thonga any more than the Thonga could be through Sesotho. They needed their own scriptures. Harries comments on the missionary conviction of the importance of a literary language in a rather curious Marxist way, belabouring them for imposing a written language on people who did not need it: 'Unlike the European bourgeoisie, the people defined as Tsonga-speakers had no need for a common language: their pre-capitalist economic activities were too restricted and localised to require the development of a language that would facilitate and defend their commercial transactions.'[8] Tell that to King Alfred. In reality such African developments were not dissimilar in context to translations into English in ninth-century Wessex.

The dilemma was a profoundly serious one. On the one hand, coastal Ronga in the south proved far more different from inland Thonga than Berthoud was willing to admit. Use of the inland Thonga was simply blocking the mission's immediate development.

On the other hand, as Berthoud argued, a double literature involved double costs, differences could be overcome with time, and two literary languages would mean two peoples. The long-term social advantage in not playing up regional dialectical differences was more important than the short-term evangelical advantage in doing so. The coastal missionaries insisted nevertheless in going ahead in accommodating to local needs. Within a few years Ronga and Thonga had become clearly recognised as distinct languages and then, in apparently inevitably consequence, as distinct peoples.

In 1934 Junod's son, Henri-Philippe, wrote critically of his father and in defence of the position of Berthoud:

> If Henri Junod had been able to understand the problem in its entirety . . . it is probable that we would today have one single language. In fact the passage of time allows us to pay homage to Henri Berthoud. He had understood that the Ba-Ronga only formed a small part of the great Tsonga tribe, and that this eccentric dialect could not reasonably be allowed to grow at the expense of the fundamental unity of a language spoken by more than one million individuals.[9]

In 1971, on the other hand, Martha Binford, an American anthropologist, confirmed the completion of the process of separation: 'The Ronga are a tribe because they have a delimited territory, a common language, common political structure, cultural unity; and an awareness of themselves as a distinct group.'[10]

This story has many lessons for us but it should not be used to bash missionaries. It is far more complex than that. It was certainly advantageous to Africa and the survival of African culture in an age of high colonial pressure to develop literary languages out of oral ones. But such a policy forced decisions where the criteria of choice were far from obvious. Junod was not initially opposed to the use of Thonga on the coast. It was the degree of difference between it and the coastal language which convinced him, as in similar circumstances numerous other missionaries up and down Africa were being convinced, that more and more different translations of the Bible were needed. It was reasonable enough to retranslate the scriptures into Ronga and there was little alternative if one saw the process of Christianisation as an urgent necessity to be achieved in only one or two generations. The Berthoud approach was the long-term, not the 'now now' one, and it corresponded with the pre-modern European practice – provide a single written form for the German scriptures and the language generally and let it exist side by side with dialects so different as to be mutually incomprehensible.

The medieval/Berthoud approach needed time; given time it would generate genuine nations transcending dialectical differences. Junod's approach on the other hand was more characteristic of the modern missionary and modern linguists in general. Their literalisation of as large a number of dialects as possible – the Bible Society ideal is to have the Bible in every discoverable dialect – must in the long run diminish the social significance of each and every translation. The Ronga may have become a people, consciously different from the Thonga, but, the more such people there are, the less a literature or an educational system is ever likely to develop in the language of any of them. The more African languages were recognised the less each could be used and the more society needed to depend indefinitely on a colonial language for its educational, economic and political needs. Nevertheless when Harries concludes that this is 'a classic instance of ethnic differences whose roots may be traced to an obscure linguistic debate between two Swiss missionaries',[11] one may again demur. The roots were there in genuine linguistic and cultural differences, inevitable when people lived some way apart, and the debate was far from obscure. The issue was whether in the move from orality to literacy one gave more weight to the dialectical divergence or the long-term needs for a larger social unity. What is important for us is that Harries has provided so clear a late nineteenth-century case study in just how 'nations' emerge out of biblical translation, demonstrating both the fluidity of the pre-literary situation and the long-term social consequence of a vernacular Bible. Once the Junod line was followed, the distinct social identity of the Ronga became inevitable.

If we now turn to Buganda and its neighbours we have a rather different story. Nineteenth-century observers encountering the Baganda were profoundly impressed by the scale, power, cultural confidence of their society. If there existed one nation-state in nineteenth-century black Africa, Buganda would have a good claim to be it. It had grown over centuries; it had a strong sense of its own history, centralised government, an effective territorial division in counties (*Saza*) and possessed in its clan organisation a horizontality of social consciousness to balance the verticality of royal and bureaucratic rule. Michael Wright, in his fascinating *Buganda in the Heroic Age*, based largely upon oral evidence obtained around 1960 from elderly informants, had one particularly impressive witness to the Buganda of the late nineteenth century, Kalikuzinga, whom he interviewed on eighty-three occasions. What Wright carried away with him, he tells us, from those interviews, was Kalikuzinga's 'sense of commonalty; his feeling for the unity of all Baganda', his recognition that 'even the most powerful Kabaka (king) was never greater than Buganda and lived his life, like his people, under custom'.[12] That seems to me to suggest the sort of horizontality we expect of a nation.

In most African societies translation of the scriptures, hymnbooks and elementary school texts defined a language and the people who used it in new ways but seldom led to any immediate literary response on the African side. Not so in Buganda. Here a society capable of using it was already in existence and anxious to do so. What was striking was both the mass desire to read and write – unrelated at the time to any work prospects – and the very considerable early use of written Luganda by Baganda themselves. Luganda literature in the early twentieth century is unparalleled in any other east or central African people and expressed a quite self-conscious national identity thriving through the uses of literacy but no less dependent upon an already existing mesh of custom, language and territoriality.[13] The late nineteenth-century Luganda Bible, in the translation of which leading Baganda were very active participants, together with much other early Catholic and Protestant religious literature, give the impression of carrying the Baganda across a line they had already nearly reached dividing ethnicity from nationhood. The impressive histories of his people written by Apolo Kagwa, their prime minister, symbolise the way in which a political identity and oral history are bound together through the development of literature, grounded on scripture translation, to stabilise a specific national consciousness.

Here again it is striking how early missionary attempts to use their original Bible translation among neighbouring ethnic groups broke down in every case. The Bantu peoples both west and east of Buganda possessed similar languages and the use of Luganda in their early evangelisation was neither impossible nor unreasonable. Just as

Buganda had incorporated Buddu in the eighteenth century and Kkooki in the nineteenth, so now it might have gone on, under the leadership of warlords like Semei Kakungulu, to take in a great deal more. If the power of Buganda had been unbroken for several generations, and if the scriptures had only been translated into Luganda, then one might have seen a single written language accepted from Mount Elgin in the east to Ruwenzori in the west. A strong central ethnicity would have become the core of a nation with many dialects but a single, shared literature. Buganda would have been the Wessex of central Africa.

It was not to be. Resistance to the use of Luganda texts was obvious everywhere, even in areas linguistically least different: Ankole cried out for its Lunyankole Bible, Bunyoro its Lunyoro Bible and so forth. The diversity of ethnicities was not invented by missionaries. On the contrary, at first they hit their heads against it. After a heated missionary discussion it was concluded that Christian faith would have to be taught in what Dr Cook, the mission's doctor, called the 'heart language' of every people and in Toro that was not Luganda but Lunyoro. The decision to use Lunyoro had the result, a missionary claimed in 1905, that 'the work has gone forward in leaps and bounds'. Evangelically that was undoubtedly the right decision; politically, however, it prevented closely related societies from being merged within a 'Greater Buganda' and instead hardened the lines between a series of petty societies which would, in consequence, find no common medium other than English.[14] These ethnic diversities were in no way invented by missionaries or colonialists. They were there, but undoubtedly in the purely oral state many of them were more fluid than they became once the written word had canonised their differences. It would be unwise to dismiss the sense of distinction these peoples already possessed, but equally unwise to regard the tribal divisions that existed at the moment of colonial conquest and missionary language-learning as in all or most cases separations of great antiquity. In fact that between the kingdoms of Toro and Bunyoro was only happening at that exact moment and might not have lasted if colonials and missionaries had not stabilised the schism.

We cannot generalise. The history of Buganda went back, quite verifiably, for centuries before the missionary advent. It was no longer an identity easily open to change as, indeed, a hundred years of subsequent history have proved again and again. The stability of Buganda can be set against the fluidity of Toro or the Ronga, where new identities dependent on territorial separation and the ups and downs of chiefly politics could come and go. Buganda's stability depended on the density of its population, the precise definition of its territorial basis along the northern coast of Lake Victoria, the comradely experience of its armies and its fleet. Even without the Bible it looked almost like a nation-state.

Our final African case study is that of the Yoruba, a group of closely related peoples and towns in western Nigeria, that is to say in pre-colonial terms west of the kingdom of Benin and east of the kingdom of Dahomey. They shared a good deal with both those kingdoms but the characteristics of the Yoruba were to dwell in a number of large autonomous towns, each surrounded by a swathe of territory and ruled by kings who seem to have been far from absolute. Yoruba claimed a common origin in the city of Ife. They shared a common cultural core – the essentials of language, religious system and political organisation – and for much of the eighteenth century most of the Yoruba kingdoms had been within the empire of Oyo, one of the most powerful of Yoruba states. If Ife represented Yoruba unity from the viewpoint of myths of origin, Oyo did from another, that of recent political history. Yet effectively the Yoruba were far from united and often at war with one another. It would be hard to claim that this decentralised group of city states formed a nation in the mid-nineteenth century. They did not, in fact, even have a common name for themselves. They had neither political nor social unity and yet they shared a common underlying consciousness at once historic, linguistic and religious.

It was once more the coming of Christianity with its concomitant of a vernacular literature which brought the Yoruba into full consciousness of being a single people.[15] Samuel Ajayi Crowther, translator of the Yoruba Bible, as well as Anglican Bishop on the Niger, was a figure of immense importance in triggering national consciousness, the sense of sharing the name of Yoruba, whether you lived in Ibadan or Ilorin, Ife or Oyo. It was another Anglican priest, Samuel Johnson, who in the 1890s composed *The History of the Yorubas from the Earliest Times* (though it was published only in 1921), doing for his people something of the job that Bede had done for the English. The Yoruba Bible, with its concomitant dictionaries, grammars and readers, created a written language transcending the boundaries of spoken dialects. It would not be unreasonable to claim that this group of Yoruba clergy, Samuel Crowther, Samuel Johnson, James Johnson and their colleagues, formed the intellectual avant-garde, principally responsible for transforming a group of closely related ethnicities into a single, self-aware nation, a feat all the more remarkable in that Christians by no means dominate among the Yoruba. The power of such works in a sort of literary vacuum, coming at a moment when literacy seems all-important, can be overwhelming, good examples of the way imagining one's nation is assisted by books. The moment was right, the books were right and yet they depended for their effectiveness upon articulating a shared ethnic identity which already existed, and which, by the horizontality which characterised this self-confident, decentralised, urban, rather collegial society, was already intrinsically well on its way to possessing many of the criteria for nationhood. Yet only Christianity could do it. There are more Muslim Yoruba than Christian Yoruba, but they had no comparable effect. Islam advances trade, education and even state-formation as well as monotheism and religious devotion but it does not advance nations or national languages. On the contrary its specific socio-cultural impact, noticeable throughout Africa, is to draw people into a single, far more universalist, community whose sole language of direct encouragement is Arabic and whose consciousness is fuelled by pilgrimage to Mecca. Every genuine example of nation-construction one can find in Africa seems dependent upon Christianity and biblical translation, never upon Islam.

One would have expected to see a twentieth-century Yoruba nation-state, as also a Buganda nation-state, and, for that matter, a Kongo nation-state, corresponding to the ancient Kongo kingdom. Yet no such thing has been allowed to come to fruition. The politically correct nationalisms of Africa have taken another form, leaving historians glibly to describe Yoruba, Ganda or Kongo as sub-nations, tribal separatists. We need now to consider why the nation-making process at work in Africa with its close affinity to European nation-making of an earlier age was stopped in its tracks by a quite different process, one which lacked almost any ethnic foundation, but which purported to produce nations out of the hat of European imperialism and borderlines established by the Congress of Berlin.

Unsatisfactory as the colonially devised 'nation-states' of modern Africa are in so many ways, one has first to admit that the process of their construction was not entirely unreasonable. The Yoruba and the Baganda were decidedly unusual in late nineteenth-century Africa as plausible candidates for nationhood. Ethiopia did make it. Ashanti, the Zulu kingdom and a number of others might have done so as well but the political gap between the large majority of Africa's ethnicities and nineteenth-century western requirements for a sensible state seemed impossibly large. If Brittany, the Basques, Naples and Hanover were discounted as candidates for viable nationhood, how much more the Ronga and the Thonga. Even an entirely benign colonialism set upon the modernisation of Africa could hardly have based it upon the multitude of diverse ethnicities that appeared to exist. If there had been a few more centuries of internal development, maybe the map would have been simplified through the incorporation of neighbouring peoples by the more powerful states. In the real world, however, the countries of Europe, still attracted in the late nineteenth century by the imagined profits of overseas rule and faced with an almost complete power vacuum in Africa and, moreover, almost completely ignorant of its ethnic composition, inevitably divided it up quite otherwise, marking out various large parcels, defined in the simplest of geographical terms. The political map of Africa, decided in the 1880s and 1890s by non-Africans for their own purposes, has remained almost unaltered ever since. While it could not, for instance, conceivably be claimed that the mix of peoples inhabiting the British colony of Kenya, such as Lwo and Masai, Kikuyu and Turkana, had any ethnic, linguistic or historical reason to be regarded as a nation, such they were now expected to become. Only in one or two cases, such as that of the Shona in Rhodesia/Zimbabwe, was there the slightest correspondence between a colonially constructed state and a pre-colonial ethnicity or monarchy. The Shona as the core constituent of Rhodesia/Zimbabwe and the smaller examples of Lesotho, Swaziland, Rwanda and Burundi are very much exceptions. Yet the new states were imagined both by encouraging colonial officials and by most members of the first generation of African political leadership – almost entirely educated on European Christian lines – as necessarily nation-states, according to the standard political orthodoxy of the twentieth century. Here, if anywhere, we have examples of 'nations' being produced out of a process of state-formation. The steady functioning of a colony or an independent state with its internal economy, communications system and capital, its own schools and universities, even churches self-geared to enhancing the identity of this particular unit, all contributed to push together a range of diverse ethnicities and persuade their members to think of themselves as now no longer Lwo, Kikuyu or Kamba but Kenyan.

That was the idea but there were little more than sixty years in which to make it work. In most places the process hardly even began until well after the First World War and only started to impinge upon most ordinary people well after the Second World War. Can you create new nations in a generation? Surely not. While Black Africa's prototype 'nation-state' of Ghana had a far longer unitary history – at least for its southern core – and some real ground to justify such a description, few if any of its successors could conceivably be described as nation-states when they became independent in the 1960s. As Chief Awolowo, one of Nigeria's leading nationalist politicians, remarked in 1945, 'Nigeria is not a nation. It is a mere geographical expression.'[16] Whether some can be fairly so described fifty years later may be more debatable. 'Nation-building' has been a favourite theme of African politicians just because nations in most countries manifestly did not exist. Both constructive and destructive factors have been at work. On one side one needs to remember how very malleable ethnicities can often be, how quickly social identities can change, how new languages can be adopted and loyalties created. I suspect that in terms of nation-building Nyerere's Tanzania has been easily the most successful case, assisted by the absence of any one dominant ethnicity, and, even more, by the official adoption of Swahili. Here once more language may be the decisive factor. Most African countries have no common or official language, other than the universal languages of English, French and Portuguese, none of which is the spoken language of any but a handful of people. Latin could not create medieval England, and one may question whether English can do so for modern Nigeria, but Swahili may well have done so for Tanzania.

Elsewhere the pretence of the nation-state where none exists may rather have exacerbated underlying ethnic tensions. It remains possible that, eventually and apart from a few exceptions, states will create their nations. Nigerian, Kenyan, Ugandan identities may genuinely prevail. But the question for us is not one of the future but of the past and present. It remains absurd to pretend that at present Baganda, Lugbara and Teso belong to a common Ugandan nation. Thirty years ago we talked of African nationalism as an undoubted reality but we linked it unhesitatingly with European-created entities. Movements which were, on the contrary, clearly related to some pre-existing people were regarded as tribal, reactionary or at best 'sub-national'. This made very little sense in terms of the genus of nationalism. To describe every anti-colonial or anti-western movement as 'nationalist' is simply an abuse of terms, customary as it has certainly been.

For a good example of this sort of politically correct interpretation of the African political scene of thirty years ago, one could take Professor Pratt's study of 'the Politics of Indirect Rule' in Uganda. While admitting that for the Baganda 'Buganda, not Uganda, was their nation'[17] his analysis could not get beyond depicting them as 'separatists' following 'tribal influences' and 'disruptive tribal loyalties' in contrast with 'Uganda nationalists' upon whose efforts a democratic future must depend.[18] Quite apart from the question as to which side deserved most sympathy, the fact is that Pratt's 'nationalists' related to no real nation whatever, while his proponents of 'tribal separatism' were pretty genuine nationalists whipping up the sentiments of an all too self-aware nation. The pretence that non-nations were nations was a piece of convenient western make-believe, a delusion almost bound to lead onto the huge political confusions of post-Independence Africa.

The 'nationalist' movements of the 1950s in fact drew what strength they had – which was often not so great – either from far narrower ethnicities or from a far wider Pan-Africanism. The colonial state was hardly a state at all – more, simply, an extension of services of one or another European country, and loyalty to these states or any real 'imagining' of their national reality was extremely limited. Movements for independence mostly prevailed not because of any inner strength they possessed in the consciousness of an oppressed nation but because the colonial rulers under UN and American pressure threw in the towel in the belief that if they did not do so 'nationalist' movements would turn Communist and open the door to the USSR. In consequence, once Independence was achieved, nationalist sentiments, movements and parties quickly faded away, leaving little more than a western-style bureaucracy and a multitude of African ethnicities to fill the gap.

African nationalism, I am suggesting, has hardly existed except where it has been ethnically based, linguistically held together and biblically watered. Even apparent state-linked nationalisms can turn out to be ethnically based, though their public image has been appropriately widened. Thus Kenyan nationalism grew out of Kikuyu nationalism and the Mau Mau struggle. Zimbabwe is a very good example for the analysis of genuine African nationalism because it went through a far tougher struggle, and nations are largely created out of wars of liberation. But at the heart of the Zimbabwean struggle were two ethnic identities, the Shona and the Ndebele, and even during the struggle they were pulling apart. One came to be represented by ZANU, the other by ZAPU and the secret history of post-Independent Zimbabwe was of a civil war between them, won inevitably by ZANU because the Shona formed 80 per cent of the country. It is the strength of Zimbabwe that its nationalism is grounded on a single central ethnicity and language, and a great deal has now been written in Shona. Zimbabwe has almost all the characteristics of classical nationalism: a considerable continuity between ethnicity and nation, the myth of national heroes such as Nehanda and Kagubi whose statues now adorn the parliament building, a national language which has already produced a varied literature, and a lengthy war of liberation. Whether the Ndebele can be effectively incorporated within what is in reality a Shona-based nation or whether many among them will continue to pursue a separatist course may depend upon great mutual forbearance. It is not unlike the relationship of Scotland to Britain and it is bound to take time.

Go further south and it is hardly surprising that nationalism there too appears to have the most fanatical endurance where it is most ethnically grounded. Nowhere has black nationalism had a longer history or a more intense struggle. The general urbanisation of South Africa and the tribally mixed society of many urban areas, coupled with the wide use of English, have contributed to provide a context in which a nationalism not grounded in a narrow ethnic base could become an enduring reality. The length of the struggle has been of great formative importance. Nevertheless even here the common front required to overcome white domination has been deeply under threat once that domination began to tumble. The linguistic division is not unimportant, even though Zulu and Xhosa are not so much more apart than Angle and Saxon or Croat and Serb. Can they now at short notice, having overthrown the white state, overcome also the inherent divisiveness of a resurgent ethnic nationalism, to maintain and deepen a territorially based nationhood? In particular, if the Zulu kingdom was for long a powerful nineteenth-century state with a huge mythology of its own, it was naive for liberals, Marxists or other anti-racists to imagine that once white domination had been overthrown an ethnic Zulu nationalism would not seek to fill the power vacuum within its own area.

To say that in fragile western-constructed states a bonding between nationalism and pre-colonial ethnicities is almost inevitable is not to suggest that ethnic nationalism is likely to be less destructive in Africa than in Europe. On the contrary. The fact is, however, that territorial nations require more time to appeal to the heart than ethnic nations. While 'the colonial states could be said to represent the primacy of territoriality over ethnicity, their roots were simply too shallow, their structures and borders too recently laid down from outside to be immediately viable vehicles for deep national senti-ment. Territorial nations cannot arise at the wave of a wand. Where in Africa they have genuinely arisen or shown signs of doing so, the pattern of their formation seems fairly comparable to that of western Europe: a basis in ethnicity, a hardening and maturing of that base through the development of an oral vernacular into a literary language, a development frequently dependent on the translation and use of the Bible, and a process of state-formation, usefully assisted by a prolonged war of liberation. Where there is no shared ethnicity, no literary vernacular, no experience of war, it is highly unlikely that either a nation or any attendant nationalism will genuinely exist.

Most African ethnicities have much in common with their neighbours. Merging across generations into a larger nationhood is as feasible for them as for Angles and Jutes in England or Scots and Picts in Scotland. It is happening in many places but it is also failing to happen in others. What is important for us is to attempt a typology of why ethnicities merge or fail to merge and even, in failure, become acutely hostile to one another. Factors of size, relationship to government and capital, and religion can all be involved. The multi-ethnic state in which one ethnicity, without necessarily constituting a majority, is yet far larger than any other and in a position to dominate, is a situation in which other ethnicities, instead of accepting a larger national identity, are likely to produce conflict and even a desire to secede. If the major ethnicity also controls the capital, the alienation of other groups is likely to be enhanced. If Tanzania may well present the best model for a healthy merging of small ethnicities into something fairly describable as a nation, it has been assisted by the absence of a single large group, by the fact that the larger and richer ethnicities have been geographically peripheral to the state, but above all by the development of a national language. What makes Tanzania unique in national terms, despite its being a large colonially constructed state, is that the common woman can everywhere understand Swahili. Tanzania's one obvious major source of division, the religious one between Christians and Muslims, has not at least as yet come into serious political play. This is all the more remarkable because in many parts of Africa Christian–Muslim tensions have become a central anti-national force. In Tanzania the religious divide does not correspond at all closely with an ethnic divide and Swahili, despite its Islamic cradle, is now as much a Christian as a Muslim language. It was the Christian adoption of Swahili – despite some early missionary misgivings – which may well have been crucial for the successful construction of Tanzanian national identity. It began with Bishop Steere's Swahili Bible in the late nineteenth century, but the deciding moment was probably the 1960s when, in the wake of the Second Vatican Council, the Catholic bishops agreed that mass should normally be celebrated everywhere in Swahili and not – as in virtually every other African country – in a multitude of different local languages. The Catholic Church is the one non-governmental community present throughout the whole country and its self-imposed Swahilisation stands at the heart of Tanzanian nation-formation, however much the social analysts have managed to overlook it. It does, of course, closely cohere with the aspirations of Julius Nyerere, himself an exceptionally devout Catholic, the King Alfred of twentieth-century Africa, with his Swahili translations of *Julius Caesar* and *The Merchant of Venice*.

In much of this Tanzania resembles the otherwise very different society of Yorubaland, comparably divided between Christians and

Muslims. But Tanzania is recognised as a nation-state, Yorubaland is not. If a religious divide does not necessarily undermine national unity, a religious community does not necessarily ensure it. A common Catholicism has had strangely little effect on merging Tutsi and Hutu in Burundi or Rwanda. Here as elsewhere one must not exaggerate the effect of religion, particularly a newly adopted religion, in shaping the political map. Where Christian–Muslim tension is reflected, as in the Sudan or the Biafran war, in the near total breakdown of a state, the underlying reasons are generally to be sought in racial and regional rather than religious factors, although it cannot be questioned that a particularly intolerant strand of northern Sudanese Islam has also much to do with it. In general, religion has not, however, been a major factor in African national consciousness and nation-formation in the second half of the twentieth century, largely because the characteristic Christian approach to the enhancement of ethnicity at work in the late nineteenth and early twentieth centuries was undermined by European policies and the need to grant a hasty independence to arbitrarily constructed states. In Africa it was clearly impossible for all the hundreds of ethnicities that did, and mostly still do, exist to turn into nations. Yet some were on their way to doing so and a few may still be inclined that way. While the process of nation-construction is quite certainly not a case of every 'primordial' ethnicity becoming in due course a nation-state, it is all the same exceedingly difficult to arrive at the latter without in some way building upon the former.

CHAPTER SEVEN

Ethnicity further considered

Our pursuit of the rise of nations, national consciousness and nationalism in medieval and early modern Europe, as well as in Africa, has led back time and again to pre-existent ethnicities out of which nations have been wholly or partially constructed. But what really do we mean by ethnicities, in what did they consist, why did they exist, and how durable were they? It is currently fashionable to be sceptical about their very existence, but, in point of fact, as John Lonsdale insists, 'ethnicity is a world-wide social fact'.[1] The point at which to start is that of observable character, not that of origin, whether claimed or hypothesised.

By ethnicity, I mean the common culture whereby a group of people share the basics of life – their cloth and clothes, the style of houses, the way they relate to domestic animals and to agricultural land, the essential work which shapes the functioning of a society and how roles are divided between men and women, the way hunting is organised, how murder and robbery are handled, the way defence is organised against threatening intruders, the way property and authority are handed on, the rituals of birth, marriage and death, the customs of courtship, the proverbs, songs, lullabies, shared history and myths, the beliefs in what follows death and in God, gods or other spirits. All this as shared through a spoken language. Ethnicity and the spoken word go most closely together. But within every ethnicity are sub-ethnicities – recognisable small diversities in everything we have listed – just as a spoken language varies across quite short distances of place, class and profession. The distinction between these two types of difference was clear enough although in ordinary daily life the inner differences might often seem to matter more than the outer ones. Nevertheless the larger shared community of identity, that on which one primarily relies for marriage partners, defence and the security of a common law, remains far more significant than its inner subdivisions, often talked up almost playfully.

Ethnicity defines the group within which one is normally expected to marry. Even that affirmation may, nevertheless, appear to raise a problem: rules of exogamy may forbid one to marry within one's own – quite extended – clan. Could it not be argued that the clan is the ethnic unit and, therefore, the truth is precisely the opposite to the one I have proposed? At least in most African cases the answer is no. A man may not marry his sister, but that does not bring into question their single ethnicity. Clan exogamy rules should be taken as an extension of that prohibition. 'Clans' of this sort are essentially subgroups within a people without their own separate territory. Such divisions do not separate one ethnicity from another: they constitute on the contrary an internal characteristic of a specific ethnicity just as a division between elders and others is one within ethnicity. The distinction between those lasting human categorisations which tend to separate ethnicities and those which instead, like functions and classes, exist within an ethnicity is a crucial one. Both are socially important but in quite different ways. There can, indeed, be so-called clan divisions which derive from distinct ethnicities of the past, just as regional divisions within an ethnicity may be in part the survival of past ethnic divisions. But the essential point being made here is that a rule of exogamy may be needed precisely because intermarriage can be so basic to the preservation of some ethnicities.

Every family needs to exist within a safe intermarrying society considerably wider than itself, a society sharing a common concept of marriage, its preparation, obligations and celebration. All this relates primarily to one's ethnicity not to the state. Control by the latter comes in at a much later stage of political development, actually a very late stage – in Britain, for instance, that of Hardwick's Marriage Act of 1753.

If an ethnicity is an intermarrying society then it will have common ancestors and, undoubtedly, tends to define itself in terms of its common ancestors and very often some specific 'myth' of origin or of this particular land. Of course, there is some central truth in that type of definition, in regard to the tracing of a central line of historic consciousness, from the present to the far past. Such a tracing is certainly not to be despised or rejected as bogus. It represents the principal public memory of an ethnicity and as marriage over the generations gives us all an incredibly large number of potential ancestors – some 40,000 for each of us within a single generation for, say, the mid-sixteenth century, and well over a million for a couple of centuries earlier – it is obvious that any group of people that has lived together for centuries must share to a very large extent a collective ethnic origin.

Beyond this rather obvious fact of the consequence of marriage across the generations in a relatively stable society, how far can we regard an ethnicity as in origin a genetic unity constituted by a shared genetic origin? Hobsbawm speaks of 'influential theories or pseudo-theories identifying nations with genetic descent'[2] with some disdain. Of course such theories are often oversimplified, very much so in regard to nations, but also even in regard to ethnicities. Nevertheless they represent a necessary core of original truth. An ethnicity is in origin constituted by, more than anything else, a genetic unity, partly real, partly mythical. If we take the Gypsies, or indeed the Jews, it is quite implausible to think that anything else could explain their survival as a cultural community in diaspora over many centuries except a shared genetic origin, reinforced by insistence upon endogamous marriage. An ethnicity without a sure territorial base, political protection or language area can preserve itself only by the closest adherence to an original charter providing a distinct genetic identity. But of course such genetic unity is protected by a cultural unity of specific customs including a way of life, work, belief, language. Yet we have to be careful here. The Gypsies do indeed have a language of their own but many of them have largely abandoned it, in favour of the language of the people they live among, just as they accepted rather easily the latter's religious practices. Nevertheless their clear identity as an ethnicity survives, rooted in a genetic base and protected by a customary life-style very hard to define. The survival of Jewish diaspora identity is relatively easier to explain, linked as it has been with a very rigid system of religious belief and practice.

These examples are important because they do, I believe, enable us to peer rather deep down into the constitution of ethnicity and its long-term survival, with a view unaffected by the protection and blurring inevitably provided by territorial or political control. In most cases, however, ethnicities are not cut off from control of a specific territorial area or even from local control of the levers of power. A territorially based ethnicity politically controlling its own, at least local, government may retain a mythic sense of genetic unity, but is likely to bother far less about the reality of genetic unity.

A basic reason lies in the static nature of territory but the mobile nature of populations. Many people do marry someone of another ethnicity – because of war, trade or just the proximity of small groups of people ethnically different. Moreover groups of people often do not stay in the same place. Large-scale migrations are not a merely modern phenomenon; a migratory people may take over political control of an area or merely enter it in a manner subservient to its existing order. But in every case migration tends not to produce a wholly new people for a specific territory, but a mix of new and old, a mix in which, however, the mythic origins may well become fused into one. In cold historical fact it is seldom that any developed and territorially stable ethnicity has a single genetic origin, but it often has a sole dominant mythological genetic origin. Throughout Africa there are numerous examples of peoples, now seen as one but in fact with a composite ethnicity, who have adopted an 'official' mythological origin, a journey from somewhere else, when this – one can be pretty sure – is historically based on the relatively recent arrival of a small minority which then came to dominate the existing inhabitants. Yet such myths are often balanced by a mysterious role in the validation of the ruler left in the hands of religious representatives of a submerged people. Thus kings of Scotland were crowned in the Pictish shrine of Scone, kings of the Kongo required for their election the endorsement of the *mani Vunda*. In these and other cases, rituals and myths, religion and political roles are interwoven in such a way as to integrate previously distinct ethnicities and tone down the more brazen implications of conquest.[3]

In Rwanda and Burundi, the case was rather different, with hindsight calamitously so. Here the Tutsi immigrant pastoral conquerors were unusual in that, while adopting the language of the previous Hutu occupants and to some extent even intermarrying with them, they failed to achieve an effective ethnic fusion; either because the time-scale was too short, the physical and occupational differences between the two groups too large or, even, because the relative number of the Tutsi may have been more considerable than in most such cases. Whatever the reason, the distinction between them remained and was actually hardened by colonialism, in both social and political terms. In post-colonial circumstances it has led to fearful disaster for both groups. But more often this does not happen. There is in time fusion of the two, so that the social division disappears and, very often, awareness of dual origin. Slavonic tribes settling in what used to be Yugoslavia – areas now described as Serbia, Bosnia, Croatia and Montenegro – undoubtedly swallowed up a large pre-Slav population, but their languages, historical origins and any sense of pre-Slav existence simply disappeared as it did for the British population of most of England. In later invasions of England the opposite happened. Quite quickly the Norman conquerors, while their own myths of origin and of triumphant conquest in 1066 were not forgotten, came to be swallowed up in the identity, history and language of the conquered.

It may well be that it is a matter of the relative numbers involved, though in most cases we can only surmise what they were. The Norman conquerors of England were really very few indeed in comparison with the English conquered. In France one may well compare the south, where the institutions, language and religion of the conquered Gauls remained so much more firmly in place, and the north, where the immigrant Germanic conquerors dominated. The identity of the south remained Gallic, we may say, that of the north Frank. France has never quite known whether its primary mythological ancestors were the Franks who entered Gaul in the fifth century or the Gauls who had already been there for many centuries. Monarchical France tended to identify with the former, Republican France with the latter – even though Republican France was at least as anxious as its dynastic predecessor to impose upon the Gallic south the language and culture of the Frankish north.

In an initially not so different case, that of Egypt, the Arab conquest of a Coptic country was also that of one world religion, Christianity, by that of another, Islam. Here for many years the conquered Christian Copts remained a majority; little by little by pressures of one sort and another the majority became a minority, abandoning the domestic – though not liturgical – use of its own language. It became a single Arab society though, in terms of a narrow ethnicity, its ancestors were overwhelmingly not Arabs; but it remained divided sharply between the two communities of Muslim and Christian, and this was far more than a religious divide. It was, in a larger sense, one of ethnicity, although the majority of modern Egyptian Muslims are in genetically ethnic terms Copts, and culturally many Coptic customs, such as female circumcision, have passed across to Muslims while much Muslim influence over and above the adoption of the Arab language has affected Christians. But the more complex a nation, the surer it is that, however mono-chrome its genetic ethnicity may be claimed symbolically to be, in reality it is complex and highly mixed. Intermarriage across many generations may, nevertheless, ensure an effectively shared genetic root.

Even in quite simple societies the difference between real genetic origins and mythical genetic origins could be recognised without difficulty. Strangers could be prisoners of war or individual wan-derers, adopted and absorbed into lineage or clan. There is nothing strange or modern in overlooking a gap between the real and the mythical. The latter establishes the necessary moral unity of a group. In adopting the ancestors and gods of one's hosts, one's conquerors or even those one has conquered, one is adopting their *mores* and a shared moral community which leaps beyond any genetic bond, without, however, disallowing the latter's symbolic meaning. The recognition of ancestry pretends, 'imagines' if you like, a genetic origin which may not be biologically correct. It remains socially correct, however, and even morally necessary to define the social mythically in terms of the genetic. It is perhaps only when an ethnicity develops into, or becomes part of, a territorial nation that it becomes possible to throw aside the claim to genetic unity and glory instead in a multiplicity of origins. Thus it is evidence of the national maturity of the English by the twelfth century that they could willingly admit to a diversity of real or mythical origins, Trojan and Roman, British, English, Danish and Norman. It helps demonstrate that their country, in the words of the constitutional historian J.E.A. Jolliffe, 'had already made the transition from the tribal to the territorial state'.[4] The tolerant ethnic pluralism of a mature nation presupposes a confident territoriality.

There are, however, limits to the credibility of adopting the ancestors of someone else. France carried its policy of assimilation from its own provinces to its empire. It became part of the process of assimilating French West Africa that its children too were taught to say 'our ancestors the Gauls'. This was to cross the frontier of the absurd. In no way could Ivory Coast or Togo really become a province of France yet it was an extension of what had happened again and again in human, and particularly French, history. If the Bretons could learn to be French, why not the Togolese? It was at least a strategy which declined to accept any absolute character of 'the other' and which also declined to define ethnicity in terms of blood.

Ethnicity is a shared community of culture of the sort I have described, but in different ethnicities different elements are taken to provide the decisive criteria of belonging. There can be, as I have already suggested, enduring sub-ethnicities which may be based on area, linguistic differentiations, religion or a history based on partial assimilation of some additional group. It is hard to define what constitutes an internal differentiation which is significant in itself but not divisive of a single ethnicity, for example religion – Catholic or Muslim – among Albanians. Nevertheless the persistent survival of a diversity as significant as this within a group which still sees itself as socially one would seem to be a major factor in the construction of the latter as 'nation' rather than as 'ethnicity'. The degree of social self-consciousness required for the acceptance of such diversity within one's group is properly a characteristic of nationhood.

The point is that two or more ethnicities can grow into one but it takes a lot of time; equally one ethnicity can grow into two under political, economic or geographical pressure. The Low Countries split into a predominantly Protestant and independent Netherlands and a predominantly Catholic and – for long – not independent Belgium, but in the mid-sixteenth century Antwerp and Ghent could just as well have gone the way of Amsterdam and Utrecht. Ethnicities do not have hard edges. They are socio-cultural realities, not legal ones. What normally constitutes the core of their community as experienced from within is the sharing of a single spoken language, though it may well include a wide range of dialectical variety. In principle it is probably true that the two are indeed interchangeable. When dialectical difference becomes so considerable as to constitute a separate language, ethnicity too may be said to be different. An ethnicity produces and is reflected in its particular language: the minutiae of culture are necessarily reflected in oral speech and vocabulary so closely that it is hard to imagine separation between the two. Nevertheless that judgement does not entirely cohere with the ups and downs of history. For two reasons. The first is that an ethnicity can be divided fairly sharply by political action from outside. Once its two parts are subject to different political regimes they may become ethnically distinct quite fast, while their language does not alter with the same speed. Flemish remains on both sides of the Dutch–Belgian frontier. This is particularly the case once a vernacular is to any great extent written down. Writing impedes diversification. Language and ethnicity, then, can move apart. A written language cannot characterise ethnicity to the extent that oral language does. Even Americans can still speak English! If they had taken a merely oral language with them across the Atlantic, it would soon have been vastly different from the English of England. The printed word prevented this from happening.

There is, moreover, no precise way to 'decide' when one language is different from another or when the two are dialectal forms of a single language. This is manifestly true of hundreds of Bantu languages in central and southern Africa. Only their (mostly missionary) encapsulation in writing has resulted in either merging or separation, often to much local dissatisfaction. Today it has become the fashionable orthodoxy of ex-Yugoslavia that there are three languages, Bosnian, Serb and Croat. That is official. Twenty years ago no one spoke Bosnian and the language of the three areas was officially described as 'Croatoserbian/Serbocroatian' or, at the next mention, 'Serbocroatian/Croatoserbian'.[5] Anything within that was a dialect. At one time one spoke even of 'SerboBulgar' wishing to incorporate an even further range of 'dialects'. That did not work. But 'Croatoserbian/Serbocroatian' did – for a while. Today the stress is instead upon the diversities within the dialects which require their recognition as distinct languages. It was a moral and political, as much as a scientific and linguistic, judgement that Scots and English were one language in 1603. If it had been politically opportune the opposite could still have been the case.

The main point to be made from all this is that of language fluidity, particularly in societies where literature is absent or limited. In this it simply reflects the fluidity of ethnicity in general. The universality of ethnicity as our point of departure is never the same thing as the stability of any particular ethnicity. Once literacy arrives, not only does the fluidity diminish, but so does the bond between ethnicity and language.

The relationship of ethnicity to religion is very similar to that with language. In a situation prior to the arrival of a universalist religion with extensive sacred texts, religious experience and formalisation was essentially ethnic or local. Anthropologists are not wrong in finding that an account of the core ideas, practices, roles and morals in a society has to a very considerable extent to be an account of a religion, and that each religion differs fairly significantly from that of its neighbours. Dinka and Nuer are neighbours, sharing a common pastoral economy, closely related in language and in most of their customs. There is obvious similarity between their religious systems but, equally, they are clearly distinct – distinct enough for both Dinka and Nuer to recognise and point out differences to outsiders, while also recognising underlying commonalities.[6]

Such forms of ethnic religion were certainly never ring-fenced. There was always intermarriage between tribal groups – if produced simply by raiding women from one's neighbours. Such women brought their spirits with them. An established territorial shrine like that of Mbona in southern Malawi could serve and be venerated by members of a range of related peoples. As I have suggested already, such peoples were not ring-fenced either in any other aspect of their ethnicity. There were always movements of universalisation derived from long-distance trade, the sharing of words and artefacts, movements which did not prevent an alternative tendency to new particularisations, new insistences on what differentiated some particular territorial area. But just as Mwari in the Matopos could bring Venda, Shona and Ndebele together in the late nineteenth century in a cult and beliefs which were definitely inter-tribal and universalistic, so more widely there was a tendency to sharing a single name of God. The spread of Mulungu/Mungu in eastern Africa, Leza in the centre, Nzambi more to the west signifies a certain de-ethnicisation of God. But, of course, the same peoples shared many other common words of importance too.

Religion provided both the mythic core in the particularisation of each local ethnicity, and a universalising bridge in its networking with wider ethnic circles. In unwritten religions the former role seems primary, the latter almost hidden. This balance was entirely reversed when a universalist, world religion burst upon the scene.

Once a people had become Muslim or Christian, its religion ceased in principle to be part of its ethnic mix, just as later when it started to buy Coca-Cola or European beer its drink ceased to be ethnically specific and, when it bought cheap crockery made on wholesale western lines, its tableware ceased to be ethnic too. Ethnicity in each case was pushed back into a more restricted area by the advance of forces shaped on non-ethnic lines.

As regards religion, this was often, in practice, only partially the case because specific peoples or areas came to be characterised by different world religions or churches within them. The Swahili, the Yao or the Hausa might become identified as Muslim, the Igbo, the Chagga, the Bemba as Christian. The new religion thus became to some extent another form of ethnic identity. This had long been outstandingly the case for the Amhara, the core group of the Ethiopian Orthodox state. Nevertheless the diversity of religious adherences within modern African societies has largely removed religion from the area of ethnic specificity. Baganda Catholics might struggle bitterly with Baganda Protestants, but both were Baganda; even Baganda Muslims were Baganda, though I remember an elderly, highly intelligent Muganda priest, thirty years ago, emphatically denying to me that a Muslim was still a Muganda. For him, Ganda ethnicity was now a Christian one, and a Muslim was simply excluded, *ipso facto*, from the people. But that, I think, was an idiosyncratic view and I suspect I can still see the twinkle of humour in Yohane Ssewajje's eyes as he vigorously affirmed it.[7]

When Saxons and Angles became Christians they were none too happy to have to admit that their British enemies were Christian already. Bede takes care to undermine the significance of this by stressing the corruption of Welsh Christianity. Nevertheless the fact was that Saxon, Briton and Dane had ethnicities distinguishable in part by their religious beliefs, the gods they appealed to, before Christian conversion, but lost a basic religious specificity for ethnic difference through Christianisation. Christianity certainly did not make them one people, but it undermined part of the reason for their not being so, it created something of a larger community and in the case of any closely similar separate Teutonic groups it set them on the fast route for ethnic fusion.

To turn to politics. Ernest Gellner maintained that 'Perhaps the central, most important fact about agro-literate society is this: almost everything in it militates against the definition of political units in terms of cultural boundaries.'[8] This is, I think, likely to be misleading. If we want to understand in its origins the relationship between ethnicity and the political, we need to recognise that the latter is an inherently natural part of the former. By the political we mean basically the response to crime within a society, the enforcement of custom in relation to property, and defence from external attack, together with the expansion and institutionalisation of those originating needs. It would be quite impossible to describe the cultural institutions of an African society as a whole while leaving out their political dimension, and as culture changes, so does the latter. It is as integral an element in culture as religion. Even where a society is stateless, it still remains intrinsically a political society and has a specific way of coping with a political agenda, as Evans-Pritchard showed so well in his brilliant study of the 'political institutions' of the Nuer. This does not mean that cultural boundaries define political boundaries in any easily recognisable modern way, and the likelihood was that a larger cultural area was for long broken up politically into far smaller units. Political needs could be catered for microcosmically rather than macrocosmically. All that needs to be asserted at this level is that political construction is intrinsic not extrinsic to normative ethnicity.

However human history is not one of ethnicities existing on their own, but of their ceaseless interaction and interpenetration, in which politically stronger units impose themselves upon weaker ones. Once a monarchy was established, in consequent control of a larger pool of human, economic and technical resources, it tended to enforce its suzerainty over smaller, weaker, more or less stateless neighbours. Some stateless peoples successfully defended their independence but in many cases a recognition of suzerainty meant at first little more than an annual tribute to secure one against raiding. As centralised states grew in size, in bureaucratic effectiveness and the impact of a literary class, this meant that while the state in its central institutions reflected the culture of its own core ethnicity, it was divorced from the ethnic identity of its subject provinces. Cultural boundaries had ceased to appear reflected in the political field; instead, as empires grew larger and larger, based essentially on the ability of a few to monopolise the machinery of war, ethnicity and the political moved somewhat apart. Nevertheless the substructures of power in any particular area remained for a large part culturally and religiously specific to that area, enforcing its own particular law and custom. They mediated between high power and the local community, ensuring that the culture of the latter was seldom upset too painfully by the decrees of the former. When such upset did occur, as happened from time to time, popular rebellion was the natural result and when the decrees were not withdrawn such rebellion could in some circumstances lead to the pursuit of independence, to a popular commitment to draw back political power within the circle of local ethnicity. One may see it in William Tell or William Wallace, many Irish rebellions against England, even the Dutch rebellion against Philip of Spain. Such movements were seldom successful for long, if they were not reinforced by an intellectual and literary proclamation of a cultural identity which called for political identity; this inevitably appealed not only to immediate grievances but to myths of origin and a distinct history, yet it was basically rooted in the human requirement for relatedness between cultural ethnicity and political power, a requirement grounded in the truth that the latter is in principle intrinsic to the former.

It seems, nevertheless, inevitable that as social development occurs literary language, political power, economic control and religious belief all tend to move away from local models, if at different speeds, while leaving behind a residue of kinship systems, vernacular speech, agricultural practice, folklore and rites of one sort and another which then – in a larger feudal, imperial or federal state – come to be identified as the constituents of a new, more narrowly defined, ethnicity. In our earlier model religion was intrinsically ethnic – the religion of the Nuer distinguishably Nuer and different from, however similar to, that of the Dinka. When Christianity or Islam replaces such localised rituals and beliefs, the world religion will undoubtedly be for long home to important surviving elements within it; nevertheless the relationship between ethnicity and religion will lose the central significance it has held hitherto, just as the relationship between ethnicity and politics will be loosened in the same way. But just as the larger political power will need not to offend local ethnic sensitivities too painfully, so will the religious authorities. Catalan or Basque Catholicism will not be quite the same as Portuguese, Austrian or Bavarian Catholicism. While the differences may be much smaller than heretofore, popular adherence to those differentia may remain, somewhat irrationally, strong.

I take it as a given of human history that in all fields there is a tendency to move from smaller to larger units, that, in modern times, this has greatly accelerated and that nationalism is very often in large part a reaction against this of groups of people threatened with the hasty erosion of traditional identity. The movement from smaller to larger cultural, economic, religious and political communities is based very largely on a development in means of communication. If walking is the only way of travel then units will be smaller than if the horse is much used. Canals and railways make a big difference, the motor car and the aeroplane each establish a further stage towards global villagisation. The same is true of writing, printing, radio, telephone, television, the Internet. Writing without printing was a better tool for the world religion than for the world empire, and religion was in fact largely detached from ethnicity at an earlier date than politics. But a world religion either insisted upon a single sacred language or encouraged the standardisation of meaning across authoritative translations in a way that also affected the relationship of language to society in general and to political authority in particular.

The Arabic Qur'an and authoritative Christian translations of the Bible into a limited number of languages contributed profoundly to the universalisation of a single ethnic–religious–linguistic community in the Muslim case and to the distinction between major written languages and dialectic vernaculars in the Christian case. While the Islamic socio-political impact was thus in principle almost entirely anti-ethnic and anti-national, the Christian impact was more complex. Its willingness to translate brought with it, undoubtedly, a reduction in the number of ethnicities and vernaculars, but then a confirmation of the individual identity of those that remained: Christianity in fact helped turn ethnicities into nations.

Let us consider the nature of such a transition. Numerous ethnic identities existed in the past and many still exist but while we might describe pre-modern society as characterised by a multitude of ethnicities, we might well describe modern society chiefly in terms of a far smaller number of nations. Nineteenth-century Africa could stand for the one model, twentieth-century western Europe for the other. How one gets from one to the other, the 'transition', is what has frequently concerned us in earlier chapters, but it is a dangerous concern if it implies that the modern world must be composed of nations and that each ethnicity must either turn itself into a nation, indeed a nation-state, or perish. The central cultural challenge facing society in Europe, in Africa or elsewhere is, on the contrary, how to find a way of safeguarding ethnicity in a non-national way.

It is so obvious that all ethnicities do not turn into nations that it does not need stressing. Groups of smaller related ethnicities can grow together naturally unless there is some specific factor to divide them; yet once a particular ethnicity has hardened with its own characteristics and written literature, it may be almost impossible for it to fuse ethnically with a neighbour. After that some sort of federal government becomes necessary, if sooner or later an ethnicity is not to see itself as a full political nation, requiring the independence of sovereignty. If one considers the numerous ethnicities of the old Austro-Hungarian Empire, it is not over-helpful to insist that the Empire had not a German identity. With its capital in Vienna and its ruling dynasty German-speaking, the relationship German-Empire and, say, Croat-Empire was a quite unequal one. The Habsburg Empire was implicitly constructed of first-class ethnicities and second-class ethnicities, and it becomes almost inevitable that people in the latter group should sooner or later become dissatisfied and pursue a political status which could not be judged inferior. Even theoretically democratic states can do the same, privileging certain ethnicities over other ones. Northern Ireland has been permanently run on such a basis. It seems almost impossible in the modern world that any ethnicity, once it has developed a modern educated leadership, will be content with a status experienced as politically inferior to that of its neighbours. There is an inherent tendency within a world ceaselessly described as one of nation-states for an ethnically identifiable community to attain the consciousness and the aspirations of a political nation. Nevertheless the fact remains that most ethnicities do not and cannot become nations. Many may be called but few are chosen. Yet they do not easily disappear. The multiplying of 'nations' to reflect the multiplicity of ethnicities in modern Africa could well be a huge political disaster. Nigeria alone contains more than two hundred distinct ethno-linguistic groups. What is needed there as everywhere is rather to focus upon a diversity of ways in which ethnicity can survive and thrive quite apart from any transformation into nation-state.

We have now surveyed a wide range of examples of the relationship between ethnicity and nationhood in Britain, Europe and Africa. In their variety they must surely deny us any easy generalisation. On the one hand, overwhelming evidence makes it absurd to deny that the shaping of a modern nation may be traced in some cases a very long way back indeed. Yet it is obvious too that many ethnicities which once existed have merged into something so different that no continuity is traceable, and that those which do go forward to nationhood and even to nation-statehood do so along a wide variety of paths. If the Picts disappeared so long ago and Northumbria and even British Cumbria were merged inextricably into the English nation, we are still after more than a thousand years not quite sure where the Welsh stand – an ethnicity within Britain or even, as at one time seemed the case, within England, a nation in a multi-nation-state, even (still to come) a nation-state of their own?

If we had looked at Yugoslavia fifteen years ago, how many of us would confidently have argued that there was no Yugoslav nation and no alternative to a multitude of little states, narrowly restricting their self-definition in ethnically pure terms or hovering on the brink of yet further disintegration? Who can be sure if Zulu and Xhosa will really create with whites, Asians and coloureds a single multi-ethnic South African nation, whether the Ndebele will really lie down in a Shona-led Zimbabwe or go on seeing their country as nationalists see Scotland? Who can say whether Nigeria will continue to be a multi-ethnic giant, a bit like the Soviet Union, or will fall apart into three or four great sections which would still, of course, be far from ethnically monochrome? Who can say how many of the hundreds of languages spoken today in Africa will be spoken by anyone in fifty years' time and, if they are, how their speakers will understand the social significance of that? Who can say whether in fifty years' time the whole of western Europe will be so much of an EC that our nation-states, constructed so painfully across the centuries, will seem no more distinct than Wales or Scotland seemed inside Britain to our Victorian ancestors?

What does seem to be generally true for past, present and future is that overemphasis upon a single level of social-political community is uniformly disastrous. It is rather through recognition of the possibility of a shifting diversity of levels – ethnic, provincial, national, international, religious – for both individuals and communities that room is left for people to breathe freely, for cultural diversity, for the acceptance of a necessary ambiguity in social and political identity. Our politicians like frequently to describe Britain as a 'nation-state' and to harp on the theme of sovereignty. We are only very ambiguously a nation-state and most other so-called 'nation-states' are much the same, while sovereignty is no less a dangerous myth if it is thought to be necessarily indivisible. It is precisely the evil of nationalism, when it is fully blown, to deny both the divisibility of sovereignty and the reality of a plurality of loyalties and identities within a healthy world. What we should rather look for are ways of ensuring that movements, at present so clamant, towards both ever larger and ever smaller units of power (for instance, the EC on one hand, an independent Scotland on the other) do not undermine either the diversity of local ethnicities or the sense of far wider communions.

The pressures of modern government, imposing uniformity in area after area of life, are inherently destructive of many of the particularities which constitute a recognisable ethnic culture. Unless that process can be restrained, it must produce either the erosion of cultural diversity or the stimulation of new ethnic-based nationalisms. Either way, society is the poorer. If ethnicities can relate both to nations and to states in a diversity of ways, we need to focus not only on the way they grow into nations or are dissolved by the impact of nationhood but also on the way they can continue to function, and the support they provide, inside larger political unities. Ethnicities not only contribute to the formation of nation-states, they also survive, grow, even start to exist within such states in ways that appear largely apolitical but which may still – if they are attacked or suppressed – turn political once more and become the source of new nationalisms. The multi-ethnic state may be a healthier reality than the multi-nation-state. It deserves encouragement, not suppression, but it may well be that we who live in western Europe are now irreversibly entering a new kind of multi-nation-state which will engender as bitter a wave of nationalist reaction as any of the empires of the past, unless we can think far more positively than anyone has managed hitherto about the role of ethnic and national sub-communities within a larger state.

The speaking of Cornish has barely survived in England, but there are numerous Hindi, Punjabi and Gujerati speakers. The survival of ethnicities derived from large-scale migration within existing states depends very largely on factors of language, religion, education and a community of distinct customary behaviour, or the freedom in significant areas of life to be nonconformist as a group. British Jews do not form a separate nation from the British or the English but they do possess an ethnicity of their own. Similarly Bosnian 'Serbs' and Bosnian 'Croats', if they are Bosnians at all, are Bosnian by nationality, their Serb or Croat character becoming a matter of ethnicity. We inevitably lose our nationhood, but not our ethnicity, once we become full citizens of a nation-state distinct from that to which our previous nationhood was related. While new ethnicities in circumstances of migration are likely to stress very strongly their non-political character, they can no more remain wholly unpolitical than any other large interest group. As they grow more confident, their politicisation grows as well – a mix between a defence of the cultural rights of their distinct ethnicity and loyalty to the state of which they now form part. Norman Tebbit's cricket test of British loyalty is, of course, an inappropriate one. It is as unacceptable to require a British citizen to support the English team as to require her to be a member of the Church of England. Why, anyway, should the Welsh not prefer the Australians to win? There is a criss-cross of loyalties in every mature national community. It is only when one is frightened that one imposes tests over this or that. That is itself a sign of nationalism, the aggressiveness derived from an uncomfortable sense of threat. A strength of Britain in the past lay in the acceptance of a large measure of collective ambiguity as to the real relationship between its members. The Englishness of the Danelaw or Cornish-men or, after they were allowed to return, the Jews, or indeed of a Catholic in a country somehow committed to Protestantism, was seldom questioned but it was also not defined, any more than was the relationship of Welshness to Englishness within Britain. Again, one did not doubt that immigrants could become very British indeed, and yet no sensible person imagined that they did not retain other strong loyalties as well in many cases and that, at times, such loyalties might seem to conflict with one another.

Preoccupation with the national narrows the mind and the heart. It is exhilarating to sing *Rule Britannia* at the right moment, but

comes to a study of nationhood itself it is Christian peoples that have been under discussion. The reason is not simply that our discussion has been largely restricted to Europe. There is more to it than that. The nation and nationalism are both, I wish to claim, characteristically Christian things which, in so far as they have appeared elsewhere, have done so within a process of westernisation and of imitation of the Christian world, even if it was imitated as western rather than as Christian.

The only real exception I would admit to this claim is that of the Jews. Indeed they may well be called the true proto-nation in that the Old Testament provided the model in ancient Israel which Christian nations have adopted. Yet from the fall of Jerusalem in the first century until the establishment of Israel in the twentieth, the Jews were so far from being a nation-state or a political entity at all that they had really ceased to look like a nation in the terms in which we are speaking. The huge paradox of Jewish history is that the people who gave the world the model of nationhood, and even nation-statehood, lost it for itself for nearly two millennia and yet survived. If they lost state, land and in consequence after a while any sort of nationalism, becoming for the most part intensely apolitical, they retained the core identity of a nation through the exercise of collective memory, the usages of religion based upon a specific literature. Whatever their spoken language, Jews were held together by the Hebrew Bible and related texts. Furthermore, they were in consequence held together as a nation rather than an ethnicity. Indeed, different ethnicities, such as Ashkenazim and Sephardim, emerged within it. It was extraordinary that so numerous a people containing within it so many educated and even wealthy people should neither have a state of their own nor be incorporated into any other state except rather marginally. The marginality was ensured by the Christian or Islamic foundation of the states in which they lived. It is the deprivation of politics that strikes one most forcibly about pre-twentieth century Jewish existence, yet in secularised states not grounded upon ethnic nationalism that was neither absolute nor irremovable. The American example here is paradigmatic. But the more the political order around them nationalised itself in an ethnic way during the nineteenth century, the more anomalous the Jewish position again became and the more inevitable the rise of Zionism. Zionism was not a religious movement. Jewish religion was fully acclimatised in a diaspora existence and was in fact for long highly unsympathetic towards Zionism. Zionism was a nationalist movement stimulated by the pressure of other nationalist movements within the European world. Its goal like theirs was the creation of a nation-state and it is lamentable that studies of nationalism regularly avoid its consideration. Here, if anywhere, the basic order runs: nation, nationalism, nation-state. Yet it is also true that before the nationalism the nation could seem almost invisible. Indeed for many individual Jews their Jewish identity could be correctly classified as ethnic and religious while their national identity was English, French or German.[1] For some this is still the case.

The long hiatus in Jewish national history, and the fact that modern Jewish nationalism and nationhood come at the end rather than at the start of a chain, is why it has seemed acceptable to start a study of the construction of nations and nationalism with England, seen as effectively the world's proto-nation within the continuities of modern history, even though in terms of Christian history England is also preceded by the more isolated examples of Ethiopia and Armenia.

The third branch of the Abrahamic monotheistic tree is Islam, a world religion which shares so much with Judaism and Christianity. But on this point it has remarkably little in common, as I will hope to demonstrate. Christianity has of its nature been a shaper of nations, even of nationalisms; Islam has not, being on the contrary quite profoundly anti-national. A great deal of vague discussion about the relationship between religion and nationalism is blighted by the easy assumption that every religion is likely to have the same sort of political effect. It is not so.

To turn to the religious stimulation of nationalism. This seems normally an overspill from one or another aspect of the religious contribution to the construction of nationhood itself. The more influential religion was in the latter, the more it is likely also to influence every expression of the former, whereas a nation whose basic construction owes little to religious factors is far less likely later to generate a nationalism with a religious character to it. We need then, primarily, to review the different, if inevitably overlapping, ways in which Christianity has shaped national formation, and I propose to do so under seven heads: first, sanctifying the starting point; second, the mythologisation and commemoration of great threats to national identity; third, the social role of the clergy; fourth, the production of vernacular literature; fifth, the provision of a biblical model for the nation; sixth, the autocephalous national church; seventh, the discovery of a unique national destiny.

Shaping and canonising origins. We have a fascinating recent example in France – the controversy over how suitably to commemorate the baptism of Clovis at Reims by St Remigius in 496. The link between the Frankish kingdom of Clovis and modern France may seem somewhat tenuous but the fact is that Clovis's conversion did effect a stabilisation of identity near the origins of an historical development going from there to here. It successfully fused the Franks with Catholicism to the great benefit of both parties, over against the Arianism of the Visigoths, and it did it at Reims, which became the crowning church for French kings. Important as this event was, it cannot quite evade the implication of a sort of secondariness in the Frankish kingdom itself. The Bishop of Reims was clearly there well before Clovis and, important as all this undoubtedly made Reims, it did not overturn the primacy of the see of Lyons, a primacy symbolising the fact that the Gauls were there before the Franks and continued to be there. St Remigius was reputed to have given Clovis the power to touch for the king's evil. The Franks became the right hand of the Catholic Church, their king *rex christianissimus*, and if the French nation – probably more than any other western European nation – grew out of a state created by a monarchy, then Clovis, his baptism and Reims Cathedral must remain in some special way constitutive of what makes France France. It is not the genetic descent of peoples, but their descent as a collectivity from some defining moment in public history, which really matters. Hence not only did the reactionary nationalism of *Action Française* claim Catholicism to be a necessary component of Frenchness but even a secular republic finds that the baptism of a king fifteen hundred years ago cannot easily be overlooked.

We have seen in chapter 2 how decisively in a number of ways Christianity shaped the origins of the English. Canterbury and its metropolitan authority united England before there was an England to unite, while Bede made the point clear by writing a history which was at once that of the church and of the nation, when there were still half a dozen different kings up and down the land. Alfred, with his strongly ecclesiastical identity, the translator into English of both

Pope Gregory's *Pastoral Care* and Bede's *History*, became effectively England's first king, the heir of Bede and of Augustine of Canterbury quite as much as of Ine or Offa.

When we turn to Ireland or to Serbia, we have a rather different type of foundation charter with the dominant figure of a single saint, Patrick or Sava. No one quite comparable is to be found in England or France and it may be that the absolutely decisive figure of a single founder, apostle and saint, had a more lasting potency for the conception of national identity in religious terms than did the more mixed and regal processes at work elsewhere. It certainly survives the age of Republicanism more easily. Yet almost everywhere at the heart of the early development of Christian nations is to be found a succession of canonised kings. It is the case for Russia and Ethiopia but hardly less – at least in Aelred of Rievaulx's eyes – for the Kings of England. Christian conversion in the medieval world again and again constructed national identity around a particular kingly line and particular holy places, precisely through the closeness of the church's identification with royal power. It elevates, consecrates and stabilises that power, but is also effectively subordinated to it. A new national identity is thus produced by a sort of religious injection. If Clovis hereafter has the power of touching for the king's evil it is because St Remigius has given it to him but his successors have it ever after. While the immediate recipient of all this is a king rather than a nation, the nation subsequently develops its identity from occupying the imaginative space produced around the king, as Israel existed around David or Solomon, though England is a little different in that the kings, despite Aelred, actually matter rather less, the national identity having been established to a quite considerable extent ecclesiastically before it was realised regally. In Ireland that is still more the case. The national supremacy of Patrick derives both from what he undoubtedly himself achieved, little as we know about him, and from the lack of a significant line of sacralised kings, whereas Sava, important as he was personally, is not separable in his nation-forming role from the royal line to which he belonged.

Sava was a far more political figure than Patrick, one very easily appropriated by nationalists whereas Patrick's greatness lies in setting so powerful a mark on a country's identity while appearing as unpolitical as Christ. Celebrating St Patrick's Day is, doubtless, often a highly nationalist affair, but the connection has not the near inescapability there is in celebrating St Sava's.

A different type of religious influence upon a nation's origins comes when it has arisen directly out of religious conflict. Holland is a classic case. One can argue about the degree of distinctiveness of the northern Netherlands in pre-Reformation times, but what determined its independence, separation from the south and basic character was a religious struggle of Protestants against Catholic Spain. The sixteenth-century Dutch predicament was closely similar to that of Elizabethan England and Holland might, indeed, not have survived without the help of an English expeditionary force, but while English nation-statehood already existed, the Dutch did not. Dutch national consciousness and nationalism were, in consequence, still more closely tied to the Protestant identity which caused them to emerge. Compare that with the Portuguese – again, a nation which grew out of religious war, this time the Crusades. Portuguese nationhood was characterised in consequence for centuries by a particularly militant type of Catholicism, aggressive, nationalist, anti-Islamic. The commitment to Christian reconquest of the Iberian peninsula was no less crucial in the construction of Spanish nation-hood. For both a militant nationalist Catholicism remained a significant force well into the twentieth century.

These examples suggest that one wide-ranging context for the religious shaping of nationalism is that of a contested frontier. Where a number of countries share the same form of religion, their national character is likely to develop without the sort of continuing religious input which a frontier atmosphere requires: Catholics facing Muslims, Orthodox facing Catholics, Protestants facing Catholics. Whenever a people feels threatened in its distinct existence by the advance of a power committed to another religion, the political conflict is likely to have superimposed upon it a sense of religious conflict, almost crusade, so that national identity becomes fused with religious identity.

This leads on to our second factor, the mythologisation of threats to national identity. I am thinking of such things as the Gunpowder Plot, the siege of Derry, the Battle of Kosovo, or the career of Joan of Arc. Here we have episodes in which national salvation is, or seems to be, at stake. There is nearly always a traitor in the story – Colonel Lundy, Vuk Brankovic, Guy Fawkes, Bishop Cauchon –

and this sharpens up the sense of 'us' and 'them', the absolute duty of loyalty to the horizontal fellowship of 'us', and the moral gap separating us from the other, from the threat to our 'freedom, religion and laws' that they constitute – whether Muslim, Catholic or just the time-serving bishop willing to do a job for his foreign masters. God is on our side most clearly in such events, even if that may only be seen to be the case a lot later on.

Seldom were such events at the time really so decisive. Meaning has largely been read back into them but that does not make it necessarily a false meaning, even in historical terms. It is rather that in retrospect a large process became simplistically symbolised in public memory by a single event or hero figure calculated best to reinforce a special identity. Most events are simply forgotten or cease, at least, to be emotive. If the siege of Derry or Gunpowder Plot becomes ritualised, it is to ensure that each subsequent generation is socialised into a certain us/them view of the world, a view at once nationalist and religious. It is the quasi-religious manner in which these really quite secular events are remembered which seems to make so heavy a load of meaning credible. Such events and their ritualisation do far more than maintain nationhood; they are potent instruments for the promotion of nationalism. Nelson Mandela describes in his autobiography the electrifying effect of the recital of a praise poem to Shaka on detainees in South Africa's first Treason Trial: 'Suddenly there were no Xhosas or Zulus, no Indians or Africans, no rightists or leftists, no political or religious leaders; we were all nationalists . . . In that moment we felt the hand of the great past . . . and the power of the great cause that linked us all together.'[2]

Our third religious factor in the affirmation of nationhood is the clergy. Not, of course, always or everywhere. An early medieval, localised, almost uneducated priesthood may not have fulfilled this role, though it is worth noting that Aelred of Rievaulx, coming from just such a background – the inherited village priesthood of Hexham – shows himself quite remarkably nation-conscious in his works on the *Genealogy of the English Kings* and the *Life of Edward the Confessor*.[3] What a clergy with some education and status did in most medieval and early modern societies was to mediate identity between rulers and ruled. In expressing a scepticism about the existence of national consciousness, Hobsbawm remarked that 'it is clearly illegitimate to extrapolate from the elite to the masses, the literate to the illiterate, even though the two worlds are not entirely separable'.[4] Just because Croat nobles saw themselves as some sort of a nation, he insists, it does not at all mean that 'the rank and file of the common people', Croat peasants, shared the same sort of consciousness.[5] Why should peasants 'identify with a "country" that consists of the community of the lords who were, inevitably, the chief targets of their discontents?'[6] There is, doubtless, some truth in such a contrast, though I suspect it implies an untenable social analysis in which class identity is simply presumed to precede communal identity. Have many of us not continued to identify ourselves as British, however much over long years our rulers, Margaret Thatcher and John Major, have been 'the chief target of our discontents'? But an intrinsic weakness within Hobsbawm's class analysis here seems to me that for traditional Europe it leaves out a third class, the clergy. It was the lower clergy who, living in their parishes throughout Europe, relatively poor, literate, educated in cathedral schools or from the thirteenth century on increasingly in universities, in regular touch with both the landed and the peasantry, fostered a sense of shared local, provincial or national identity. If the very earliest universities were distinctly European, the more they multiplied the more national and even nationalistic in ethos they became. Already in 1214 the students at the university of Paris spent a week celebrating the victory of Bouvines. It is not surprising that Owen Glyn Dur wanted to open a couple of Welsh universities. From the sixteenth century seminaries fulfil the same role. They are indeed at times hotbeds of nationalism, but their universal role is to prepare men to teach the illiterate or the barely literate in the vernacular and to do so they themselves needed vernacular religious literature.

The requirements of their work and of the church forced the clergy to think in local, vernacular and, increasingly, national terms. This is most evident from the sixteenth century on, not only with the Protestant clergy publicly committed to vernacular scriptures and services, but also with the Catholic clergy, French, Spanish or Irish. But it in fact began much earlier and the need for it was one of the factors pushing priests into Lollardy or the like. But quite apart from the Lollard case, the pastoral task of the church required an increasing use of the vernacular and of vernacular literature as soon as it became feasible. This is not a reformation development. We see it already in tenth-century England, in the mission of Cyril and Methodius and probably in every country of western Europe. Linking the classes as the clergy did (and they were often very numerous), they had an inevitable role, through their shared existence as well as through their ministry, in ensuring something of a collective consciousness between rich and poor, literate and illiterate, nobles and peasants. They were not in a narrow way simply teachers of religion, but also of history and much else. Thus Layamon, an obscure priest in a Worcestershire village of the late twelfth century, composed the poem *Brut*, the first history of England in English to include Arthur, Lear and Cymbeline. Doubt-less Layamon was unusual in his literary skill but not in the sort of social role he fulfilled. Village priests ensured that the articulation of a nation was shared by every class. This contribution was greatly enlarged through the printing of a vernacular literature even in a pre-Protestant church. Eamon Duffy in *The Stripping of the Altars* has demonstrated how printing in England between its introduction in the 1470s and the 1530s was devoted overwhelmingly to the production of 'a vast range of devotional and didactic tracts, designed to promote traditional piety' of a wholly orthodox kind. Most of this was in English and 'printing gave an enormous impetus to the movement for vernacular religious instruction'.[7] Many of the texts had in fact already been circulating in manuscript since the four-teenth century. In chapter 4 I have suggested how influential this was in seventeenth-century France, and in chapter 5 its impact for Croat identity. The point for us in this is that it is indicative of the central way in which the clergy simply by doing their job enhanced national consciousness through the widespread diffusion of vernacu-lar literature. It was, I believe, this process going on all across Europe, which, far more than anything specifically political, stabi-lised the main national identities, as societies separated by their literatures. In the course of the nineteenth century this role of the lower clergy was increasingly taken over by primary-school teachers, or even by university professors.

This brings us to our fourth factor, the encouragement of literature in the vernacular. Any extensive vernacular literature proper to a particular people is intrinsically likely to have the effect of stabilising a conscious sense of national identity. To understand the significance of this for the relationship between religion and nationhood in the European context, it is necessary to explore further, first the nature of Christianity as a religion of translation and, second, the intrinsic relationship between being a bearer of the Bible, both Old and New Testament, and the fostering of nationhood. Benedict Anderson has claimed the rise of nations and of nationalism only to be possible when the influence of religions with their 'sacred languages' declined. It is a great misconception. Christianity never had a sacred language. If it had one it would presumably have been Aramaic, that spoken by Jesus, the 'Word made Flesh', but Christians quickly abandoned its use as they moved out from Palestine, though a few still use it. But it has never been seen as sacred. Even Greek, in which the New Testament was written, has not been. Only a sort of fundamentalism can make language sacred within the Christian tradition but to do so goes against the whole nature of the religion. What is striking about its history is the willingness again and again to translate – into Syriac, Armenian, Coptic, Ethiopian and Latin in the early centuries, then Slavonic and finally almost numberless other languages. Undoubtedly there were periods of intransigence and linguistic conservatism on the part of authority, especially of the papacy, but it would be quite mistaken to see the centrality of translation to the Christian enterprise as merely a Protestant characteristic; or to doubt that the attempt to make Latin of all languages into a sort of 'sacred' language on the part of Roman clerics was other than a deviation from the Christian norm. The speed with which the vernaculars of western Europe – Welsh, Irish, English, German, French, Dutch and the rest – were colonised by Christian writers is striking and it derives from the nature of Christianity, the absence of any writing by Jesus himself and the commitment to universality which is so clear in the New Testament, to make disciples of all the nations (Mt. 28.19). The Pentecost text in Acts 2 which can be taken as representing the foundation myth of the church stresses precisely a diversity of language – Parthians, Medes, Elamites and the rest, 'we hear them preaching in our own language about the marvels of God' (Acts 2.11). Christianity had, then, the use of the world's vernaculars inscribed in its origins. Neither Hebrew, Greek nor Latin had any special claim on its loyalty and it was quickly recognised that sacred texts remained equally sacred in translation. The early tradition that Matthew's Gospel was first written in Aramaic and then translated into Greek is evidence of that, as are the translations into Latin and Syriac already in the second century. Christianity did, then, take a culture of translation for granted. It also had in the New Testament numerous references to the world as one of 'peoples' and 'nations', and in the Old Testament it offered a model of what a nation looked like. Regino of Prüm writing his *Chronicon* about the year 900, set out what may be called the normative Christian view of human society as follows: 'Just as different peoples (*diversae nationes populorum*) differ between themselves in descent, manners, language and laws (*genere, moribus, lingua, legibus*) so the holy and universal church throughout the world, although joined in the unity of faith nevertheless varies its ecclesiastical customs among them.'[8] Here the unity and universality of the church is not in question; it inevitably limits the degree of specifically religious diversity acceptable between nations but it takes the existence and differences of the latter for granted and does not rule out a diversity of ecclesiastical custom reflecting national differences.

Within the unity of Christian faith, the full diversity of nations, customs and language comes simply to be taken for granted. No one reading the New Testament as a primary guide to the way the world is could have much doubt of that. This brings us to our fifth factor – the Bible as the mirror though which to imagine and create a Christian nation. In central New Testament terms nations might be encouraged but there could be no place for a single chosen nation. It is the church itself which is the New Israel. Nevertheless the Old Testament provided a detailed picture of what a God-centred nation would look like and of the way God would treat it if it was faithless. Why should God behave differently now? Why should one's own, New Testament-sanctioned nation not be vouchsafed an Old Testament style providential role? One finds already in writers like Bede the application to their own people of what one might call Old Testament political economy, an economy that included belief in divine predilection for a particular people. John Barbour, the four-teenth-century Scottish poet, saw national resistance to the English in terms of the story of the Maccabees. Such comparisons seemed so natural and even so apparent in one's own case. Theologically one might be held back from suggesting too special a status for a particular people but in terms of some sort of political or historical destiny it could be hard to deny it, and the more the Old Testament was translated into the vernacular and accessible to a theologically untrained laity, the greater the likelihood of claiming for one's own nation a divine election, so powerful was the Old Testament example working on the political imagination of a Christian people. We have seen this particularly at work in medieval France and seventeenth-century England, but it is curiously revealing to find that even Rousseau, secular prophet of the new nationalism, when lecturing to the Poles on how to be a nation, appealed to the example of Moses, as the ideal nation-builder.

This tendency was enormously stimulated by our sixth factor, the development of autocephalous state churches, primarily within the Orthodox tradition, especially among the Slavs, but also in Protestantism. The total ecclesiastical autonomy of a national church is one of the strongest and most enduring factors in the encouragement of nationalism because it vastly stimulates the urge to tie all that is strongest in God's Old Testament predilection for one nation and New Testament predilection for one church contemporaneously to one's own church and people.

All the aspects considered hitherto can easily coalesce under our final heading, a nation's holiness and special destiny. Once a Christian history has been constructed for a nation from the baptism of a first king and on through great deliverances, a history of a people's faith and divine providence, once the Bible is meditated upon in one's own language with all the immediacy this could bring, once one's own church is fully independent of any other and identified in extent with that of the nation, the more it seems easy to go the final step and claim to be a chosen people, a holy nation, with some special divine mission to fulfil. The Old Testament provided the paradigm. Nation after nation applied it to themselves, reinforcing their identity in the process.

Hobsbawm devotes a couple of interesting pages to the concept of 'Holy Russia', following Michael Cherniavsky's *Tsar and People*.[9] With Russia Hobsbawm briefly links 'holy Ireland' and 'holy Tyrol'. Why should they be holy and why stop there? For Cherniavsky a land could not be holy 'unless it could put forward a unique claim in the global economy of salvation'[10] which Russia could do as the heir to Byzantium which made of Moscow the 'Third Rome'. That is fair enough but, as Hobsbawm suggests, Russian peasants hardly needed such an ecclesiological argument to convince them that Rus was

God's chosen land. Such a conviction derives rather from a popular theology of creation and incarnation biblically reweaving themes of primal religion, the sacredness of local space. Such intuitions are caught up in the life of the Christian Church, in its liturgical round at once seasonal and biblical, to provide the conviction that this people, our people, has been chosen by God as Israel was chosen. We find in the Ethiopians, as I suggested in chapter 6, an excellent early example, symbolised by the wonderful myth of the carrying off of the Ark of the Covenant by Menelik from Jerusalem to Aksum. Ethiopia becomes in consequence the true, Christian, Israel. Undoubtedly, in Frankish eyes, the French were little less. And, in English eyes, the English. In Serb eyes, the Serbs. And, finally, the Americans, though 'finally' may prove the wrong word. Each people sees its 'manifest destiny' clearly enough. Why precisely the Tyrol should do so, I do not know but, doubtless, they have a good reason.

Once, as I was walking along Offa's Dyke, I stopped at a cottage, remote from anywhere, to ask for a glass of water. As I was drinking it, the old woman who had offered it, and a cup of milk as well, asked me, a little hesitantly, whether Offa might be one of the kings we read of in the Bible. The Bible is so easily indigenised. By its very nature and the church's retention of such lengthy Israelite histories it hints at a continuity of more than a theological kind between it and us. The whole concept of a 'Holy People', divinely chosen but enduring all the ups and downs of a confusing history, seems so very applicable to life nearer home. Of course for the early Christian and for the universal church's permanent theological vision that concept is realised in a universal community of faith and by no means in any one nation, but for ordinary Christians, lay and clerical, that can seem too remote, too unpolitical. Even as good a theologian as Bede can help renationalise the universal.

Anthony Smith[11] has denied that German National Socialism is properly to be recognised as a nationalism on the rather odd grounds that it is incompatible with a nationalist vision of a plurality of free nations. But can one really define the membership of the nationalist club in such polite terms and is it not actually very anti-historical to do so? Does any powerful nationalism ever really hold that other nations matter equally with one's own? I would argue that at this point the German National Socialist type of nationalism, despite its particularly violent character, is in principle quite close to normative nationalism, a norm with a biblical background. The root of the more extreme wing of European nationalism lies precisely here, in a widely held Christian assumption that there can only be one fully elect nation, one's own, the true successor to ancient Israel. The contrariness of this to Christian belief is something we shall return to later, but what matters now is to recognise how powerful it has been in Christian experience. It seems too that the more powerfully one identified one's own nation as chosen, the more one might want to eliminate the first chosen nation, the Jews, from the face of the earth. The more intense nationalisms within the European sphere have grown out of a series of such identifications, one often reacting to another, even if they have mostly, though not entirely, adopted a secularised form of it in the modern era. What one must not be deceived into thinking is that modernised, secularised forms of nationalism in any way represent its beginning. Moreover the hard religious rock which led to such identifications in the past still provides enormous strength to national struggles at the popular level.

Because of the lack of evident political concern in the New Testament as also within the early Christian community, Christianity does not start – as Islam did – with any clear political model of its own. As a consequence when Christians came to power they were able to go in two very different directions. The one, the nation-state; the other, the world empire. Each appears very early within Christian history. The first state to become Christian was Armenia in the late third century and the survival of the Armenian national identity from then until now is surely one of the more remarkable things in human history. The kingship did not survive, what did do so was the Armenian Bible, liturgy and related literature. The Ethiopian case is closely parallel. One would not expect small kingdoms of that period to survive in any shape or form across fifteen centuries. The key to their national survival seems to me the way that Christian conversion produced both a vernacular literature and the idea of a nation out of which grew a real nation able to endure across the political vicissitudes of the centuries.

II

We have seen the national model recur again and again, yet if one looks at some of the central areas of Christian history, one also sees a quite different one – acceptance of a world empire, the continuation of Rome. Here, Christians were able to feel no less at home. A world empire corresponded geographically and politically to the sort of religious society they saw themselves to be, and they were just as able to find providence at work in Roman imperial history as other Christians found it at work in the development of Armenia, France or England. There was no theological reason to think that because the Jews had had a nation-state, Christians should live in nation-states. Nations exist divided by language and culture, according to numerous New Testament texts, but they can do so within the empire of Rome. Nations, then, but not nation-states. Read Eusebius or Lactantius for the glorification of Constantine and of the providentiality of the empire.

While, in the west, the empire soon after collapsed, the idea of it did not. Its revival by Charlemagne and fitful continuation both as the Holy Roman Empire and as a papal empire across the medieval and early modern centuries into the beginning of the nineteenth never produced a stable international unity. What it did produce was, on the imperial side, a rather decentralised federation of provinces and cities, and, on the papal, a highly influential unity of canon law. The former never in any way included England; it was soon reduced to little more than Italy and Germany, and then to Germany and contiguous areas alone. Yet it held the heart of Dante. One of the reasons why the medieval empire failed was that it could not work with the papacy, each appearing to threaten the other, yet in point of fact empire and papacy were agreed in asserting a Christendom which was more than a collection of nation-states. And while the final political achievement of neither may appear very considerable on the positive side, on the negative they helped to ensure the lack of development of nation-states until a very late date in both Germany and Italy. The tendency is to ask why these two countries, central to Europe, were so backward in this great 'modernising' development which made so much more progress in rather marginal areas like England and Spain. The best answer seems to be that they had been too deeply affected by a different, and larger, conception of the state, a conception for which in practice the time had not yet come but which, at least arguably, grew more harmoniously out of core Christian experience, the New Testament vision of 'neither Jew nor Greek . . . but all are one in Christ'

(Galatians 3.28) than did the Old Testament inspired nation-state. It is a conception which in our time is coming back into its own.

If the Habsburg Empire was, in its multinationality, the last survival of the central political experiment of the first fifteen hundred years of the Christian Era, the European Community can fairly be seen as its resurrection. Great cities like Cologne and Bologna have spent most of their history happily enough outside nation-states but inside a sort of decentralised empire. For them experience of the nation-state over little more than a hundred years has been sufficiently disastrous to suggest the moral that other ways of structuring sovereignty may be preferred. It seems hardly surprising that they do not feel the kind of antipathy to the European Community which so many people do in England where we have had the longest nation-state history and one which, until recently, proved notably successful in political and economic terms.

The point we need to insist upon is that while the nation-state was largely shaped by a Christian and biblical culture so that without the latter it is hardly imaginable, it was not the only political option consonant with Christian culture or the European tradition and, indeed, in its full form it flourished particularly within Post-Reformation culture. Even though the Middle Ages actually nurtured it, it was at the same time antipathetic to the central political traditions of Catholicism, whether papal or imperial.

But it is far more antipathetic to Islam. Here there was from the start a political model – the world empire based on the *umma*, a community of faith, but based also on the possession of a single, and genuinely sacred, language. Not only was the explicit model of Islam together with its early history opposed to anything like a multitude of nation-states, unlike Christianity, it was also opposed to linguistic diversity. Its culture was not one of translation but of assimilation. This is a point which Lamin Sanneh has made effectively in his much-discussed work *Translating the Message*[12] but, interestingly, it was made already by an observant Arab in the sixteenth century who became a Christian and a monk of Dabra Libanos in Ethiopia. Enbaqom wrote his *Anqasa Amin*, 'The Door of the Faith', in 1540 during the Jihad of Gran. It was an apologetic work comparing Islam and Christianity to prove the superiority of the latter and one of his most interesting arguments was that the Qur'an is the book of a single language, Arabic, while the Bible exists in twenty languages and he cites many of them to prove that Christianity can be at home anywhere.[13] Enbaqom put his finger on a quite crucial divergence between the two religions. The Muslim attitude to the Qur'an made translation almost impossible. For the religious person it has to be read, recited out loud five times a day, or listened to in Arabic. In consequence the whole cultural impact of Islam is necessarily to Arabise, to draw peoples into a single world community of language and government. And this is what it did. Even the language of Egypt disappeared before it, except as a Christian liturgical language. Nations are not constructed by Islam but deconstructed. That is a fact of history but it is a fact dependent upon theology. Recognition of it should make it all the clearer that the construction of nations within the Christian world was not something independent of Christianity but, rather, something stimulated by the Christian attitude both to language and to the state.

While both Muslims and Christians recognise their Abrahamic inheritance, Muslims did not incorporate the Hebrew scriptures into their own as Christians did. This meant that Muslims were never affected by the Old Testament state example in the way that Christians have continuously been even into the twentieth century. While Christianity in consequence has always been politically ambivalent between nation-state and universal state, Islam has never been. It is in every way in principle far more politically universalist and exercises in consequence a religious restraint upon nationalism which Christianity has often failed to do. This does not, of course, mean that Muslim societies cannot develop into nations, only that their religion does not help them to do so, directing them instead towards different social and political formations.

Arabisation has been resisted by Iranians and Turks as by all the people east of Iran. A single political and linguistic community for the world was impossibly premature a thousand or five hundred years ago, though maybe not now. Arabisation itself might be regarded as a large example of nation formation, comparable to Frenchification, and indeed it has been so judged by some. Given the preoccupation of the modern world with nation-states it is inevitable that some modernisers have imagined an 'Arab nation' stretching from Morocco to Iraq, but it is mistaken to do so and only the imposition of western categories has made it plausible or seem desirable to Arabic speakers. Arab 'nationalism', like Turkish or

Egyptian 'nationalism', dates only from the twenty years or so before the First World War, a time when the impact of European thinking was at its highest and most uncriticised point in the Middle East. It was essentially a western, Christian-rooted, concept quite foreign to Islam, one closely linked with secularisation – as also with the presence of a considerable native Arabic-speaking Christian population, notably in Egypt and Palestine. It remains theoretically possible that the sharing of Arabic will still create an Arab nation but it seems unlikely, any more than the sharing of English does so.

The following quotation from Kalim Siddiqui expresses the specific Islamic approach to the nation with the starkest clarity. In terms of history it may be a simplification, but in terms of Islam's central political and religious ideal it is entirely accurate.

> Today we come face to face with perhaps the greatest evil that stalks the modern world – that of nationalism . . . The path of the *mmah* and that of the Islamic movement within the *mmah* is blocked by nation-states. These nation-states are like huge boulders blown across our path by the ill wind of recent history. All nation-states that today occupy, enslave and exploit the lands, peoples and resources of the *mmah* must of necessity be dismantled.[14]

As Christianity split into a diversity of ecclesiastical streams, the dualism implicit within its political agenda – nation-forming on the one side, universalist on the other – was further accentuated. The classical eastern orthodox form stressing the power of the emperor was in principle universalist enough in its vision of Constantinople as the 'New Rome', but in practice Byzantium became a rather narrowly Greek empire, alienating non-Greeks in Egypt, Syria or the west. This combined with its considerable degree of Caesaro-papism led to the generation of a type of church–state relationship characteristic of eastern autocephalous churches of a highly nationalist type.

In the west, on the contrary, the central Catholic tradition under papal influence has always veered towards a universalist dimension to the structuring of society, opposed to absolutist claims of national sovereignty. While the Catholic Church has in practice often under-girded nationalism – in Spain, France, Ireland or Poland – there are limits to its national enthusiasm, at least within areas effectively influenced by the papacy. Where, in the early modern period, the

Catholic Church was most completely controlled by a national monarchy as in Spain or France, there the nationalist dimension of Christianity could be allowed as free a rein as in Anglican England, but where, as in nineteenth-century Ireland, the bishops were ultramontanes answerable to the Pope – whose concerns could be as much to placate the British government as to support the grievances of Irish peasants – the Catholic Church was of its nature a restraining rather than inflaming influence upon nationalism.

That is to speak at an institutional level. At a personal, popular or communal level things could be different. The lower clergy could in Ireland be more nationalist than the bishops, though in Fascist Italy or Nazi Germany the opposite could be the case, and ordinary priests often stood out against the new nationalism more firmly than their superiors. The point is that Catholic Christianity, understood in a wide sense, was both incarnationalist and universalist – it tended both to identify closely with particular communities, cultures and nations, and to insist upon a communion transcending such particularities. It oscillated, one might say, between Old and New Testament sources of inspiration. It would be quite wrong to think of Christianity's relationship to the nation in terms of only one of these two characteristics, particularly western Christianity with its long commitment to dualism – the distinction of the two swords in classical Gelasian theory, church and state, pope and emperor. The shrine of Edward the Confessor, saint and king, was central to the royal church of Westminster but the still more popular shrine of Thomas Becket, archbishop and martyr at a king's hands, was central to the Cathedral of Canterbury. Unsurprisingly Thomas's shrine was destroyed with particular ferocity by Henry VIII. Thomas Becket, nevertheless, expressed a dualism central to Christianity which distinguishes the claims of God from those of Caesar and brings with it a necessary restraint upon the claims of sovereignty, not only that of Caesar but of nationalism too. In the words of another Thomas, whom Henry beheaded: 'The king's good servant but God's first'.

The Reformation was fuelled in part by repudiation of just that: both the Catholic Church's more universalist claims and any sort of dualism, under pressure from rulers anxious to monopolise power, temporal and spiritual, within their own dominions. In the later Middle Ages the nationalisation of the church had developed almost uncontrollably pace by pace with the hardening of national identities through language, literature and state formation. Christianity was entering a new kind of world, which it had itself done so much to engender, but which it was almost powerless to restrain or even to understand. The Rood was removed in English parish churches from its central place above the chancel arch and the royal arms put in its place. The more the monism of Caesaropapism came to prevail within any ecclesiastical tradition, the more the church has subsequently given almost unlimited support to nationalism as well. Within the Protestant world this has been especially the case for Anglicanism and Lutheranism. The political compromise with which the Wars of Religion came to an end in the seventeenth century, *cuus regio eus et religio,* was little less than an abdication of the universalist essence of Christianity in the face of a triumph of state sovereignty, particularist in principle and often nationalist in inspiration. Such a principle was too absurd to work and it led on, inevitably, to a new freedom, though more quickly in some places than others. Protestantism has, however, frequently been pressed along a nationalist road not only by erastianism but also by according greater weight to the Old Testament than Catholicism is prepared to do in the shaping of the Christian mind. Christians in general have always tended to use the Old Testament, especially its historical sections, as providing a set of precedents, pairing a situation there with one here. This leads on only too easily to identifying the general experience of one's people with that of Israel, in a way productive of nationalism and it long made much Protestant thinking naively nation-affirmative. 'It is by God's appointment that nations exist', wrote William Temple in 1915, and their existence is in consequence an 'instrument' of the 'divine purpose'.[15] For Temple as for Rousseau, Moses was the great nation-builder. Temple had been five years before an usher at the Edinburgh Missionary Conference of 1910 where it was affirmed in the Report of its first Commission that 'Christ never by teaching or example resisted or withstood the spirit of true nationalism.'[16]

Modern Protestantism has found it quite hard to disentangle itself from this sort of rather soft use of national categories for political and moral analysis, though the most thoughtful assembly it ever mounted on political issues, the 1937 Oxford Conference on Church, Community and State, wrestled with the ambiguous nature of the nation and nationalism with a maturity far beyond Edinburgh 1910 or the William Temple of 1915.[17] Those who have often led the way here are some of the Free Churches, though not always. Evangelical Protestantism has frequently combined a strongly universalist loyalty in highly spiritual terms with a very particularist loyalty in political terms. In chapter 3 we saw how easily early Methodists reverted to a very nationalist attitude towards Ireland.[18] But it is undoubtedly within this constituency that the most creative efforts have been made to free Protestantism and Christianity with it from nationalist bondage. It is groups like the Mennonites and the Quakers which have produced a Christian spirit most impervious to nationalism. Thus small non-state churches and very large, highly international, churches are those least affected by nationalism. It was the established state church in east and west which most completely succumbed to it. With time national churches have been increasingly discredited and, of course, some of them, perhaps most notably *Ecclesia Anglicana*, have been transformed instead into international fellowships. Only in eastern Europe has this development, central to modern Christianity, still hardly got under way.

III

Nationalism owes much to religion, to Christianity in particular. Nations developed, as I have suggested, out of a typical medieval and early modern experience of the multiplication of vernacular literatures and of state systems around them, a multiplication largely dependent upon the church, its scriptures and its clergy. Nation-formation and nationalism have in themselves almost nothing to do with modernity. Only when modernisation was itself already in the air did they almost accidentally become part of it, particularly from the eighteenth century when the political and economic success of England made it a model to imitate. But nations could occur in states as unmodern as ancient Ethiopia or Armenia and fail to happen in Renaissance Italy or even Frederick the Great's Prussia. If Christianity on one side fostered this development, both creatively and disastrously, it always had another side – whether papal, imperial or free – struggling to reach the surface. Certainly that is the side which those of us who share in the western ecumenical experience mostly prefer to encourage. If religion in the past did so much to produce, for example, Ireland's present divisions, so that they still appear to be religious divisions, it is no less true that most of what is alive in religion today in Ireland is extremely committed to their overcoming. Yet the churches are not only still intensely nationalist in many parts of the world, they also continue elsewhere to reinforce myths and practices which produce the alienation between communities upon which rival nationalisms inevitably feed. To give just one example. I recall listening to a memorable speech by Garret Fitzgerald, at the time Minister for Foreign Affairs in the Irish Republic, at an international consultation on inter-church marriage in Dublin in September 1974.[19] He spoke as a Roman Catholic layman pointing out that intermarriage breaks down social and political barriers while religious segregation, stimulated by Roman canon law, reinforces nationalism, and applied that message to Ireland. I too find it hard to believe that the conflicting nationalisms of modern Ireland would have remained so intense if there had been a wider practice of Catholic–Protestant marriage.

Intermarriage can undoubtedly in some circumstances threaten the very existence of a community, just as in others it can threaten its purity and act as a red rag to a bull in actually exacerbating an existing nationalism. If there was little inter-religious marriage in Belfast, there was a very great deal in Sarajevo. It was seen as a threat to Serbdom and one of the aims of Dr Karadzic's brand of ethnic nationalism was precisely to bring it to an end, to prevent further pollution of Serb blood. Freedom to marry across boundary lines is anti-nationalist. In hegemonic situations, the Sharia and Catholic canon law have both been systematically applied to make of intermarriage an effective instrument for the suppression of a minority community. Only when a relationship of genuine recipro-city is admitted can intermarriage contribute, as it is of its nature shaped to do, to the bonding of contiguous communities.[20] The fact remains that intermarriage across ethnic borders strengthens territor-ial nationhood but threatens ethnic nationhood and is anathema to ethnic nationalists. Intermarriage and nationalism remain practical contraries and if one wishes to diminish the latter one will not discourage the former. In that charming song, *The Old Orange Flute*, Bob Williamson, a Protestant Dungannon weaver, betrayed his people and their national identity:

> This treacherous scoundrel, he took us all in,
> He married a papist, named Bridget McGinn
> Turned papist himself and forsook the old cause
> That gave us our freedom, religion and laws.

A riot resulted and Bob and Bridget fled to Connaught. If he and others like him had stayed in place and multiplied, would not the interweaving of family relationships across the two communities inevitably have created from the bottom up a sense of single nationhood? It was doing so in Sarajevo until ethnic nationalism had to bring such dangerous communion to an end.

I would like to end this discussion of the shaping of nations as of their restraining through a larger vision by appealing to two people, one English, one Irish, in a way I hope appropriate for an Englishman invited to lecture in Ulster. My Englishman is William Shakespeare. I briefly discussed his rather nationalist historical plays in chapter 2, but will now, in returning to him, call attention to a very different work.

The nationalist plays, from *Richard II* to *Henry V*, were written in youthful vigour during the 1590s when English nationalism was particularly vigorous too, the years of the Spanish war at its fiercest. They are ebullient, robust, emphatically English, even if there is at times an underlying, more self-questioning, message, particularly about the relationship of crown to people. But near the close of his active life Shakespeare returned to our theme in a quite other key. *Cymbeline* is a play about Britain not about England. It was, of course, written after James VI of Scotland had become James I of England and the Spanish war was over, thus providing circumstances in which Shakespeare could perhaps think of the nation and the world more ecumenically: there is, despite the almost impossibly complicated strains of the personal story, a sense of tranquillity in Cymbeline, of peace regained. It is, nevertheless, the story of an irrational and nationalist Britain, set upon being 'a world by itself', where refusal to pay formal tribute to Rome and the disruption of domestic harmony have been produced by the machinations of a thoroughly evil queen. Remembering Spenser's *Gloriana*, it is hard to discount the suspicion that in this firmly nameless queen Shakespeare is hinting at Elizabeth. Cymbeline's own Roman-named sons have long ago been hidden away in a cave in the mountains of Wales by another Roman, ill-used by Britain, who has appropriately disguised himself under the name of Morgan. Rome, that universal place where exiled Britons can mix with Frenchmen, Spaniards and Dutchmen, sends her 'gentry' to return Britain to the European fold, and Imogen, Britain's glorious princess, disguised as a boy, is part of the European army. In battle Cymbeline is defeated and captured until rescued by Morgan and his supposed sons. The Romans, captured in their turn, are about to be executed, contrary to all civilised norms, until the wickedness of the queen is at last revealed to Cymbeline together with the identity of his sons. The destructive blindness of nationalism falls from British eyes. Through Wales the true *Romanitas* of Britain is revealed once more and, though victor in battle, Cymbeline promises to restore the payment of 'our wonten tribute'. Thus an exaggerated nationalism is overthrown and peace re-established between Caesar and Cymbeline, Brussels and London, Wales and England, the international community and the nation-state, perhaps even Catholicism and the national church. But it is the British, rather than the English, dimensions of our identity which have made that possible. The path from Rome lies via Milford Haven. The symbolism in this, Shakespeare's final testimony to his fellow countrymen in regard to the matter of nationhood, is mysteriously emphatic, woefully overlooked as it mostly is.

My Irishman is St Comgall, who founded the abbey of Bangor, only a little outside modern Belfast, in the middle of the sixth century, forty years before Augustine first arrived in Canterbury. Almost everything I have been endeavouring to delineate in these lectures as somehow characteristic of the healthier tensions within the European tradition may find some sort of origin in Comgall's Bangor. It was undoubtedly the most lively centre of learning in Ireland at that time and it looks as if the origins of Irish vernacular literature may well be located in and around Bangor, here in Ulster, that is to say the first step in the stabilisation of national identities. In this Ireland actually leads the way in Europe. Yet Bangor was no less a universalist place. Columbanus had been a disciple of Comgall and dwelt here for many years before setting out for the continent, to found the great monasteries of Luxeuil and Bobbio. Columba was here too and Comgall joined him for a while at Iona in the conversion of the Picts. There is then nothing narrowly nationalist in the legacy of Comgall's Bangor. On the contrary, it points each way, to the maturing both of Irishness and of an international catholicity.

Yet again, if Comgall's Ireland was already very much one, in language, myth, religion and law, it was also a divided island even, we may say, a little provocatively, between north and south. Let me give an example.[21] There is a story recorded in later centuries of how when Cormac, son of Diarmuid, King of Leinster, resigned his crown to become a monk, he went north to Ulster to join the community in Comgall's Bangor. Columbanus too had come to Bangor from Leinster and at much the same time. After a while, we are told, Cormac could no longer bear to be absent from his fatherland and Comgall permitted him to return to the South. On the journey he fell asleep on a hillside and in a dream saw all the beauties of Leinster and its people. When he woke up it was enough and, returning to Comgall and Bangor, he stayed there till he died. There can be no question that there was a real unity of Ireland already in Comgall's time just as there can be no doubt of Ireland's already belonging to a still greater community stretching across Europe. But there can also be no doubt that the political model of Irishness, then as for centuries afterwards, allowed Ulster to be sufficiently distinct from Leinster to give Cormac's story its point. I am not wanting to suggest that fidelity to Ireland's most ancient traditions requires the indefinite maintenance of a border between Ulster and the South, but only that the narrowly unitary model of a nation-state which England has marketed seems foreign to the Irish genius. For the latter it would seem natural that at one level Ulster and Leinster are separate realities, at another Ireland is a single national community, at a third the confines of a territorial nation are quite transcended and Irishmen can be at home in Iona, Bobbio, Rome or Brussels. Shakespeare was surely suggesting much the same when he ends *Cymbeline* with Britain's voluntary decision to pay tribute once more to Europe. The king's final command is clear enough:

> Let
> A Roman and a British ensign wave
> Friendly together.[22]

What better conclusion can there be to a study of nationalism?

Notes

I THE NATION AND NATIONALISM

1 E.J. Hobsbawm, *Nations and Nationalism since 1780* (Cambridge University Press, 1990)

2 John Breuilly, *Nationalism and the State*, 2nd edn (Manchester University Press, 1993); Ernest Gellner, *Nations and Nationalism* (Oxford: Blackwell, 1983); Benedict Anderson, *Imagined Communities, Reflections on the Origin and Spread of Nationalism* (London: Verso, 1983).

3 Keith Stringer, 'Social and Political Communities in European History: Some Reflections on Recent Studies', in Claus Bjørn, Alexander Grant and Keith J. Stringer (eds.), *Nations, Nationalism and Patriotism in the European Past* (Copenhagen: Academic Press, 1994), pp. 23 and 33.

4 At the beginning of the eighteenth century, Anthony Ashley Cooper, the Third Earl of Shaftesbury, defined a 'People' or 'Nation' in his *Characteristics of Men, Manners, Opinions, Times* (London, 1714, III, 143n) as follows: 'A multitude held together by force, though under one and the same head, is not properly united: nor does such a body make a people. It is the social league, confederacy, and mutual consent, founded in some common good or interest, which joins the members of a community and makes a People one. Absolute Power annuls the publick; and where there is no publick, or constitution, there is in reality no mother-country or Nation.'

5 Liah Greenfeld, *Nationalism: Five Roads to Modernity* (Harvard University Press, 1992), p. 23. This constitutes, of course, a precise denial of Renan's claim for France: 'Le principe des nations est le nôtre', *Qu'est-ce qu'une nation?* (Paris, 1882), p. 10.

6 Hobsbawm, *Nations and Nationalism since 1780*, p. 11.

7 Anderson, *Imagined Communities*, p. 111.

8 R.R. Davies's presidential addresses to the Royal Historical Society for 1993 and 1994: 'The Peoples of Britain and Ireland 1100–1400: I

Identities', *Transactions of the Royal Historical Society*, 6th series, vol. 4 (1994), pp. 1–20, and 'The Peoples of Britain and Ireland 1100–1400: II Names, Boundaries and Regnal Solidarities', *Transactions of the Royal Historical Society*, vol. 5 (1995), pp. 1–20; Susan Reynolds, *Kingdoms and Communities in Western Europe 900–1300* (Oxford: Clarendon Press, 1984); Bjørn, Grant and Stringer (eds.), *Nations, Nationalism and Patriotism in the European Past*; Simon Forde, Lesley Johnson and Alan V. Murray (eds.), *Concepts of National Identity in the Middle Ages* (Leeds Texts and Monographs, 1995); Thorlac Turville-Petre, *England the Nation: Language, Literature and National Identity 1290–1340* (Oxford: Clarendon Press, 1996).

9 Anthony D. Smith, *The Ethnic Origins of Nations* (Oxford: Blackwell, 1986); see also *National Identity* (Penguin, 1991), and John Hutchinson, *Modern Nationalism* (London: Fontana, 1994).

10 Greenfeld, *Nationalism: Five Roads to Modernity*, p. 14. Another wide-ranging American study which significantly deviates from full modernist orthodoxy is John A. Armstrong, *Nations before Nationalism* (Chapel Hill: University of North Carolina Press, 1982). Despite its title it has nevertheless little to say about nations, being rather a discussion of the construction of ethnicity. Verbally at least the author appears to accept the modernist thesis that there are no nations before nationalism and no nationalism before the eighteenth century. He also strangely avoids serious consideration of almost any of the older nations of western Europe. Furthermore while claiming to 'provide an overview of Eastern and Western Christendom and Islamic civilisation' (p. 3) he does not appear to realise how profound is the difference between Christianity and Islam in relation to nationhood. Despite its richness of material, it is in consequence a confused and confusing book.

11 Greenfeld, *Nationalism: Five Roads to Modernity*, p. 42.

12 Joseph R. Strayer, *Medieval Statecraft and the Perspectives of History* (Princeton University Press, 1971), p. 347 (the essay in question first appeared in 1963).

13 Elie Kedourie, *Nationalism* (London: Hutchinson, 1960).

14 Gellner, *Nations and Nationalism*, p. 55.

15 Ernest Gellner, *Thought and Change* (London: Weidenfeld and Nicolson, 1964), p. 168.

16 Hobsbawm, *Nations and Nationalism since 1780*, p. 10.

17 *Ibid.*, pp. 5 and 9–10.

18 *Ibid.*, p. 14.

19 Gellner, *Nations and Nationalism*, p. 55.

20 Yet he has to admit in his far too brief analysis of the English experience of the sixteenth and seventeenth centuries that 'the idea of the nation

was not radically distinct from the idea of the state'. Breuilly, *Nationalism and the State*, p. 85.

21 Anderson, *Imagined Communities*, p. 46.

22 *Ibid.*, p. 81, n. 34.

23 *Ibid.*, p. 191 and n. 9.

24 Liah Greenfeld provides the explanation: in essence it was not new at all – 'the story of the emergence of the American nation' represents a realisation of 'the promise of original English nationalism', *Nationalism: Five Roads to Modernity*, p. 401.

25 Almost the only recent study of nationalism to take its biblical basis seriously is that of Conor Cruise O'Brien, *God Land: Reflections on Religion and Nationalism* (Harvard University Press, 1988), a book which appears to have been largely ignored.

26 Rogers Brubaker, *Citizenship and Nationhood in France and Germany* (Harvard University Press, 1992).

27 Hobsbawm, *Nations and Nationalism since 1780*, p. 17.

28 Edmund Burke, 'On Conciliation with the Colonies' (1775), *Speeches and Letters on American Affairs* (London: Everyman, 1908), p. 89.

29 Paul Williams (ed.), *The Life of Olaudah Equiano, or Gustavus Vassa the African* (London: Longman, 1988), p. 4.

30 *Areopagitica* (1644), *Complete Prose Works of John Milton* (Yale University Press, 1959), II, p. 551.

31 'Considerations touching a war with Spain inscribed to Prince Charles (1624)', *The Works of Francis Bacon* (1778), II, p. 318.

32 William Shakespeare, *Henry IV, Part II*, Act I, Scene 2.

33 Samuel Daniel, *Musophilus* (1599), line 957.

34 Oxford English Dictionary, 2nd edn, 1989, 'nation'.

35 Sherman M. Kuhn and John Reidy, *Middle English Dictionary* (University of Michigan Press, 1975), 'nacioun'.

36 J. Forshall and F. Madden (eds.), *The Holy Bible . . . in the Earliest English Versions made from the Latin Vulgate by John Wycliffe and his Followers* (Oxford, 1850), I, p. ix.

37 H.R. Bramley (ed.), *The Psalter or Psalms of David and Certain Canticles with a Translation and Exposition in English by Richard Rolle of Hampole* (Oxford, 1884), p. 387.

38 Forshall and Madden, *The Holy Bible . . in the Earliest English Versions*, IV, p. 511.

39 As, e.g., Kedourie, *Nationalism*, pp. 13–14, Hobsbawm, *Nations and Nationalism since 1780*, p. 16, Greenfeld, p. 4, etc. Probably the rest depend on Kedourie.

40 Davies, 'The Peoples of Britain and Ireland 1100–1400: I Identities', p. 10.

41 Bramley, *The Psalter or Psalms of David*, p. 406.

42 The translation of 'gens/gentes' is further complicated (and confused) by the fact that a word in English was developed to fill this gap in a specific theological context – 'gentiles', with a connotation 'heathen/non-Jew'. So, if we compare the translations of Acts 2.5 and 22.21 – the every nation under heaven of Pentecost and Paul's mission to go afar unto the nations – we have 'ethnos' for both in Greek, 'natio' for both in the Vulgate and 'nacioun' for both in Wyclif, but Tyndale switches to 'the Gentyls' for the second which is retained in the Authorised Version. However, where the early sixteenth-century versions switched widely from 'nations' to 'Gentiles', the King James moved back in some cases such as Psalm 117, quoted above. In the earlier sixteenth-century translations, issuing in the 'Great Bible' of 1539 (the first to be printed in England), we have 'Praise the Lord, all ye heathen: praise him, all ye nations'. Undoubtedly in this the Vulgate was a better translation to which, essentially, the Authorised returns. But the point remains that the two sixteenth–seventeenth-century translations both manage to use the word 'nation' in this verse though one uses it in the first phrase, the other in the second!

43 George Garnett, *The Journal of Ecclesiastical History*, vol. 47.1 (January 1996), p. 140.

44 V.H. Galbraith, 'Nationality and Language in Medieval England', *Transactions of the Royal Historical Society*, vol. 23 (1941), p. 117.

45 Ruth Finnegan, *Oral Literature in Africa* (Oxford: Clarendon Press, 1970); Jack Goody, *The Myth of the Bagre* (Oxford: Clarendon Press, 1972); Tomás Ó Crohan, *The Islandman*, translated from the Irish with a foreword by Robin Flower (Oxford: Clarendon Press, 1937).

46 Ian Green, *The Christian's ABC* (Oxford: Clarendon Press, 1996), p. 175.

47 Ian Green, *Print and Protestantism in Early Modern England* (Oxford: Clarendon Press, forthcoming).

48 Anderson, *Imagined Communities*, p. 7.

49 Eugen Weber, *Peasants into Frenchmen* (London: Chatto and Windus, 1977), p. 493.

50 Anderson, *Imagined Communities*, p. 81.

51 Greenfeld, *Nationalism: Five Roads to Modernity*, p. 14.

52 The argument over the function of language in the basic formation of nations can be well illustrated with reference to the particularly strong case of Wales by the following two quotations. Hobsbawm, whose general scepticism on the subject goes so far as to conclude that 'languages multiply with states; not the other way round' (*Nations and Nationalism since 1780*, p. 63), dismisses the unity of Welsh with a

reference to 'jokes about the difficulties of North Walians understanding the Welsh of those from South Wales' (p. 52). In contrast R.R. Davies stresses that 'dialectical differences − such as those which characterised the men of Gwent − were recognised; but they were of small significance compared with the broad linguistic unity of Wales' already in the twelfth century (*Conquest, Coexistence and Change, Wales 1063−1415* [Oxford: Clarendon Press, 1987], p. 17). Hobsbawm's argument here as elsewhere depends on focusing upon differences in the oral mode whereas the key to stable nation formation lies not here but in the power of the written form.

53 A. Hastings, 'Africa's Many Nationalisms', *Worldmission* (Fall 1955), p. 351; Pierre de Menasce's article, 'Nationalism in Missionary Countries' first appeared in the *Neue Zeitschrift für Missionswissenschaft* in 1947.

54 Hobsbawm, *Nations and Nationalism since 1780*, p 12.

55 *Ibid.*, p 13.

2 ENGLAND AS PROTOTYPE

1 Patrick Wormald, 'The Venerable Bede and the "Church of the English"', in Geoffrey Rowell (ed.), *The English Religious Tradition and the Genius of Anglicanism* (Wantage: Ikon Publications, 1992), p. 26.

2 James Campbell, 'The United Kingdom of England: The Anglo-Saxon Achievement', in Alexander Grant and Keith J. Stringer (eds.), *Uniting the Kingdom? The Making of British History* (London: Routledge, 1995), p. 31.

3 William Stubbs, *Select Charters*, 9th edn, revised by H.W.C. Davis (Oxford: Clarendon Press, 1946), p. 70.

4 Dorothy Whitelock, 'The Anglo-Saxon Achievement', in C.T. Chevallier (ed.), *The Norman Conquest: Its Setting and Impact* (London, 1966), p. 38.

5 Charles Plummer (ed.), *Two of the Saxon Chronicles* (Oxford, 1892), p. 140.

6 Gavin Bone, *Anglo-Saxon Poetry* (Oxford: Clarendon Press, 1943), pp. 27−36.

7 Mary Clayton, 'Aelfric's *Judith*: Manipulative or Manipulated?', *Anglo-Saxon England*, vol. 23 (1994), p. 215.

8 Cf. Anthony Smith, 'National Identities: Modern and Medieval', in Simon Forde, Lewsley Johnson and Alan V. Murray (eds.), *Concepts of National Identity in the Middle Ages* (University of Leeds, 1995), p. 27, and elsewhere in his numerous writings.

9 John Gillingham, 'The Beginnings of English Imperialism', *Journal of Historical Sociology*, vol. 5 (1992), pp. 392−409; 'Henry of Huntingdon

and the Twelfth-Century Revival of the English Nation', in Simon Forde, Lesley Johnson and Alan V. Murray (eds.), *Concepts of National Identity in the Middle Ages* (Leeds Texts and Monographs, 1995), pp. 75–102; 'Foundations of a Disunited Kingdom', in Grant and Stringer, *Uniting the Kingdom?*, pp. 48–64.

10 See R.R. Davies, *Domination and Conquest* (Cambridge University Press, 1990), p. 13.

11 Stubbs, *Charters*, p. 480.

12 Basil Cottle, *The Triumph of English 1350–1400* (Blandford Press, 1969), pp. 16–17.

13 Stanley Hussey, 'Nationalism and Language in England c. 1300–1500', in Claus Bjørn, Alexander Grant and Keith J. Stringer (eds.), *Nations, Nationalism and Patriotism in the European Past* (Copenhagen: Academic Press, 1994), pp. 96–108.

14 May McKisack, *The Fourteenth Century, 1307–1399* (Oxford: Clarendon Press, 1959), p. 524.

15 As already remarked (chapter 1, n 11), one of the large weaknesses of John A. Armstrong's study of *Nations before Nationalism* (Chapel Hill: University of North Carolina Press, 1982), is apparent ignorance about so many of the prime examples – England, Scotland, Wales, Ireland and Denmark among others. A striking instance is his discussion of the role of capitals and the comment that 'Cairo is an outstanding example of the single dominating city such as Europe did not know until the eighteenth-century expansion of London and Paris' (174). Perhaps he should start by reading that late fifteenth-century poem, formerly attributed to William Dunbar, 'London, thou art of townes A per se', or reflecting on the inclusion of the Mayor of London among the twenty-five 'barons' appointed to ensure the fulfilment of Magna Carta, or on the absolutely decisive role of London in the seventeenth-century Civil War. Despite the existence of many other flourishing towns, the far greater size of London, its unique mix of population, its commercial power and literary activity made it a very dominating national capital long before the eighteenth century. Note particularly London's near monopoly of printing and publishing books.

16 J.-P. Genet, 'English Nationalism: Thomas Polton at the Council of Constance', *Nottingham Medieval Studies*, vol. 28 (1984), pp. 60–78.

17 'Unus Anglus perimet Scoticos quam plures', T. Wright (ed.) *The Political Songs of England* (Camden Society, 1839), p. 175.

18 Barnaby Keeney, 'Military Service and the Development of Nationalism in England, 1272–1327', *Speculum*, vol. 22 (1947), pp. 534–49.

19 T. Wright (ed.), *Political Poems and Songs* II, Rolls Series (1861), p. 124.

20 McKisack, *The Fourteenth Century*, p. 150.

21 In Froissart's account of a speech of the Sire de Clisson, Froissart, viii, 302, quoted by McKisack, *The Fourteenth Century*, p. 151.

22 T. Wright (ed.), *Political Poems and Songs* II, *Rolls Series* (1859), pp. 26 and 35.

23 W. Stubbs, *Constitutional History of England* (1874), I, pp. 532 and 637.

24 J.C. Holt, *Magna Carta* (Cambridge University Press, 1965), p. 187.

25 The Remonstrance of May 1642, Andrew Sharp, *Political Ideas of the English Civil Wars 1641−1649* (London: Longman, 1983), p. 37.

26 Conrad Russell, *The Causes of the English Civil War* (Oxford: Clarendon, 1990), chapter 6, 'The Rule of Law: Whose Slogan?'

27 'Qui representant totam communitatem Angliae', Stubbs, *Charters*, p. 505.

28 May McKisack, *The Parliamentary Representation of the English Boroughs during the Middle Ages* (Oxford University Press, 1932), pp. 24 and 44.

29 R.R. Davies, *Domination and Conquest* (Cambridge University Press, 1990), p. 16.

30 *Ibid.*, p. 18.

31 R.W. Chambers, *Thomas More* (London: Jonathan Cape, 1935), p. 341.

32 Anthony D. Smith, 'National Identities: Modern and Medieval?', in Forde, Johnson and Murray, *Concepts of National Identity in the Middle Ages*, p. 35.

33 The only ground for such a claim might be the impact of printed works in English from the 1470s, cf. H.S. Bennett, *English Books and Readers 1475−1557* (Cambridge University Press, 1969). The number of books printed in English before 1530 is fairly limited and it would be highly implausible to claim so rapid an effect on the 'sense of national identity'.

34 *Political Poems and Songs* II, p. 178.

35 *Political Poems and Songs* II, p. 188.

36 E.J. Hobsbawm, *Nations and Nationalism since 1780* (Cambridge University Press, 1990), p. 75.

37 *Henry V*, 3.6.

38 *Henry V*, 4.7.

39 *Richard II*, 2.1; *Henry V*, 3.1.

40 *Complete Works* of John Lyly (Oxford, 1902), II, 205.

41 *Areopagitica, Complete Prose Works of John Milton* (Yale University Press, 1959), II, p. 552.

42 Carol Z. Wiener, 'The Beleaguered Isle. A Study of Elizabethan and Early Jacobean Anti-Catholicism', *Past and Present*, no. 51 (May 1971), p. 35. For seventeenth-century English anti-Catholicism, see also Robin Clifton, 'The Popular Fear of Catholics during the English Revolution', *Past and Present*, no. 52 (August 1971), pp. 23−55.

43 William Haller, *Foxe's Book of Martyrs and the Elect Nation* (1963).

44 Eamon Duffy, ' "Englishmen in Vaine": Roman Catholic Allegiance to George I', in Stuart Mews (ed.), *Religion and National Identity, Studies in Church History* 18 (Oxford: Blackwell, 1982), pp. 345–65; see also chapter 3, 'A Tradition of Dissent', in my *Church and State, The English Experience* (University of Exeter Press, 1991).

45 F.S. Siebert, *Freedom of the Press in England 1476–1776* (University of Illinois Press, 1952), pp. 191, 203.

46 Don M. Wolfe (ed.), *Leveller Manifestoes of the Puritan Revolution* (London: Frank Cass & Co., 1967), p. 56.

47 See Peter Furtado, 'National Pride in Seventeenth-Century England', in Raphael Samuel (ed.), *Patriotism* (London: Routledge, 1989), I, pp. 44–56.

48 Edward Chamberlayne, *Angliae Notitia, or the Present State of England* (London, 1669).

49 Linda Colley, *Britons, Forging the Nation 1707–1837* (Yale University Press, 1992), p. 8.

50 *Ibid.*, p. 373.

51 A.O.H. Jarman, 'Wales and the Council of Constance', *Bulletin of the Board of Celtic Studies* 14 (1950–2), pp. 220–2.

52 Robert Southey, *Life of Nelson* (1813).

53 R. Coupland, *War Speeches of William Pitt* (1915), p. 35.

54 David Livingstone, *Missionary Travels and Researches in South Africa* (London: Ward, Lock & Co., 1857), pp. 583–4, and for a schoolboy's adulation of 'England's missionary explorer, Livingstone' as 'the greatest' among 'England's heroes', see Margery Perham, *Lugard, The Years of Adventure* (London: Collins, 1956), p. 34.

55 *The Letters and Diaries of John Henry Newman* XXV (Oxford, 1973), p. 166.

56 David Cannadine, 'British History as a "New Subject": Politics, Perspectives and Prospects', in Grant and Stringer, *Uniting the Kingdom?*, p. 16.

57 Colley, *Britons, Forging the Nation*, p. 374.

58 *Ibid.*, p. 6.

59 Edward Norman, *Anti-Catholicism in Victorian England* (London: George Allen and Unwin, 1968); D.G. Paz, *Popular Anti-Catholicism in Mid-Victorian Britain* (Stanford University Press, 1992).

3 ENGLAND'S WESTERN NEIGHBOURS

1 R.S. Hawker, *The Song of the Western Men*, re-using lines first composed in 1688, on the imprisonment of Bishop Trelawney.

2 R.R. Davies, *Conquest, Coexistence and Change: Wales 1063–1415* (Oxford: Clarendon Press, 1987), p. 385.

3 R.R. Davies, 'Law and National Identity in Thirteenth-Century Wales', in R.R. Davies *et al.* (eds.), *Welsh Society and Nationhood. Historical Essays Presented to Glanmor Williams* (Cardiff: University of Wales Press, 1984), pp. 51–69; Davies, *Conquest, Coexistence and Change*, especially chapter 1, 'Wales and the Welsh'.

4 Keith Robbins, 'Religion and Identity in Modern British History', in Stuart Mews (ed.), *Religion and National Identity, Studies in Church History* 18 (Oxford: Blackwell, 1982), p. 483.

5 Dauvit Broun, 'The Origin of Scottish Identity', pp. 35–55, and Alexander Grant, 'Aspects of National Consciousness in Medieval Scotland', pp. 68–95, in Claus Bjørn, Alexander Grant and Keith J. Stringer (eds.), *Nations, Nationalism and Patriotism in the European Past* (Copenhagen: Academic Press, 1994).

6 F.M. Powicke, *The Thirteenth Century* (Oxford: Clarendon Press, 1953), p. 421.

7 Davies, *Conquest, Coexistence and Change*, p. 352.

8 Gywn A. Williams, *When was Wales?* (London: Black Raven Press, 1985), p. 121.

9 Carl Bridenbaugh, *Vexed and Troubled Englishmen 1590–1642* (Oxford: Clarendon Press, 1968), p. 402.

10 *Ibid.*, p. 401.

11 Cotton Mather, *Magnalia Christi Americana*, ed. Kenneth Murdock (Harvard University Press, 1977), p. 92.

12 *Ibid.*, p. 67.

13 Perry Miller, *The New England Mind: From Colony to Province* (Harvard University Press, 1953), p. 371.

14 Carl Bridenbaugh, *Mitre and Sceptre: Transatlantic Faiths, Ideas, Personalities and Politics, 1689–1775* (New York: Oxford University Press, 1962), Part Two, 'No Bishop, No King'.

15 29 August 1773, Charles Metzger, SJ, *The Quebec Act* (1936), p. 39.

16 *Ibid.*, p. 60.

17 Bridenbaugh, *Mitre and Sceptre*, p. 339.

18 Daniel J. Boorstin, *The Americans: The Colonial Experience* (New York: Random House, 1958), p. 278. I am much indebted to Boorstin's treatment of this theme.

19 *Ibid.*, p. 290.

20 Liah Greenfeld, *Nationalism: Five Roads to Modernity* (Harvard University Press, 1992), p. 407.

21 W.J. Bate (ed.), *Selected Writings of Edmund Burke* (Westport, Connecticut: Greenwood Press, 1960), p. 151.

22 *Ibid.*, p. 134.

23 Elie Kedourie, *Nationalism*, 4th edn (London: Hutchinson, 1993), p. 74.

24 Quoted Greenfeld, *Nationalism: Five Roads to Modernity*, p. 410.

25 Abraham Lincoln, The Gettysburg Address, 19 November 1863, R.P. Basler (ed.), *Collected Works of Abraham Lincoln* (1953), vol. VII, p. 23.

26 Claude Halstead Van Tyne, *The American Revolution 1776–1783* (New York, 1905), p. 71.

27 The point of the joke in the altercation between Fluellen and Macmorris in *Henry V*, III, 2, over the former's slighting remark about 'your nation' and the latter's reply, 'What ish my nation? What ish my nation?' would seem to lie precisely in English awareness of Irish sensitivity about the subject in Shakespeare's own time.

28 See J. Stanley Leatherbarrow, *The Lancashire Elizabethan Recusants* (Manchester: Chetham Society, 1947), especially pp. 112–24; compare this with Helen Walshe, 'Enforcing the Elizabethan Settlement: The Vicissitudes of Hugh Brady, Bishop of Meath, 1563–84', *Irish Historical Studies*, vol. 26 (1989), pp. 352–76. The situation in Meath looks remarkably like that in Lancashire.

29 Frank Kermode, *Shakespeare, Spenser, Donne* (London: Routledge and Kegan Paul, 1971); Michael O'Connell, *Mirror and Veil, the Historical Dimension of Spenser's Faerie Queene* (Chapel Hill: University of North Carolina Press, 1977); Patricia Coughlan (ed.), *Spenser and Ireland: An Interdisciplinary Perspective*, (Cork University Press, 1989); John N. King, *Spenser's Poetry and the Reformation Tradition* (Princeton University Press, 1990).

30 *Spenser's Prose Works.*, ed. Rudolf Gottfried (*The Works of Edmund Spenser, A Variorum Edition*, Edwin Greenslaw *et al.* (eds.), (Baltimore: Johns Hopkins Press, 1949)), p. 148.

31 *Ibid.*, p. 240.

32 *Ibid.*, pp. 243–4.

33 Winston S. Churchill, *A History of the English-Speaking People*, II (1956), p. 232.

34 *Ibid.*, p. 221.

35 Geoffrey Keating, *Foras feasa ar Éirinn; the history of Ireland*, ed. David Comyn and P.S. Dinneen (London: Irish Texts Society, 4 vols., 1902–14); see also Bernadette Cunningham, 'Seventeenth Century Interpretations of the Past: the case of Geoffrey Keating', *Irish Historical Studies*, vol. 25 (1986), pp. 116–28.

36 For Bedell, see especially Desmond Bowen, *History and the Shaping of English Protestantism* (New York: Peter Lang, 1995), pp. 73–84, and Gordon Rupp, *William Bedell 1571–1642* (Cambridge University Press, 1971).

37 Brian Ó Cuív, 'Irish Language and Literature, 1691–1845', in T.W. Moody and W.E. Vaughan (eds.), *A New History of Ireland*, IV, *Eighteenth-Century Ireland*, (Oxford: Clarendon Press, 1986), p. 376.

38 Roy Foster, *Modern Ireland 1600–1972* (London: Allen Lane, 1988), p. 51.

39 David Hempton and Myrtle Hill, *Evangelical Protestantism in Ulster Society 1740–1890* (London: Routledge, 1992), p. 15.

40 David Hempton, *Methodism and Politics in British Society 1750–1850* (London: Hutchinson, 1984).

41 *Parliamentary Debates (Ireland)*, xii, pp. 134–5, quoted in Thomas Bartlett, *The Fall and Rise of the Irish Nation. The Catholic Question 1690–1830* (Dublin: Gill and Macmillan, 1992), p. 143.

42 William Mollyneux, *The Case of Ireland's being Bound by Act of Parliament in England Stated* (Dublin, 1725), p. 15.

43 There is no serious consideration of Ireland in Hobsbawm's *Nations and Nationalism since 1780*, Anderson's *Imagined Communities*, Breuilly's *Nationalism and the State*, Armstrong's *Nations Before Nationalism* or Greenfeld's *Nationalism: Five Roads to Modernity*. So sustained an avoidance of Europe's most continuously active nationalist volcano is surely noteworthy.

4 WESTERN EUROPE

1 Liah Greenfeld, *Nationalism: Five Roads to Modernity* (Harvard University Press, 1992), pp. 160–88.

2 Ian Wood, 'Defining the Franks: Frankish Origins in Early Medieval Historiography', pp. 47–58, and Alan V. Murray, 'Ethnic Identity in the Crusader States: The Frankish Race and the Settlement of Outremer', pp. 59–74, in Simon Forde, Lesley Johnson and Alan V. Murray (eds.), *Concepts of National Identity in the Middle Ages* (Leeds Texts and Monographs, 1995).

3 Joseph R. Strayer, *Medieval Statecraft and the Perspectives of History*, ch. 19, 'France: The Holy Land, the Chosen People and the Most Christian King' (Princeton University Press, 1971), pp. 300–14.

4 Bull, *Rex gloriae*, 1311, quoted in Strayer, *Medieval Statecraft*, p. 313.

5 J.E.J. Quicherat, *Procès de condemnation et de rehabilition de Jeanne d'Arc* (Paris, 1849), V, p. 127.

6 Charles T. Wood, *Joan of Arc and Richard III* (Oxford University Press, 1988), p. 146.

7 Greenfeld, *Nationalism: Five Roads to Modernity*, p. 99.

8 *Ibid.*, p 107.

9 Nancy Lyman Roelker, *One King, One Faith* (University of California Press, 1996).

10 Robert Palmer, 'The National Idea in France before the Revolution', *Journal of the History of Ideas*, vol. 1 (1940), p. 104.

11 E. Weber, *Peasants into Frenchmen* (London: Chatto and Windus, London, 1977), p. 72.

12 Weber, *Peasants into Frenchmen*, pp. 70 and 73.

13 Arthur Young, *Travels During the Years 1787, 1788 and 1789* (London, 1792), pp. 146–7.

14 For a good recent review of France, Germany and Italy too see Ralph Gibson, 'The Intensification of National Consciousness in Modern Europe', in Claus Bjørn, Alexander Grant and Keith J. Stringer (eds.), *Nations, Nationalism and Patriotism in the European Past* (Copenhagen: Academic Press, 1994), pp. 177–97.

15 Greenfeld, *Nationalism: Five Roads to Modernity*, p. 277.

16 Susan Reynolds, *Kingdoms and Communities in Western Europe 900–1300* (Oxford: Clarendon Press, 1984), p. 289.

17 Peter Linehan, 'Religion, Nationalism and National Identity in Medieval Spain', in Stuart Mews (ed.), *Religion and National Identity* (Oxford: Blackwell, 1982), pp. 161–99.

18 See Norman Cigar, *Genocide in Bosnia, The Policy of Ethnic Cleansing* (Texas A & M University Press, 1995).

19 Quoted by R.R. Davies, 'The Peoples of Britain and Ireland 1100–1400: I. Identities', *Transactions of the Royal Historical Society*, 6th Series, vol. 4 (1994), p. 12.

20 Ernest Renan, *Qu'est-ce qu'une nation?* (Paris, 1882), p. 10.

21 Diana M. Webb, 'Italians and Others: Some Quattrocento Views of Nationality and the Church', in Mews, *Religion and National Identity*, p. 257.

22 J. Forshall and F. Madden (eds.), *The Holy Bible . . . in the Earliest English Versions made from the Latin Vulgate by John Wycliffe and his Followers* (Oxford, 1850), I, xiv.

23 Reynolds, *Kingdoms and Communities in Western Europe*, p. 252.

5 THE SOUTH SLAVS

1 H. Kohn, *The Idea of Nationalism* (New York, 1944), p. 546.

2 Woislav Petrovitch, *Serbia, Her People, History and Aspirations* (London: Harrap, 1915), pp. 7–12.

3 *Ibid.*, pp. 241 and 158. By contrast a modern Croat scholar can accuse Croat leadership in 1918 of 'political lunacy . . . determined to commit national suicide', Stanko Guldescu, *The Croatian–Slavonian Kingdom 1526–1792* (The Hague: Mouton, 1970), p. 154.

4 R.W. Seton-Watson, *The Southern Slav Question and the Hapsburg Monarchy* (London, 1911), pp. 336 and 339–40.

5 Harold Temperley, *History of Serbia* (London: G. Bell, 1917), pp. 1 and 3. Amazingly, Temperley listed the components of the Jugo-Slav race as follows: 'the Serbo-Croats of Croatia, the Serbs of Dalmatia, the Bosnians, Montenegrans and the Serbians of Serbia proper' (p. 2).

6 Hugh Seton-Watson, *Nationalism – Old and New*, (Sydney University Press, 1965), p. 7.

7 Mateja Matejic, *Biography of Saint Sava* (Columbus, Ohio, 1976).

8 I have mostly followed the careful analysis in John V. Fine, *The Late Medieval Balkans* (University of Michigan Press, 1994), pp. 408–27.

9 Thomas Emmert, *Serbian Golgotha, Kosovo, 1389* (Columbia University Press, 1990), p. 46.

10 Noel Malcolm, *Bosnia: A Short History* (London: Macmillan, 1994), pp. 55, 70–3.

11 See Wayne S. Vucinich and Thomas A. Emmert (eds.), *Kosovo, Legacy of a Medieval Battle* (University of Minnesota Press, 1991), especially Radmila J. Gorup, 'Kosovo and Epic Poetry', pp. 109–21, and Vasa D. Mihailovich, 'The Tradition of Kosovo in Serbian Literature', pp. 141–58.

12 Emmert, *Serbian Golgotha*, p. 128.

13 *Ibid.*

14 Ivo Banac, *The National Question in Yugoslavia: Origins, History, Politics* (Ithaca: Cornell University Press, 1984), p. 100.

15 *Ibid.*, p. 102.

16 *Ibid.*, p. 81. Croatian nationalist scholars almost prove Karadzic right when, to distance Croatia from Serbia, they repudiate what is shared. Thus Guldescu (*The Croatian–Slavonian Kingdom*, p. 276), declares Čakavian 'the only really authentic Croatian speech', by implication denying the Croat authenticy of Štokavian-speaking Dubrovnik. See also Bette Denich, 'Dismembering Yugoslavia: Nationalist Ideologies and the Symbolic Revival of Genocide', *The American Ethnologist* (May 1994), pp. 367–90.

17 Rogers Brubaker, *Citizenship and Nationhood in France and Germany* (Harvard University Press, 1992), p.12.

18 The extent of Serbia was to be defined not just by Štokavian but by the presence of the popular epic ballad, the *pjesme*, something in fact common to all the peoples of the area. Thus *The Frontiers of Language and Nationality* by Leon Dominian (New York: American Geographical Society, 1917) includes the following amazing passage: 'The *pjesme* voices Serbia's national aspirations once more in the storm and stress of new afflictions. Its accents ring so true, that the geographer, in search of Serbia's boundaries, tries in vain to discover a surer guide to delimita-

tion. For Serbia extends as far as her folk-songs are heard. From the Adriatic to the Western walls of the Balkan ranges, from Croatia to Macedonia, the guzlar's ballad is the symbol of national solidarity. His tunes live within the hearts and upon the lips of every Serbian. The *pjesme* may therefore be fittingly considered the measure and index of a nationality whose fibre it has stirred. To make Serbian territory coincide with the regional extension of the *pjesme* implies the defining of the Serbian national area', p. 322.

19 R.G.D. Laffan, *The Guardians of the Gate* (Oxford: Clarendon Press, 1918), p. 20.

20 Dominian, *The Frontiers of Language and Nationality in Europe*, p. 191.

21 *Ibid.*, p. 182.

22 H.A.L. Fisher, *A History of Europe* (London: Edward Arnold, 1936), p. 1090.

23 In an address to the Norwegian Refugee Council, Kjell Arild Nilsen, *Bosnia Report*, 11, June–August 1995, p. 4.

24 Branko Franolic, *Croatian Glagolitic Printed Texts Recorded in the British Library General Catalogue* (London: Croat Information Centre, 1994).

25 Carole Rogel, *The Slovenes and Yugoslavism 1890–1914* (Columbia University Press, 1977).

26 We have already seen Serb examples of this. For a Croat example, claiming 'the Croatian character of Bosnia', see Francis Eterovich and Christopher Spalatin (eds.), *Croatia, Land, People, Culture* (University of Toronto Press, 1964).

27 Vinko Puljic, *Suffering with Hope: Appeals, Addresses, Interviews* (Zagreb: HKD Napredak, 1995), p. 8.

28 Ivan Lovrenovic, 'The Deconstruction of Bosnia', unpublished paper, p. 8.

29 Banac, *The National Question in Yugoslavia*, p. 132.

30 Mirko Grmek, Marc Gjidana and Neven Simac, *Le nettoyage ethnique: Documents historiques sur une idéologie serbe* (Paris: Fayard, 1993) provides the basic documentation covering both the nineteenth and the twentieth century.

31 Hugh Seton-Watson, *Nationalism – Old and New*, 1965, p. 16. A close African parallel to this can be found in two remarks of President Banda of Malawi: (1) 'So far as I am concerned, there is no Yao in this country; no Lomwe; no Sena; no Chewa; no Ngoni; no Nyakyusa; no Tonga; there are only "Malawians". That is all.' (2) 'I am a Chewa', Leroy Vail (ed.), *The Creation of Tribalism in Southern Africa* (London: James Currey, 1989), p. 151.

32 Branka Magas, *The Destruction of Yugoslavia* (London: Verso, 1993), pp. xx, xii and xxiii.

33 Philip J. Cohen, *Serbia's Secret War: Propaganda and the Deceit of History* (Texas A & M University Press, 1996).

34 Michael A. Sells, *The Bridge Betrayed: Religion and Genocide in Bosnia* (University of California Press, 1996).

6 SOME AFRICAN CASE STUDIES

1 Leroy Vail (ed.), *The Creation of Tribalism in Southern Africa* (London: James Currey, 1989).

2 Terence Ranger and Olufemi Vaughan (eds.), *Legitimacy and the State in Twentieth-Century Africa* (London: Macmillan, 1993), pp. 62−111, criticising his earlier 'The Invention of Tradition in Colonial Africa', in Eric Hobsbawm and Terence Ranger (eds.), *The Invention of Tradition* (Cambridge University Press, 1983), pp. 211−62.

3 John Lonsdale, 'Moral Ethnicity and Political Tribalism', pp. 103−30 of Preben Kaarsholm and Jan Hultin (eds.), *Inventions and Boundaries: Historical and Anthropological Approaches to the Study of Ethnicity and Religion* (Roskilde University Press, Denmark, 1994).

4 Compare P.T.W. Baxter's remarks about Oromo ethnic identity: 'In my experience Oromo exiles feel their sense of ethnic identity very, very strongly indeed; it really does have intense, even passionate, "moral value" for them . . . the essence of Oromo identity is active involvement in Oromo cultural values through local ritual and social performances', 'Ethnic Boundaries and Development: Speculations on the Oromo Case', in Kaarsholm and Hultin, *Inventions and Boundaries*, pp. 247−60.

5 I. Shalid, 'The Kebra Nagast in the Light of Recent Research', *Le Muséon*, vol. 89 (1976), pp. 133−78.

6 Kay Kaufman Shelemay, 'The Musician and Transmission of Religious Identity: The Multiple Roles of the Ethiopian Däbtära', *Journal of Religion in Africa*, vol. 22.3 (1992), pp. 242−60.

7 Patrick Harries, 'The Roots of Ethnicity: Discourse and the Politics of Language Construction in South-East Africa', *African Affairs*, vol. 87,346 (January 1988), pp. 25−52. See also his parallel study, 'Exclusion, Classification and Internal Colonialism: The Emergence of Ethnicity among the Tsonga-Speakers of South Africa', pp. 82−117 of Vail, *The Creation of Tribalism*; Nicolas Monnier, 'Stratégie missionnaire et tactiques d'appropriation indigènes: La Mission romande au Mozambique 1888−1896, *Le Fait Missionnaire*, vol. 2 (December 1995, Lausanne), pp. 1−85, and G.J. van Butselaar, 'The Ambiguity of (Cross-Cultural) Mission: Swiss Missionaries and Tsonga Christians in the Context of South Africa', *Missionalia*, vol. 24 (1996, Pretoria), pp. 63−77.

8 Harries, 'The Roots of Ethnicity', p. 41.

9 *Ibid.*, pp. 51−2.

10 *Ibid.*, p. 52.

11 *Ibid.*, p. 52.

12 Michael Wright, *Buganda in the Heroic Age* (Nairobi: Oxford University Press, 1971), p. 204.

13 J. Rowe, 'Myth, Memoir and Moral Admonition: Luganda Historical Writing 1893−1969', *Uganda Journal*, vol. 33 (1969), pp. 17−40.

14 Tudor Griffiths, 'Bishop Tucker of Uganda', unpublished manuscript.

15 P.F. de Moraes Farias and K. Barber (eds.), *Self-Assertion and Brokerage: Early Cultural Nationalism in West Africa* (Birmingham, 1980); J.D.Y. Peel, 'The Cultural Work of Yoruba Ethnogenesis', in E. Tonkin (ed.), *History and Ethnicity* (London: Routledge and Kegan Paul, 1988), pp. 198−215; Toyin Falola (ed.), *Pioneer, Patriot and Patriarch: Samuel Johnson and the Yoruba People* (Madison, 1993).

16 Richard Sklar, *Nigerian Political Parties* (Princeton University Press, 1963), p. 233.

17 D. Anthony Low and R. Cranford Pratt, *Buganda and British Overrule 1900−1955* (Oxford University Press, 1960), p. 253.

18 *Ibid.*, p. 349.

7 ETHNICITY FURTHER CONSIDERED

1 John Lonsdale, 'Moral Ethnicity and Political Tribalism', in Preben Kaarsholm and Jan Hultin (eds.), *Inventions and Boundaries: Historical and Anthropological Approaches to the Study of Ethnicity and Nationalism* (Roskilde University Press, Denmark, 1994), p. 131. My understanding of ethnicity is very much that of John Lonsdale and of Richard Jenkins, 'Ethnicity, *etcetera*; Social Anthropological Points of View', *Ethnic and Racial Studies*, vol. 19 (1996), pp. 807−22.

2 E.J. Hobsbawm, *Nations and Nationalism since 1780* (Cambridge University Press, 1990), p. 104.

3 See Anne Hilton, *The Kingdom of Kongo* (Oxford: Clarendon Press, 1985), pp. 36−7, 46−7, 219−21; Victor Turner, *The Ritual Process* (London: Routledge and Kegan Paul, 1969), pp. 97−102; Monica Wilson, *Communal Rituals of the Nyakyusa* (London: Oxford University Press, 1959), pp. 24−5.

4 J.E.A. Jolliffe, *The Constitutional History of Medieval England* (London: Black, 1937), p. 100.

5 Preface to the second edition of the *Enciklopedija Jugoslavije,* 1983, pp. ix−x.

6 E.E. Evans-Pritchard, *Nuer Religion* (Oxford: Clarendon Press, 1956), pp. 287–9; Godfrey Lienhardt, *Divinity and Experience: The Religion of the Dinka* (Oxford: Clarendon Press, 1961), p. 219.

7 The underlying reason in his deeply traditional Ganda thinking was probably that a Muganda cannot be circumcised.

8 Ernest Gellner, *Nations and Nationalism* (Oxford: Blackwell, 1983), p. 11.

8 RELIGION FURTHER CONSIDERED

1 For a fascinating discussion of the relationship between Englishness and Jewishness, see James Shapiro, *Shakespeare and the Jews* (Columbia University Press, 1996).

2 Nelson Mandela, *Long Walk to Freedom* (London: Little, Brown and Company, 1994), p. 188.

3 See Rosalind Ransford, 'A Kind of Noah's Ark: Aelred of Rievaulx and National Identity', in Stuart Mews (ed.), *Religion and National Identity, Studies in Church History* 18 (Oxford: Blackwell, 1982), pp. 137–46.

4 E.J. Hobsbawm, *Nations and Nationalism since 1780* (Cambridge University Press, 1990), p. 48.

5 *Ibid.*, p. 76.

6 *Ibid.*, p. 74.

7 E. Duffy, *The Stripping of the Altars: Traditional Religion in England 1400–1580* (New Haven: Yale University Press, 1992), pp. 77 and 79.

8 Regino of Prüm, *Chronicon, Monumenta Germaniae Historica: Scriptores Rerum Germanicorum* (65), p. xx, quoted in Susan Reynolds, *Kingdoms and Communities in Western Europe 900–1300* (Oxford: Clarendon Press, 1984), p. 257.

9 Michael Cherniavsky, *Tsar and People: Studies in Russian Myths* (New Haven: Yale University Press, 1961).

10 Hobsbawm, *Nations and Nationalism*, p. 49.

11 Anthony Smith, *Nationalism in the Twentieth Century* (Oxford: Martin Robertson, 1979), especially pp. 78–80.

12 Lamin Sanneh, *Translating the Message: The Missionary Impact on Culture* (New York: Orbis, 1990).

13 E.J. van Donzel (ed.), *Enbaqom, Angasa Amin (La Porte de la Foi): Apologie éthiopienne du christianisme contre L'Islam à partir du Coran* (Leiden: E.J. Brill, 1969).

14 M. Ghayasuddin (ed.), *The Impact of Nationalism on the Muslim World*, (London: The Open Press, 1986), pp. 1 and 4.

15 William Temple, *Church and Nation* (London: Macmillan, 1915), p. 45.

16 World Missionary Conference, Edinburgh, 1910, Report of Commission I, *Carrying the Gospel to the Non-Christian World.*

17 *The Churches Survey their Task*, the Report of the Conference at Oxford, July 1937, on Church, Community and State (London: George Allen and Unwin, 1937), especially the 'Longer Report on Church and Community', pp. 188–240, significantly owed in its final form to Sir Walter Moberly, chairman of that section of the Conference. The most acute Christian analysis of the nation and nationalism dating from the Second World War period is probably Christopher Dawson's *The Judgement of the Nations* (London: Sheed and Ward, 1943).

18 The case of modern Fiji is also interesting. It is perhaps the most Methodist society in the world, and Methodism has become the core of its nationalism. When more ecumenically minded Methodists came to control the leadership of the church, they were forcibly ousted by nationalists.

19 *Beyond Tolerance: The Challenge of Mixed Marriage, A Record of the International Consultation held in Dublin, 1974*, ed. Michael Hurley (London: Geoffrey Chapman, 1975), Appendix II, pp. 188–93.

20 Adrian Hastings, 'Intermarriage and the Wider Society', *Beyond Tolerance*, pp. 1–8, reprinted in A. Hastings, *The Faces of God* (London: Geoffrey Chapman, 1975), pp. 117–25.

21 Robin Flower, *The Irish Tradition* (Oxford: Clarendon Press, 1947), p. 22; cf. Dáibhí Ó Cróinín, *Early Medieval Ireland 400–1200* (London: Longman, 1995), p. 54.

22 *Cymbeline*, 5.5.

Index